Narrow Escapes

A Memoir

Louise Nayer

SPUYTEN DUYVIL

New York   Paris

This is a true story though some of the names have been changed
to protect people's privacy.

Library of Congress Cataloging-in-Publication Data

Names: Nayer, Louise, author.
Title: Narrow escapes : a memoir / Louise Nayer.
Description: New York : Spuyten Duyvil, [2023]
Identifiers: LCCN 2022053281 | ISBN 9781956005912 (paperback)
Subjects: LCSH: Nayer, Louise--Childhood and youth. | Nayer,
    Louise--Travel--Morocco. | Nayer, Louise--Travel--United States. | Young
    women--United States--Biography. | Authors, American--20th
    century--Biography. | Women--United States--Social conditions--20th
    century--Anecdotes. | United States--Social
    conditions--1960-1980--Anecdotes.
Classification: LCC PS3564.A8937 Z46 2023 | DDC 818/.5403
    [B]--dc23/eng/20230216
LC record available at https://lccn.loc.gov/2022053281

For Jim

I wanted to be sure to reach you;
though my ship was on the way it got caught
in some moorings. I am always tying up
and then deciding to depart.
    Frank O'Hara

CHAPTER ONE

I came close to death in Marrakesh. My traveling companion, Jaclyn, went out shopping while I lay on my bunk, weak and sick, hallucinating red and yellow colors that danced and fluttered across the pea green walls at the youth hostel. Had I known this would happen, I might never have gone on this journey when school ended.

But hindsight is 2020. I was young; it was 1969. A global youth peace movement swept the world, hundreds of thousands of mostly middle-class kids, thumbs out on the endless highways of the world, entering and leaving countries they knew little about. All people are good I wanted to believe, like my heroine, Anne Frank, even as bombs dropped fire on villages in Vietnam.

. . .

"Be careful. Don't be silly, keep your traveler's checks and passport in your money belt," my mother said to me on the deck of the student ship, the *Aurelia*, before I left for France on my junior year abroad. My mother was a practical, "no nonsense" woman who always had her ducks in a row. That July morning, only a few days before the moon landing in 1969, she wore a pressed khaki skirt, white silk shirt and navy blue blazer. The daughter of a Presbyterian minister, who adopted her at nine after her biological father ran off, and a religious mother, she had pulled herself up with a Master's Degree in Nursing Education from Columbia University, unusual for a woman of her time. In 1942, she married my father, a Jewish doctor with Ivy League credentials. We had a beautiful home in Greenwich Village. My mother's impeccable dockside attire was in sharp contrast to my peasant blouse and ragged jeans, too tight for my thighs. I had gained 20 pounds drinking beer in the Yakima Valley, Washington, where I worked that summer with the American Friends Service Committee, a Quaker organization, helping in a migrant community. I almost dropped out of school and stayed in Washington, pulled like so many others towards doing community work. Plus, I had a love affair with Mateo, a lawyer and spokesperson for the migrant community. I left the Yakima Valley with a heaviness in my heart, desperately alone, travelling through three time zones, Seattle to New York City.

"I've found real work here. I'm dropping out of college," I wrote to my parents two weeks earlier, but I tore up the letter. It was scary to drop out of college, to defy my accomplished parents. I got stoned with some legal aid workers in Seattle who drove me to the airport—late. I missed my flight. But I dutifully boarded the next flight and slept through the landing and takeoff in Chicago, groggy with leaving a place I loved and scared to go on the next journey. Five days later, I stood on the deck of a huge ship that left for France.

On the deck my mother handed me a big floppy doll with brown braids and a pink flowered pinafore. "From that New England catalogue," she said, looking at me and hoping I would accept her gift, even though I was too old for a doll. I turned away for a minute, aware of her scars, and the smell of heavy cosmetics. Blobs of flesh, like silly putty, covered her face below her eyes and down her neck. You could see a thin red line where flesh from her stomach was sewn on and a crisscrossed line, like a jagged stitch on her neck flesh. Her eyebrows were drawn on with pencils, and her right eye was slightly bigger than the other. Her perfect outfits couldn't hide her reconstructed face.

An explosion in the dank cellar of a summer rental in Wellfleet, Massachusetts. I was four years old. My mother's hands and face were blackened with burns. "No hot water to wash my face," my mother said to my dad when they got home. He held the flashlight as they climbed down the rickety ladder to the musty cellar to light the pilot light on the hot water tank. Gas with no smell had escaped. My mother lit the match. Blue flames ravaged her face and hands. My father too. My mother's face would be unrecognizable. They narrowly escaped the fire.

Earlier that evening, they had passed the "gas men" on the road and waved at them, two ordinary cars passing at twilight. My last memory before she lost her face: my mother kissing me goodbye, a lavender shawl swept over her shoulders. The scent of rose perfume. Her shining eyes. A few minutes later our fate was sealed. Our babysitter, Della, let the men in to change the propane tank. A faulty valve. Nine months of separation. A perfect storm of grief.

Now, on the broad deck of the enormous student ship, my mother's smell was thick from cosmetics, covered over by Chanel perfume. I stared back at the strangers on deck who looked at her too long. "My mother is not a freak," I wanted to shout to the world.

"Thanks, Mommy." Even though I was 19, I still called her "mommy" as if I could be four years old forever, before the fire to always stay a happy little girl. I clutched the doll to me, rubbing my face over the thick brown braids. My mother stayed until the last minute, no hugs, just a quick peck on the cheek. Her white patent-leather purse slung over her shoulder, she walked briskly back onto the streets of Manhattan, away from the deep, groaning sounds of the ship about to leave port. I wanted to run after her, to cling to her skirts and shout, "Mommy don't go." I used to press my face against the windowpane of our second floor apartment, watching for her red coat coming back to me after one of her 37 operations. I tried to have faith that she'd always return, but I wasn't so sure.

Now I was the one leaving.

I took the steep steps down to my bunk, so low in the ship I didn't even have a porthole. Three days later, a morning newspaper slid under my door. Men had landed on the moon and planted an American flag on that luminescent sphere. In small print below all the fanfare about the moon landing, I saw a little boy had drowned in a stream full of reeds. Tears flooded my eyes. I felt so sad for him and his family, to die in the reeds when America was celebrating the moon landing. Deep down, I lived in this chiaroscuro world: great joy shading to great grief.

...

"Morocco." Jaclyn nervously twisted her long brown hair. "I'll have to ask my parents." Nine months had passed since my mother saw me off. Jaclyn and I sat at a wooden table on the main square of Aix-en-Provence, France. It was May. The pungent smell of lavender sachets from the nearby shops wafted through the air. I didn't know Jaclyn well. She studied at the American university, and I studied at the French university. We were 20 years old, finishing our junior year abroad. It was one of those friends-of-friends kinds of things that brought us together. My best friend, Ken, my soul mate that year, and a friend of one of my high school classmates, introduced me to her just when school was ending. She was from the New Jersey suburbs, driven everywhere in a big American car, not like me who rode

the crowded subways in New York City. I saw men expos-
ing themselves on the platforms. Sometimes in a packed
car, men pushed their groins against me, and I had to turn
away. I don't think her parents let her ride the subways.

A poetry book always lived in my messy purses or big
pockets and now inside my knapsack, my precious house
on my back. I loved to taste words, to feel them roll around
my mouth and move to my gut. I secretly wanted to be a
writer.

Jaclyn talked endlessly about boys and getting thin, so
thin she could fit into a size three, which she swore she wore
before coming to France and hitting the bakeries. I wanted
to be thin too, Vogue-thin like the long-legged models on
the glossy pages. Some women starved themselves, refusing to eat ten calories in a stick of gum. Some women died
chasing a fantasy body. I weighed myself whenever I found
a scale, taking off shoes and jewelry and mostly cringed at
the numbers. Never good enough. My mother wanted me
to look perfect, head to toe, but there was always a stain on
my shirt, or a loose thread threatening to unravel me. If she
couldn't look perfect, maybe I could.

One day I'd devour four or five cookies in one setting,
palmiers shaped like butterflies, buttery, sugary crumbs
dripping down my shirt until my stomach hurt. The next
day I'd starve myself and feel faint, dizzy and deprived. A
penance, though I wasn't sure for what. Ken helped me kick
my sugar addiction that year, at least for a while. I watched
him eat a cookie vicariously and even pretended to wipe off

crumbs from my lips. I dropped the weight I gained, but now I chain-smoked. My doctor father's talk at my high school, "Smoking is the worse form of personal pollution," was a distant memory.

Ken and I had tried to cross the border at Gibraltar three months before, but we were barred from entry. Morocco was the apex of cool. Nixon's war on drugs and the peacenik hippies was raging with its no-knock warrants. We stood on one side of the border near a shiny metal booth where the head official worked and angrily watched parades of perfect-looking families, husband, wife, and two children in shiny new Volkswagen cars, flashing moneyed smiles as the border guards smiled back and waved them through.

"The girl can come in," one border guard said, looking a bit too deeply into my eyes, but Ken pulled me close to him. I wasn't about to go there alone. We walked back through no-man's land, a breath of concrete between countries.

Morocco had it all: deserts, waterfalls, camels trekking across the beaches; Jaclyn and I could cross borders and be with the real people of Morocco, not on some fancy tour. Maybe we'd be invited into a Moroccan home? The Beatles went there. The Stones. Famous writers sipped mint tea in cafes in Tangier. I wrote dark and magical poems in my black notebooks that I hid in the bottom of my knapsack.

Ken and I never made it into Morocco. Instead, we hitch-hiked up the coast of Spain and dropped acid on a promontory in Ibiza, an island off Barcelona. Ken was a veteran, and it was my first acid trip. When my body was floating molecules, he was solid, later making sure we got the last bus back to town, "What's a bus?" I said, sitting on a rock, forgetting the world of solid objects.

"It's the last bus of the day and it's cold. Get up!" His voice was firm. I rose from the ground.

That gorgeous day of my first acid trip, sunshine splattered across the granite rocks and azure blue water. I sat on a huge gray rock by the water and looked at Ken's face and saw the capillaries inside, branches of a tree where blood pulsed through. I put my hand in the water, liquid fingers dancing into the sea, my body, the gray rocks. That night, we climbed the tall hill up to the lighthouse. All the stars were shooting in the sky, tiny, infinite explosions of light. I knew then that nothing ever dies. That we are all pulsing with light. It was the closest I came to being born again.

"Yes," Jaclyn said the next day when we met again. "I talked to my parents. I can go." We hugged and did a circle dance. We were going to Morocco, to the cool place. It was Saturday and the main square was filled with markets, people hawking fruits, vegetables, and baked goods. The café, filled with college co-eds like us, faced the square, the square that I had come to love over the past year.

Just a week before, my mom wrote me a letter. "You did so well in your classes and all in French. We'll give you money for a trip. But that's it. Budget wisely!"

I couldn't believe my luck. Morocco. With Jaclyn, I knew we would be allowed to enter. "The girl can enter," the border guard had said. *Wouldn't you know we're riding on the*

Marrakech Express. The lyrics of the Crosby, Stills and Nash song played like a loop-tape in my brain.

Neil Young's *Four Dead in Ohio* also played in my brain. My hands trembled, remembering that day, only a month before.

This summer I hear the drummin'...soldiers are cutting us down/And found her dead on the ground.

Ken and I marched with a few others to the American embassy that May 4th, horrified that young lives were gunned down by our own government. A week later, we boarded a bus to the Cannes Film Festival to see the film *Woodstock.* Among the starlets in slinky dresses climbing the grand stairs of the theater we shouted, "America out of Vietnam and Cambodia," drawing a crowd and even making the French news.

At times I ached to be back in America and part of the peace movement again. But my body relaxed in Aix: picnics in the French countryside, watching films by Truffaut and Renoir, listening to Edith Piaf, "La Vie en Rose," and other songs that my sister and I sang together for years, hiding in her back bedroom as teenagers, drawn to La Petite Rossignol, the little nightingale. She had an orphan heart.

Maybe my sister, Annie, and I had orphan hearts, too. A whole in our hearts from the long separation from our parents.

My parents returned after the fire alive but forever changed. My mother's stoic armor entered all the rooms of the house. She wanted everything to be normal. After the bombs dropped on Hiroshima, shop owners quickly put up facades to get back to business, as Oleander flowers blossomed in the blackened landscape. Nature came back, but nothing would be the same.

Aix-en Provence, my respite from the violence in America. My eyes burned when I remembered being tear-gassed, protesting Dow Chemical on our Madison, Wisconsin, campus sophomore year, October 1968—huddled with others like sardines in the Commerce Building. Dow, the makers of napalm, dropped on children in Vietnam was recruiting on our campus. I knew what burns looked like, the horrible ropey scars on my mother's face, once wrapped in bandages with only slits for eyes. We all sat at the dinner table when she was wrapped like a mummy. I was seven, trying so hard to be happy. That's what my mother wanted. She spooned tomato soup into the slit that was her mouth. We talked as if nothing was wrong even as the smell of antiseptic-laden gauze filled the dining room.

That windy October day, cops charged in with Billy clubs and beat students. Cracking sounds and blood. I ran out terrified and stood on a grassy knoll where a line of eighteen-year-old National Guard, 18-20-year-olds like us, shot tear gas into our faces, a blinding, stinging pain. Ambulances carted away friends. My eyes burned in their sockets.

The quest for peace and love exploded into bombs and terror.

CHAPTER TWO

In the sunlit square of Aix, Jaclyn and I spread out our wrinkled maps on the wooden table of the café and traced our route. To Marrakesh, of course, through Tangier, Rabat, Fez and Beni-Mellal. We'd travel back though Essaouira, Casablanca, Rabat and back to Tangier. Casablanca! I couldn't believe my luck to travel there. "Here's looking at you, kid." Humphrey Bogart spoke to me with his throaty, sexy voice. We'd ride on buses but also hitchhike. We were students. Money was tight. "Make do with what we've given you," my mother said. "You're lucky to be able to have this trip." Later on in the trip, I obsessively opened the blue plastic wallet that held my traveler's checks and counted my money at night, afraid it wouldn't be enough.

The real people, that's who we'd be with, not the pretentious bourgeois travelers, riding on huge tour buses, their sanitized printed itineraries in their laps. Joni Mitchell sang, "We've got to get ourselves back to the garden." We could rely on the kindness of strangers in this new world, open our hearts, share our lives. Just as Kerouac was on the road searching for the real America, I wanted to see the real Morocco, gracefully enter the homes of ordinary people living their lives. All of us are made of the same mettle.

"I'm sure we'll get in," I told her as we sat in the square. "They like to let women in!"

"Ken and I were turned away twice. The U.S. secretary of state wanted the borders closed to hippies. As if we were

19

going to ruin the country!" Jaclyn sipped her iced tea and then looked up at me, her eyebrows arching. She looked concerned.

I didn't tell her the next part. The third time we tried to cross, Ken demanded to talk to "the head official." A tall man dressed in a suit and tie briskly walked out of a booth. "Why can't we enter?" Ken asked. "We have money. We just want to see your country."

"We don't like your type," he said, and Ken got livid, his face red, screaming, "What type do you like?" What type do you like?" I yanked him away. Back to the desolate walk across no-man's land. We could have ended up in prison.

Two young women going anywhere in the world alone was dangerous. Maybe I was trying to prove something? My parents climbed out of that incendiary cellar and survived. I could hitchhike, face danger on the road and not get pulled under the earth, abducted like Persephone by dark forces. Young people were hitchhiking all over the world, even queuing up on street corners in Paris thumbing rides. Young women, too. It was the era of women's liberation. I wanted to have adventures like men. I wanted to be free of the anxiety that shackled me, free of the panic that lived just under my skin, free of the sound of sirens, free of thinking an accident was always about to happen.

On one trip to Greece months before, I hitchhiked with a friend on the Peloponnese and got into a truck with two Greek men who assured us they would let us off in the next town. Fatherly men, big, burly and kind. But a few minutes later, the truck drove down a dirt road to the middle of nowhere and stopped. I was in the front of the cab, stuck between the two men. The driver tried to kiss me and touch my breasts with his big, weathered hands. My friend, Valerie, in the back of the truck screamed and jumped up and down and finally leapt out of the back. I struggled free, climbed over the kinder man who didn't try and touch me and bolted out the door. Thank God we both had our knapsacks. The men drove off, dust rising under the spinning tires.

We trekked about a mile back to the main road in a thick silence, not speaking to each other, both scared for our lives. Our stomachs grumbled. Our throats were parched. We walked along the edge of the road carefully in the now pitch black, terrified of more men trying to molest us or even wild animals. Or getting hit by a car. Up the hill, the shadows of olive trees danced drunkenly. Then lights, a huge bus coming closer, and we waved it down. A bus of Italian nuns and giggling adolescent Catholic girls picked us up and drove us to a convent that night with huge stone walls and a bedroom with neatly made twin beds, ironic to be in a house of purity after getting molested by a truck driver. The girls were so excited we were Americans and rushed into our room wanting to speak English. I hadn't said my prayers since I was 14. That night when I lay down, I was so grateful for the bed, the room, and for the safe convent. I prayed that night, thanking God that he kept us safe.

On our program in France, we were warned of the white

slave trade. "You can try on a bra at a lingerie shop, and a trap door will open, and you'll be captured and sent to another country and used for sex." At least neither of us were blonde. We heard rumors that blonde women were traded for camels.

We were also told to never let go of our passports, ever. Plus, we heard that the Moroccan women only went out with male escorts. Jaclyn looked more and more uncomfortable, seeing the worry creasing my face. She shifted back and forth in her seat. She didn't ask any questions. She stared at the table. She stopped sipping her drink.

"We'll dress the part," I said, trying to soothe her fears. "Just like the bona fide moneyed tourists. They let women in—so why not us! We'll see camels." Her eyes lit up at the word camels.

Then we both laughed and agreed to iron nice white shirts and khaki pants that we'd place carefully in the bottoms of our packs and pull out in Malaga.

"Goodbye, Jaclyn, goodbye for now!"

We sang our goodbyes to each other, our voices high-pitched with excitement, our lists in our hands of what we'd bring, mostly t-shirts and shorts. We didn't think at all about how others would look at us, two young woman, scantily dressed in a country where women covered themselves head to toe.

When we hugged, I thought maybe she could be a best friend. A true friend I could count on. I missed Ken.

I felt like I had fought in a war that no one had heard

about but me. I carried an unspeakable terror inside me. My sister and I didn't talk about the fire or the burns. It was off limits, but it had scarred my heart. I needed a true friend whom I could trust.

Jaclyn and I planted our feet on the side of the road outside of Aix-en-Provence, two independent women about to hitchhike down the coast of Spain. My mother was independent for her time. She had even taken a bicycle trip in Germany, right before the war. She told me her boat was the last boat allowed back to New York from Hitler's war. She decided to wait to get off the boat so not to be in a crowd. My grandmother was hysterical, waiting and waiting until she saw her only daughter come back to her.

Now, the road was pure liberation, not knowing where we would land for the night. So completely different from our orderly lives, the lives our Depression-era parents created with their hard work and high expectations for their children: lawyer, doctor, Ph.D. professor. Our backpacks sat next to us on the ground. Sunlight bathed our bodies. Aix-en-Provence would soon be a memory.

We made it easily from Aix to Alicante, got a good ride. In Alicante, palm trees stood like proud dancers encircling the town. The cerulean sky and aquamarine water bathed the landscape in gorgeous shades of blue and green. After that ride, we stood out in the explosive heat. The straps of my backpack dug into my skin, itchy from beads of sweat. A rash sprouted under my arms and in the back of my knees. I kept trying not to scratch, but I couldn't control myself.

The sun scorched our bodies. Cars whizzed by packed with families.

Suddenly, a car screeched to a halt. It was an old car, dilapidated appearance and noisy, rusted on the outside. Jaclyn and I raced inside without even glancing at the driver. My thin white t-shirt dripped with sweat. The air conditioner blew cold air over our overheated bodies. But as soon as I climbed into the front seat and Jaclyn in back, I knew we shouldn't be there. *How stupid!* I could hear my parents' voices. What was I doing hitchhiking, and without a man to protect me? My stomach clenched with fear. I had already shut the car door. Jaclyn too. I smelled alcohol and noticed empty beer bottles at my feet. The driver scanned our bodies even as he drove. I didn't like his rusty-brown eyes. The agonizing heat would have been better.

I sat on a torn orange fabric seat, but I didn't want to sink into the upholstery. I didn't want to sink into anything.

The driver, thick build with short greasy hair, kept taking his eyes off the petrifying curves. He kept looking at me and smacking his lips. His left leg jerked up and down. Then I saw a small photo of two girls taped to the dashboard. "What sweet little girls," I said, hoping he spoke some English. "How old are they?" He didn't respond. My stomach tightened even more. A crucifix dangled from his rearview mirror. I appealed to his Christian goodness though I kept seeing images of Christ all bloodied in my mind. We were the lambs.

"We're students, seeing the world." His leg was still

shaking, but I kept talking. "My parents—my mom and dad—a doctor and a nurse, they write to me every week. I write them back on the thin stationery that I get at the post office that costs less when you send letters overseas." I told him how my mother had gone with me to the post office two blocks from my apartment in New York City so I could write to her about my adventures in Europe.

"Make sure to write a lot," she had said.

"We're going home soon," I said to him, emphasizing the word "home." The sickly smell of alcohol rose from the dirty floorboards.

I closed my eyes for a minute and imagined my parents' home, the dark wood furniture, and the blue-and-yellow flowered curtains in my room. The big portraits of me and my sister in gold-leaf frames on the living room wall. I came from someplace that existed. Someplace solid.

Did he understand anything I was saying? I kept talking in a low, reasonable tone, as if reason could save us.

I glanced back at Jaclyn. She was biting her nails. She didn't make a peep. Her eyebrows arched like they had at the café when I told her about being turned away from the Moroccan border. Her long brown hair, like mine, swayed from side to side as the car lurched around the bends.

My pearlescent string of words meant to soothe the savage beast did nothing. He kept glaring at me, taking his eyes off the road, moving his thick, hairy hand, like a spider, toward my thigh and then looking in the rearview mirror at Jaclyn. I moved my backpack to the left side of my body, all the accumulated stuff of my vagabond student life, sleeping bag, diary, Frank O'Hara poems, Sylvia Plath poems, skin cream, toothbrush, protecting my thighs from his grasp.

"You are both so pretty," he said in perfect English, touching his tongue to his lips. The calm blue water on the left spoke a different language than the insane driver, luring me into a different reality. I wanted to leap into the sea.

I inched closer to the window, but not too close in case the door swung open. *Don't rape us. Don't kill us*, I silently prayed, holding my hands together like a church steeple underneath my knapsack as the car bumped up and down, the old shock absorbers making a clinking noise. "We need to get out of the car," I mouthed to Jaclyn in the back seat. Her eyes darted from me to the window. She clutched the straps of her backpack. I did the same. I didn't want to die on some godforsaken highway in Spain. My life over, faster than birth. We had miles to go to reach our destination. *Miles to go before I sleep.* I had copied that Robert Frost poem in dark blue marker on a white poster board. It hung in my bedroom at home in New York.

Who would find us?

Would we just disappear?

The roads got busier as we entered Malaga, our destination. We heard through the grapevine that it was easier to cross here, more upscale, fewer "hippies." When the driver stopped at a light, distracted by a young woman in high heels crossing the street, I looked back at Jaclyn and mouthed, "NOW." Please God, make sure the doors aren't locked I whispered to myself, my heart racing as we leaped out of the car and landed on the concrete sidewalk. My knee stung from the fall. A burning, scraping stinging. The car sped away.

I stood up quickly, wiped some dirt off my shirt, embarrassed to be on the ground. People ambled down the street. "My arm hurts," Jaclyn said, rising slowly like a feeble old woman from the ground.

I checked her arm for bruising, then gently put my hand along her forearm and pressed lightly, seeing her reaction. No reaction. This was how my father checked me when I was hurt. Gently but concerned. When we went for lunch, I asked for a bag of ice, which she kept on and off for a half an hour, until she said, "I'm fine. Let's get the boat!" We both went into the ladies' room and changed into our pressed shirts and khaki pants.

"Keep an eye on your arm," I said, "and make sure it's okay. I can always take you to a doctor in Morocco." We had to take care of each other.

In the restaurant bathroom I wet a paper towel, put soap on it, and scraped as much dirt as I could off my knee and winced at the pain. Oozing red blood bubbled to the surface like in a cauldron. Little specks of dirt buried inside the wound like tiny bugs.

Jaclyn didn't ask me how my knee felt.

Malaga, home of the great Pablo Picasso, was booming. Under palm trees, people folded themselves leisurely over chairs in cafes sipping café con leche. We arrived at the dock just in time and strode onto the huge white ferry that would carry us into the magical land of Morocco. The sky was a gorgeous delft blue. Our family went to Europe and visited Delft, in Holland, with the "burn money" (as my mother called it), the settlement for the explosion.

Money could never bring back her face.

The sky here was as deep as the delft blue of the Dutch plates.

Jaclyn and I found a small wooden bench to sit on the top deck. A cool breeze soothed my itchy skin. I stood on the deck watching the dazzling blue-green colors of the ocean waters wash over my eyes. I looked around for men in uniforms. Would an officious bureaucrat sweep through the boat and find out I had been denied entrance before? Would our passports be checked on the boat or when we landed? I touched my hand to my money belt where my passport lived.

In our khaki pants, white button-down collared shirts, and well-brushed hair, Jaclyn and I looked like put-together young women. Put-together was something my mother loved. She grew up in Salvation Army homes. Our backpacks, though, screamed something different, stained with dirt, sleeping bags tied chaotically to the top with a bungee cord.

As I looked out over the sea, I knew I might be on the "bad" list. Teachers at my progressive school in New York City were blacklisted during the McCarthy era. I knew what the stroke of a pen could do to a life. But Jaclyn and I were dressed up as we leaned against the bow of the ship. This wasn't Gibraltar with the scores of "long hairs" as hippies were called, knocking on the door to Morocco, looking for some illusive nirvana, but turned away in droves.

Still panic coursed through my body, sticking to me like an electric web.

My first panic attack had jolted through my body right after I broke up with my boyfriend, Joe, freshman year of college; I was at a jazz concert, alone. The walls came towards me like crushing monuments. I clutched the side of my chair, embarrassed that my body was out of control, the panic a locomotive I couldn't stop.

At the first intermission I ran outside, as if outrunning a fire. I went back home to my new apartment. My two roommates were out. The house seemed too big. I felt small and lonely. I had even gotten a second-hand canopy bed, four posters holding up a peach- colored arch of soft fabric. I had always dreamed of owning a canopy bed, like a Queen, but Joe wouldn't be next to me, his long legs wrapped around mine, even in sleep. Some mornings if I had nothing to do for the day, I'd desperately call one person after the next. If no one answered, I'd hold my ear to the phone too long, the dial tone ringing like a siren.

Jaclyn walked to the front of the boat which groaned loudly as it pulled out of port. "I'm feeling panicky," I wanted to say. I wanted to talk with her about the sights. I wanted to recite a poem, the Yeats poem, "What dread beast/ its hour come round at last, slouches toward Bethlehem to be born." I wanted to be born again into this new land, to talk to her about the way the froth on the waves looked like tiny beards, or how the sun changed the water from blue to green to black—like a huge bruise. She wasn't interested in my overactive imagination or my fears.

She kept looking at men, sizing them up. I often had the feeling she was looking at my body, her eyes doing a quick survey from my face to my toes—to see how it compared with hers. Who was thinner? Who was more attractive?

Salty air rinsed over me, softening my skin, dry and cracked from the relentless sun. I loved the velvety coolness of the mist on my skin.

The boat was crowded with well-dressed tourists bedecked with gold bracelets and earrings, holding designer purses, and with Moroccan men returning home in long robes and women in headscarves as well as a few travelers like us with sleeping bags tied to the tops of their backpacks. North Africa. I tasted the words like the sweet butterscotch sundaes of my childhood, when my mother would take me to Schrafft's, the servers dressed in pink dresses with white peter pan collars. I'd eat the whipped cream first.

After forty-five minutes skimming along the sea, where the Atlantic meets the Mediterranean, turquoise, deep blues and greens swirling together in those waters—we spotted Tangier—a busy port surrounded by square white apartment buildings stacked one upon the other. Seabirds, stretching out their white, downy wings, flew nearer to the boat. The boat pulled into port in the late afternoon. My hands shook, hummingbird hands. I was nervous about what would happen. I might get sent back on the boat. *No Entry. No Entry.* The tall American man right in front of me was being questioned. Then he was permitted to enter Tangier, gone, down the plank.

"Passport, your passport, Miss," the official said. I thought of good things while he inspected my passport and then looked at me. Scrumptious donuts with thick sugar sprinkled on top. *Let me in. Please, please, let me in,* I silently prayed.

"Okay. You're okay to go." My passport was stamped. I was "in!" I wanted to run and show the stamp to Ken. I wanted a true best friend on this journey.

Ken went to my university in Madison and had been introduced to me by a friend from high school. He dropped out of college and decided to go to art school in Aix. We had been inseparable that year, often meeting at a small bakery in the early morning. We bought warm bread and a piece of chocolate that melted in the middle and walked the cobble-stoned streets. The sky in southern France was gorgeous at dawn, changing colors as the sun rose; we read poems to each other; and even sized up men together as we sat in a café on the Cours Mirabeau. "I like that one," I said.

"Oh, he's not my type," Ken would say. To look at men like that felt wrong but also liberating. As a woman I was taught to be picked like a shy flower from a corner of the dance floor. With Ken I could be different.

I was with him in his windowless top-floor studio when

he got a letter back from his father after he wrote to his parents that he was gay. His hands shook when he carefully opened the thin blue airmail letter. "I'm not surprised. We love you. We'll talk when you get back to the States," his father wrote. His mother didn't write anything. He was standing up and quiet. He put the letter down on the table. I didn't go near him at first. When he looked up, eyes teary, I gave him a big hug. We didn't say anything.

One afternoon after class, I napped at his apartment. "My hand is burned," I cried out from a nightmare. He was one of the only people I had told about my parents. That they had been burned, my mother facially disfigured. He reached out and held my hand for a long time. The feel of his hand on my hand helped the scars recede, knobby, red, ropey scars turning back to my young, 19-year-old unburned flesh. "I love you," he said as he got a Kleenex and gently wiped the tears from my eyes.

Now, I just wanted to push all the scary thoughts away. I only wanted to feel joy and freedom. To be young and free. Throw the scary thoughts into a huge dumpster, buried forever.

I didn't realize then that you couldn't bury grief.

The city of Tangier, so sparkling white, so light now I could soar into the sky like a gorgeous balloon and gaze down at all the dazzling white houses surrounded by the sea.

CHAPTER THREE

"Here, here, over here," the vendors and snake charmers shouted as Jaclyn and I walked off the boat. One man in long robes had a huge black snake in front of him curled on the cobblestones that he picked up while dancing in circles. The snake hissed into his face. I wasn't a huge fan of snakes, but I thought that was cruel, using an animal to make money. I turned away.

Two young men, dressed in tan pants and pressed, button-down white shirts, stood by the edge of a pier, looking nonchalant. They approached us. "I'm Mohammed. I'm Youssef." They must be well educated, I thought. They spoke perfect English. My parents were forever promoting education. "It's the ticket," my mother said though I knew it really didn't make any difference in a person's character. Kindness, which mattered most to me, sprung from something deeper. But it was hard for me not to get taken in by their language skills. Plus, they lived here.

Mohammed was taller with dark, sparkling eyes. Youssef was a head shorter than his friend and sturdier. He couldn't stand still and kept moving from one leg to the next. They moved closer to us. In New York City, at night, I put keys between my fingers for a weapon and crossed the street if anyone looked suspicious. I hoped I wouldn't need anything like that here.

"We're *university* students," Mohammed said in French, emphasizing the word *université*. That sealed the deal.

My parents had their diplomas beautifully framed on the walls of "the middle room" of their New York City apartment. I wondered if Youssef and Mohammed had framed diplomas.

"We can take you to the Kasbah!" I had heard of the Kasbah, where the sultan used to live, protected by high walls. They offered to carry our backpacks, but Jaclyn and I looked at each other. "No, thank you," we each said. The weight of our packs grounded us. They contained our treasures. Our passports, the most important treasures, lived in money belts tied around our waists. We followed behind them down small, packed alleyways, passing ancient buildings, once fortresses, rising a few stories out of the busy streets like granite giants until we reached the Kasbah.

Mosaics, blue and red and orange—burst with dazzling colors from ancient walls. We walked past arched doorways and cobblestoned streets. Men in long robes, women with their faces covered and others in modern dress all pressed together. The streets teemed with people—even busier than New York City.

We followed a serpentine road into the Medina, the walled part of town, which enclosed all the shops. Mohammed pointed to a sad-looking building.

"An American is in prison there for drugs. Seventeen years. That window," he said, pointing to a small, barred window. Who was it? I imagined the suffocating small cell, the smell of urine and feces and the scorching heat.

Was it some middle-class kids like us just bopping

around but with some marijuana in their pocket? Had some distraught suburban parents spent years and years and all their money on lawyers? Did they have a sister, a brother? Did they count flies on the wall to stay sane? Did they begin to love their captors?

"This way," Youssef said to me as Jaclyn and Mohammed started walking toward a café. "There's nothing you can do to save them," he said, as if reading my face.

The café was bursting with customers, noise and the pungent smells of cinnamon, ginger, turmeric and mint tea. Mohammed led the way, and we climbed up steep steps to a room sealed off from the bottom levels with wooden doors. Dark red couches lined the walls and people dozed off. I smelled marijuana, but it was a thicker, earthy smell. Would we end up in prison? I heard there were informants who arrested people. My hands turned icy.

"Second story is smoking," Mohammed said. "This café is fine. Safe. No one comes up here to check." I wasn't sure how much of a risk we were taking. But the room seemed cut off from the street, a sealed place. It was dark as we sat down at one of the large wooden tables and ordered couscous and chicken. Youssef pulled out a pipe and offered us each a puff. I had smoked marijuana with the artsy crowd quite a few times by then in Aix, rocking in a circle at my friend Catou's house to the bluesy sounds of John Mayall and poetry we read out loud to each other. Worry slipped off my shoulders, rocking and rocking as darkness fell. I had changed from the purely outdoorsy kid, with my white ski jacket splattered with blue flowers, refusing to ever buy cigarettes for my sister. "That's gross," I said, "inhaling smoke into your lungs." Now I was a heavy smoker and loved to open the Gitanes cigarette package with the figure of a woman sitting on a smoky cloud, framed by a Mediterranean sky-blue background.

During freshman and sophomore year of college, Joe and I only smoked grass once late one autumn night and made electric love while listening to *Surrealistic Pillow. Don't you want somebody to love.* We skied on nearby slopes and went on hikes. My mother liked him because he was kind and handsome. I didn't know how my father felt. But the summer after we were first together, Joe went off to work with the American Friends at an Indian Reservation. He wrote me beautiful letters with E. E. Cummings poems. One friend even asked, "Are you going to get married?" But one day at Washington Square Park, I met an artist in Greenwich Village who painted huge abstract canvases. He invited me on a motorcycle ride around Manhattan at night, and I said "Yes." We rode around the city, and he showed me the sparkling lights. When I came home, my mother said, "Joe called," and went back to her room. She didn't kiss me goodnight. Though I never saw that artist again, though I never even kissed him, part of me was pulled into a different and more difficult world. Something darker than Joe.

Joe's roommate, Eric, and I talked about French poetry, the I-Ching, and Jewish humor late into the night when Joe was working nights. We sat on a huge green couch, sometimes until 1 a.m. My mind and body began to separate. Intimacy with Joe and deep talks with Eric, talks that connected me back to my intellectual father, who loved poetry, Shakespeare, and wanted to die solving a mathematical equation.

"You're not intellectual enough," I said to Joe one day and then immediately regretted my cruel words. Tears flowed down his face.

Now, I took a deep puff and thought it was going to be passed around again. "One puff is enough," Mohammed said. A few minutes later, dizzy, I gazed at my plate of half-eaten couscous. The couscous had morphed into cotton balls, floating in a sea of sizzling, luminescent oil. My limbs, so wooden-heavy, I wanted to shrink to the floor. All the cracks in the table grew bigger, gigantic, and became cavernous holes. I glanced at Jaclyn, her hair waving like a flag in the wind, her face fuzzy with no eyes. The prison. 17 years. I had just smoked marijuana. We could be carted away.

Right now, my parents might be sitting in their comfortable black-and-white tweed chairs facing each other in a small sitting area in their bedroom, reading, unwinding from the day, martinis on the round wooden table. The house impeccably neat.

"This is Kef," Youssef said. "Very strong." The dark woody smell enveloped us.

Kef—the resin from the plant, powerful resin—I had heard about this and felt anxious. Where would we sleep tonight? My head was heavy as a watermelon. I just wanted a bed and a pillow to hug, to lay my body down to sleep.

"We can play you some authentic Moroccan music," Youssef said.

Men only want one thing. I heard my father's voice the summer day he said that to me as we walked together down 12th Street in New York City. It was 1968. The sexual revolution had swept through an entire generation. He and my mother must have thought I'd meet a nice guy, and they had big expectations for who that would be, find a career, maybe not in that order, and get married and have children.

My dad's voice sounded strained, and his body caved in as if he thought he *should* be saying this to me. Or perhaps my mother put him up to it. I was silent. I didn't know what to say back. I thought maybe I had let him down.

Women want sex, too, I wanted to say, but didn't. *We can have sex without marriage. We can use birth control. We can control our bodies!* So much had changed. Was I letting him and my mother down by not marrying Joe? Having sex without marriage? And now, smoking kef with strangers in Tangier?

Mohammed and Youssef inched closer to us, and their breaths smelled thick with a mixture of couscous and Kef. The heat from their bodies spread over me like a wind, their chairs too close. Youssef's thigh almost touched mine through his thin beige cotton pants. This could be the New York City subway. This could be anywhere, two women out alone, encountering men. Just as I knew to cross the street in New York, I knew we needed to leave.

"We're exhausted," I said, quickly moving away. "Thanks so much for showing us around." Jaclyn stood still and silent, then moved nearer to me, so we were shoulder to shoulder. I wanted her to say something, too, but she didn't. I didn't want to be in charge. My voice was sweet. I was polite. "Well brought up," my mother would say always reminding me to write thank-you notes when I was young.

"Thank you, thank you," I said moving away with Jaclyn next to me. Youssef moved back and forth again from leg to leg. Mohammed looked hurt. Specks of anger flecked his liquid brown eyes, but they didn't follow us, or try to touch us or grab us. They looked stunned as we raced down the dark wooden stairs of the café, swept into the crowds of mostly Moroccans as we were on the Arabic side of town. The European side of town had the fancy hotels. We didn't want fancy.

Jaclyn followed me as we walked through a maze of streets, now almost empty, until we found a cheap hotel. The lobby was sparse, just one green plant perched on the counter. A man snored in a chair and woke up startled as we walked in. "A place to stay, you need a place to stay?" he said, his voice groggy. "We have one room left. A good room. Twin beds."

"Yes," we both said in unison. Sleep. Sweet sleep. "Let flights of angels sing thee to thy rest." My father used to stand in the doorway of my bedroom when I was little and recite Shakespeare lines before I dozed off.

The concierge handed me the key after we paid for the

night, and we climbed slowly up two flights of stairs, our bodies worn out from traveling. Specks of dirt on the wall looked like thousands of tiny black bugs moving ever so slowly. I blinked a few times to stop the images and flopped on one of the beds. I forced myself to get up and use the bathroom and brush my teeth. Large windows overlooked the tiled roof of a mosque.

A half an hour later we both collapsed on twin beds that squeaked every time we turned or twisted. All the anxiety of that day thankfully vanished into the ether, at least for the night. Nighttime in North Africa!

The next morning, I rose early and from the window right over my bed I glimpsed the green tiled roof and old men going in and out of the mosque, sometimes sitting cross-legged on reed mats in areas shaded from the sun. How tranquil the old men seemed to be, all gathered together listening to the calls to prayer from the muezzin; singing and chants, minor key sounds that took me back to a past perhaps similar to this—my Jewish father and his ancestors, also sons and daughters of Abraham.

I was raised Episcopalian, my mother Christian, practical, determined and at times remote. I attended a progressive school which closed for Civil Rights marches. Many of my classmates' parents were Jewish and political, like my dad, fighting for equality for everyone. "Single payer healthcare." That's what we need, my dad said all the time. Mitzvahs, good deeds to do in this world, not the next one. Was I Christian, Jewish? Wasn't it all the same, to be a kind person? I often didn't know where I belonged.

Here, in the Arab section of Tangier, grief spilled into all my cells.

"I don't like anything in a minor key," my mother once said to me when I played the theme from *Exodus* on the piano, my fingers crying onto the black and white keys. She wanted me to be normal and not see my tears.

My mother's scars were on the outside, but her tears were inside her.

She wanted to soldier on.

In Tangier on the Arabic side of town, so much seemed to be in a minor key: grief was hidden in the labyrinthine alleyways and in the children with one leg, or one eye filled with pus, sitting on the streets begging. I longed to help them, to cure them. I wished I had brought the tiny tubes of antibiotic ointment my dad kept in the bottom drawer of his white wooden desk. It would take so little. I didn't want to turn away or keep walking, but I did, their sad stares and their tin cups forever etched in me.

The summer streets of Tangier teemed with people, and as we walked to a café to get breakfast, men approached us, some in slacks and shirts and others wearing long robes, offering to take us to get a drink or lead us to their houses. "Come here. I'll show you the best café. Psst—here. I have a store to show you. The best jewelry. Shirts." Everywhere, voices followed us. "Psst, psst, psst." The sounds started off softly then got loud as a hundred bees buzzing incessantly, "Psst, psst, this way, come here," as we got nearer to the stores.

How could we get away from these voices? Jaclyn and I locked arms and stood tall. Women in their culture never, ever traveled without a man. Once in Greece when I was hitchhiking, an old woman dressed in black spit on me. She was small and hunched over, her lips curling with disgust as she glared at me in my shorts and sleeveless top. She must have felt I was spitting on her culture, bopping around so freely.

We found a café, sipped mint tea, and pulled out our map, hoping no one would approach us. I sucked in my energy like I did on the streets of New York City to make myself invisible.

I looked at our crinkled map and found an area to camp the next night in Tétouan, an hour away from Tangier. We had heard of this place, so near to Tangier—a stop on the trail of "cool."

CHAPTER FOUR

We clambered up the steep steps of a bus filled with old women covered in headscarves holding squawking chickens; next to them, men in business suits perspired in the 100-degree heat. We were the only young women on the bus at that moment, and I felt overly exposed, my body an insult. Jaclyn had the window seat and fell asleep almost immediately. I lifted up my backpack and put it on my lap over my shorts. At least my legs were covered then. I folded my arms across my chest. Red raised itchy bumps splashed across my neck. All I wanted was to race into the cool water.

An hour later, we ambled slowly down to the beach in the excruciating heat, but a salty, cool breeze from the ocean misted the air and swept over our bodies. Under a wooden awning, sleeping bags littered the sand, and we searched for a space where we could sleep for the night. "Here, Louise," Jaclyn said. "Here's a space." She was excited to find us a spot, and I was grateful. We both dropped our gear down on our new home on the sand.

Some people slept; some kissed and made out under big blankets and a few people were far away on the beach, little human specks. The sand was cool under the awning, but our throats were parched. Jaclyn and I both chugged water. "I'm sleepy," Jaclyn said. "I'm taking a nap." She lay on top of her bag, her hand over her backpack, and fell asleep.

I wanted to run into the sea. Wellfleet 1954, I ran into

the sea every day. One day when my father took us to the beach, I wrapped seaweed rings around my fingers and my sister, Annie, lured by the cool water, ran with abandon into the sea. Daddy screamed, "Stop, Annie, stop," and raced into the water to rescue her.

Soon afterwards, when he was burned, he couldn't rescue us.

I crawled into my sleeping bag and put on my yellow two-piece bathing suit. When I emerged, filled with joy, about to jump into the water, I threw a thin cotton flowered dress over my suit and strode down to the water just as a camel train passed by, a man in long white pants and flowing shirt, leading four camels on the sand by the sea. The proud animals with their huge humps and spindly legs moved slowly. "Ken," I wanted to shout out. "Look at the camels!" He was far away, back in New York City.

Maybe I would ride a camel later on?

Swirling water caressed my knees. The water soothed my hot, aching calves and tunneled between my toes, my toes which were starting to get calluses, thank God. I waded for a few minutes, trying to decide whether to just run up the beach, throw my dress onto the sand and jump into the water. Everyone seemed far away, either under the awning or further down the beach. Should I go in? *Yes, no, maybe so, yes, no, maybe so.*

I couldn't feel an undertow; I didn't know about this water, this Moroccan water. Then I laughed out loud. Water is water, wet and cool and the sun was scorching.

It's time. I was just about to plunge into the sea at Tétouan when a wind swirled up, so hot and fierce I could be blown away, *really* blown away. Red dust ripped over my body and across my face. I was blinded. Dust coated the roof of my mouth. I clamped my mouth shut. I spread my legs apart for balance and anchored my toes as deeply as I could into the shifting sand, my hands protecting my face, covering it from the dusty, hot, steaming pellets. *Hold me on the earth,* I prayed.

Riding the New York City subway, scared I would knock into someone on the crowded IRT or fall on the floor, I spread my legs like this, strong as The Rockefeller Center Atlas holding up the world.

But I was not home, riding on the subway with its familiar stops. I was alone—as I began to feel more and more with Jaclyn—on a beach in Morocco. Like Dorothy in *The Wizard of Oz*, I could be whooshed into another reality. Wicked witches with green faces. Shrieking monkeys. An hourglass telling me my time was up.

I dug my toes deeper into the wet sand and hugged my arms around my waist. I closed my eyes, praying the red dust wouldn't blind me, as I wound my way back to the wooden awning. Just as quickly as it came, the fierce wind stopped. I wept with relief, dusty tears streaming down my face. Dust filled my mouth, making it hard to breathe. I had to tell Jaclyn. She was stirring in her sleeping bag, about to wake up. I wondered if she had completely slept through the Sirocco?

"That wind—there was just a huge swirling wind— the Sirocco. I read about the Sirocco—hurricane-force winds from the Sahara, stronger than the Mistral in France." Words tumbled out of my mouth. People went crazy from these winds. "Electrification of the atmosphere," I once read. Too many positive ions.

I could have been blown away, lifted on a tornado of red dust and wind. Jaclyn sat up and cocked her head, looking at me for a quick second, and then pulled out a book. Maybe she said, "Oh," but I couldn't really hear anything. We were not "sisters" together. We lived on separate planets. I don't think we even liked each other much anymore, though I couldn't bear to think that. It was just the two of us on this trip.

Ken would have given me a hug if I told him about the crazy wind. "Poor baby. Are you okay? How are your eyes? So dusty! Let's get some water." He would have seen the trickles of red dust seeping out of my mouth. Made a joke even. "You look like a dust monster!" Helped calm me down. Or at least looked up from his book for more than a few seconds. I collapsed on top of my sleeping bag. I missed Joe's arms around me at night. He tethered me to the earth when it was dark. I didn't like sleeping alone.

That night I slept badly, especially when I had to get up to pee in the middle of the night. We heard police officers raided the beaches even in the dark, huge flashlights shining into your eyes. They asked for passports and even if you had a passport, they shooed everyone away. Where would we go if that happened? Sleep on a bench?

My money belt with my passport was securely wrapped around my waist; some nights I opened the zipper and fingered the stiff, solid paper. That paper let me cross borders.

In the middle of the night, when nature called, I nearly tripped over other people in sleeping bags until I found a safe, secluded spot on the sand. Some of the pee got on my legs. When I got back to my sleeping bag, I wet a Kleenex with water and washed my legs. Oh, how I craved a warm shower.

The cold that night was piercing, not the hot, fierce wind that enveloped me just hours ago. I struggled to get warm. Sleep came in fits and starts; I held my arms together and rubbed my right foot over my left foot. I stopped saying my prayers many years ago when I decided I was a pantheist, believing God is in nature, and didn't believe in original sin or the words *We have erred and strayed from thy ways like lost sheep.* That night I felt so alone, almost as alone as the night when my parents were burned, when I slept in my neighbor's basement. The ceiling was filled with mold spores. Now, struggling to get warm, I said the prayer that my sister and I made up at the farm at four and six years old when I lived with my aunt and uncle. They sat with my sister and me upstairs on our double-bed the second night we were there. "Your parents are in the hospital," they said. "Why don't you pray for them?"

"We don't pray," my sister said but then thought about it. "Okay, we'll make up a prayer."

We each made up a line. We knew my mother was hurt the worse. We knew that they might not have her blood type in all of New York City.

We had to try and call our parents back to us.

God bless Mommy and make her better soon.

God bless Daddy.

God bless everyone.

God bless the whole world.

Dust still coating my eyes, I fell asleep.

We rose early, the sun a hot dome in the sky. Couples spooned, men and woman slept next to each other, some curled up like little babies, others on their backs, arms out, open to the world. I went to sleep missing Joe and woke up missing him. I had a crush on him in high school; we met at the American Youth Hostel on Eighth Street which organized hikes, sailing trips and ski trips and we both loved to ski, to dance down a mountain. He had a girlfriend then and once at a ski lodge I saw him lovingly help her get on her ski boots. I loved his easy kind laugh, blue eyes, tall athletic body, and was surprised and excited to see him at my university. We had both just broken up with someone so were free.

The first date he took me to an Italian restaurant with wine bottles covered with wax and Christmas lights strung permanently across the windows. "Nothing to be nervous about," he said as I nervously picked at the wax from one of the wine bottles, and it made a mess on the table. He didn't care. He looked right at me then as if he already loved me.

He was good at love.

I didn't know it then, but real love scared me. It could disappear.

Soon after that date, I woke up on his covered porch, our legs intertwined, and sunlight flooding the room. He played "Michael Wakes you Up at Dawn," Judy Collin's flute-like voice, waking us from a deep sleep. I didn't know where his body began and mine ended. He told me he loved me, all the time, not only when we made love.

I only said it back after we split up. Our last morning together we drove to *The Pancake House*. I wore a purple and black dress, and he had on his green wide-whale corduroy pants and a light blue shirt. We dressed up. We hardly talked. Later, he brought all my suitcases, and pots and pans to my new house. As he walked out the door I said, "I love you."

"Why couldn't you say that before," he said, not looking at me and shutting the door. I looked at all my stuff and burst out crying.

Weeks later we made love in the woods, a long hike in. No one was around but the trees. We climaxed at the same time and both cried. It was the last time.

Jaclyn and I rolled up our sleeping bags and shook them out. Sand coated everything and nestled between my toes, but I didn't mind. I loved the beach—salt water and briny smells.

The humans looked like beached sea animals in pods of two, four or six. Goodbye camels, I said to myself as another train made its way across the sand. We walked to the main street and again boarded a bus crowded with women, chickens, merchants, and a few other young American students. We got seats in the middle of the bus. I was glad to be next to the window. I fished through my backpack for snacks. My blood sugar spiraled up and down like my moods. I panicked until I found a stash of nuts, two oranges, some raisins and two pieces of slightly dried-out bread. Jaclyn had the peanut butter. I shared my orange and bread and dove into her peanut better.

"Protein," she said.

"Yes, protein." We needed protein as we had just made a pact. "No sugar for the rest of the trip." We shook on it like CEOs of a huge company. We could get as thin as Twiggy and wear mini skirts.

"I'm going to be a size 3," Jaclyn said. "Finally."

I wasn't so sure with my Russian Jewish zaftig thighs and backside from my father's side that I'd ever be a size three, so I didn't say anything back. Also, it was starting to feel too much like a competition.

After I ate my tiny snack, I rested my head by the window, scrunching my sweatshirt into a pillow, the thick cotton smelling of the sea.

CHAPTER FIVE

"Fez Fez," the driver shouted. Saliva coated my arm where I had rested my head for hours. People scurried to scoop up their belongings from under their seat. Jaclyn had fallen asleep, too. "We're here already?" she said, rubbing her eyes. "Where are we going to sleep? I don't see any hotels." Not many buildings right near us, and they didn't look like hotels. Small concrete houses. We were on the outskirts of town.

"We'll find something." But she grimaced and looked annoyed as if I should have reserved a spot somewhere.

It was getting dark outside. Nothing could stop that.

Where *would* we sleep?

A rotund and well-dressed man—suit, tie and pressed white shirt—was sitting across from us. "Put together." There it was again. My mother's words inside me. When the bus stopped, and we walked down the stairs and adjusted our knapsacks, he came over. "My name is Massoud. I would like to invite you as guests to our home." Welcoming guests was a central part of the culture. I knew that and hoped for this very moment, to be invited inside the house of a family who lived here.

Massoud looked at our faces (not our bodies), safe and fatherly. He clutched a black briefcase. "My wife would love to have two young American women to dinner. You can be with a family. *Real* Moroccan people." He even said the word, *real*. He was older, married. I didn't think ahead, about where we would sleep later. To eat with a Moroccan family was a dream come true. To break bread with people from a culture so different from my own.

Jaclyn looked at me, dark brown eyes searching for what to do, and I whispered, "Okay?"

"Okay," she whispered back. The Greek man that tried to rape me seemed fatherly too. But my backpack weighed me down. My skin itched under my arms and on the backs of my knees. I just wanted to wash up, eat and relax. My stomach ached for food.

We walked with him about two blocks to his home— arid land right near the bus station, a stop on a dirt road next to vendors wearing djellabas, long loose-fitting robes, while selling soft drinks and meat cooking on spigots. The rich smells made my hunger worse. His house was a huge compound. An old woman wore a long white skirt and white shirt, and sat cross-legged on a concrete patio, rocking and singing. She lifted up her head to show a toothless smile as we walked by. Women cooked in the kitchen. Exotic spices filled the air: turmeric, ginger and cumin. A few children raced by chasing red rubber balls. A small black dog barked from the second floor.

"Put down your packs. Please wash up and then come sit for a minute."

In the restroom I glimpsed my face in the mirror: slightly sunburned and sandy, especially around my ears. I washed up, ecstatic to have a restroom and feel clean, soapy suds washing away the dirt caked on my hands and stuck under my nails. Jaclyn went in next and then we came back and sat by Massoud. For the first time in a while—my muscles, my feet, even my mind relaxed. The hitchhiking, the evening with the guys in Tangier and the scary wind on the beach were all tinged with anxiety. I sank like a rock into a green-and-white-striped cushioned chair.

"You are students?" he said.

"Yes. We just finished our third year of university."

He raised his eyebrows and seemed impressed. Did any of the young women in his house have the chance to go to college? I wanted to ask but stopped myself. I already knew that many women in Morocco had no chance of an education and that they could go places only if escorted by men. We were strangers from a different world. But they had opened up their home, welcomed us into their lives.

Throw open the doors; throw open the windows. Crossing borders. Being grateful and humble. So many in our generation longed for this, a huge circle of hands of all shades and colors making peace, not war. A year later, John Lennon would write "Imagine." Years after that, my father would give me a book of poems written by Vietnam Vets who had seen too much, some who had lost their limbs. My father wrote in the opening, "To Weezie, who someday, I hope, will live in a world without war."

"We're traveling for two more weeks until we leave from Paris to go back to America," I said to Massoud. America. Even saying that word produced disparate feelings: I'd find a full-time job, probably typing through Kelly Girls, live with my parents, sleep in my old twin bed for the summer, which I didn't want to do, as I imagined a new boyfriend in my life—and there were too many things about my life they wouldn't approve of—sex before marriage, smoking grass—maybe I could afford an apartment in the East Village. A sublet might magically appear. My mind galloped from one thought to the next.

"Meet my son, Wasim, and his friend, Ali."

Suddenly two men appeared, as if spun from the air. His son, a tall and quite handsome man, shook our hands gently and then introduced his friend, a beady-eyed, overweight man whose gaze wandered down my shirt, stopping for a minute at my breasts and going even further down. I turned my body sideways, trying to avert his staring.

Damn it, I thought to myself. Where will we sleep? Nightfall was coming soon. Why weren't we shown to a room? How would we get a hotel, now? It was too late to just walk out into the darkness, two women alone.

A middle-aged woman escorted us into the eating area, where a huge, low, round table fit about twenty people, young and old, who had all gathered on the floor. The dog lay sprawled on his side on the concrete patio where the grandmother had been singing. Massoud's son and his friend were placed far away from us. I was relieved. At each place there was a water bowl for dipping our fingers. We ate with our hands—which thrilled me as dish after dish was passed around in colorful ceramic dishes—first salad, then a chicken and potato dish and then some figs. Many around the table spoke no English or French but they kept smiling at us—as others asked us in French where we were from, how long we would be in Morocco, what did we study at school.

As I sunk my hands in the warm water bowl, the fat from the chicken dripped off my fingers and I picked them out of the dish and licked them like the others did, savoring the swirling tastes in my mouth.

My mother was Miss Manners times ten. I would have never been allowed to lick my fingers growing up. When my father slurped his soup, my mother winced. "Hank, stop that slurping sound," she'd say. At 14 and my sister 16, *Tiffany's Table Manners for Teens*, two copies, sat neatly wrapped in gold paper and red bows under the Christmas tree. Annie and I just laughed when we opened the books, and my mother grimaced. I guess she had a point: to make us respectable. But it was already the beginning of the sixties. We were not going to be debutantes. The generation gap was beginning then and would get wide as a chasm.

I loved licking my fingers, one by one, my soft tongue soaking in the savory and sweet smells, then soaking my hands in the small cups of warm water like everyone else.

We were low to the earth on the colorful fabric cushions.

Massoud sat at the head of the table like a tired but proud lion, proud to show off his crew to the young American women. His wife sat next to him and looked tired. But right after tea and figs, he left abruptly without saying anything. His wife left soon after and gave us a watery smile.

Where did he go? Where did she go? *Come back. Come back. Don't leave us here.* I wanted to race after Massoud. How could he just leave us?

The compound had so many rooms, little square spaces. We could lay down our bushed bodies and spread out our sandy sleeping bags.

The women buzzed around the men. I offered to help. "No, no," one of the women said. "You are our guests."

Twilight descended through huge picture windows. My stomach was full. Jaclyn looked like she might doze off.

"Shelter from the Storm," Bob Dylan would sing just a few years later. "I came in through the wilderness a creature void of form. Come in, she said, I'll give you shelter from the storm."

We had shelter from the storm. I was even happy to be with Jaclyn, then, who had gotten up from the floor and was on the patio, throwing a ball to one of the kids and laughing. I liked her then as she and the little girl threw the ball to the dog. The dog kept chasing the ball and barking, back and forth, back and forth, delighted with all the attention. Darkness flooded the windows.

I had just done the final wash of my sticky fingers in the bowl of warm water in front of us when Wasim spoke. I was the only one left at the table.

"Only an hour's drive," he said. "An amazing landscape that you have to see. Then you can rest comfortably."

Jaclyn came back from the patio and stood next to me. I rose from the table with great effort, the effect of the long bus ride. Jaclyn looked at me nervously. I stood in front of the two men with absolutely no expression. Invisible. I'm transparent. Maybe they can see how tired we are? Exhausted.

Wasim and Ali had other ideas; no one was around anymore. The women chattered softly in Arabic in the kitchen, maybe about us. The other men, father and young sons, had disappeared. The mother was nowhere to be found. Children had been taken to their rooms, some looking back at us longingly, wanting to stay up and play. The grandmother was gone. Even the dog was gone, one or two balls still sitting silently on the floor.

It was dark. Wasim and Ali moved nearer to us.

"We insist, we insist," they both kept saying, almost in unison. "To escort you to the mountains," Wasim said. The way they said the word "escort" sounded gentlemanly. "Escort you above Fez to a wonderful hotel." They spoke English. Not crazy men drunk or on drugs. Maybe that meant something, that we'd be safe. I wanted to ask to stay here, at their family's house. Going to the mountains seemed inevitable. I didn't want to be impolite. This was their culture, not mine. They had opened their home to us, taken us in. Our stomachs were full of their food. Plus, where would we go?

"Two rooms," I said, threading my fingers together, anxious about the dark.

"Oh yes, two rooms. I'm sure of it." Ali still eyed me. Wasim was the cooler, more handsome of the two. He

glanced over at Jaclyn but didn't look her up and down as
Ali had with me.

"Jaclyn and I are tired. We'll go to sleep early." My heavy
eyelids slid downward by gravity, a blood-sucking fatigue
that spread through my whole body, especially after the
seven-hour bus ride and the meal. "We've been traveling,
all day traveling." I wanted to reinforce what I said earlier.
Wasim's father had taken us in, under his wing. Where was
his wing now?

Both men nodded. They were from *good* families. What
they said to each other in Arabic then, of course we couldn't
follow, but we had just been with the extended family. Everything felt surreal, the men's voices floating in the air,
disembodied. Unexpected. My mind did a re-run of the
past few days. Nothing bad had happened with the two
men in Tangier. Yes, they were disappointed when we left
the café, but they didn't run after us, or yell at us. We were
not harmed. I prided myself on reading people's faces.

One time freshman year at Madison, Wisconsin, I met
a man at a restaurant for a date. He was tall and thin and
always carried a book. When we sat down at a table, he
stared at me. His eyes had no depth, flat and dangerous as a
sharp blade. I excused myself and went to the restroom and
stayed there for a half an hour. Then I peeked out and when
I saw him look another way, I escaped and believed I had
escaped a terrible fate. I never saw him again on campus,
thank God. Wasim and Ali's eyes were not like that.

"Of course, of course," Wasim said. "Yes, you are very tired. Tomorrow we will go back, and you can say farewell to the family." Jaclyn and I picked up our backpacks and crawled reluctantly into the back seat of Wasim's car. A new car with leather seats. A moneyed car, so different from the clanking rusty car of the crazy man down the coast of Spain. Jaclyn and I both glared out opposite windows and didn't say anything to each other. That was the way it was most of the time. I think she thought this was all my fault, that we didn't get a room at the compound or a hotel. A few times, Jaclyn looked over at me anxiously. We could have just walked out into the night looking for a hotel. But the area was desolate around the compound. No stores. Not the crowded streets of the 24-hour city of New York.

The road up to the hotel wound through the mountains. I gazed out at the landscape but could glimpse little in the dark—maybe an outline of a mountain covered with snow. Something white glistened from far away. As if reading my mind, Ali said, "The Atlas Mountains. See the snow? Our country has snow, too," which was hard to fathom as the heat soared to almost 100 degrees during the day. If I lived here, I would have to stay inside a lot of the day or metamorphose into a reptile.

"Near Mount Zalagh," Wasim said. We passed by a lake. "Many wildflowers that you can see tomorrow," Ali said. Before it got completely dark, the higher up we traveled, I saw how lush the landscape became, so different from the beach and the dry hills and the camel trains. The hotel—a square terra cotta colored concrete building, was nestled among trees. The men walked in first. We tagged behind, lugging our overstuffed backpacks. "We can pay," I whispered to Wasim, who was filling out a piece of paper, though I was worried at how expensive it might be. I heard my mother's voice. *You're lucky to be able to travel. Many people are not so lucky. Conserve your money. Don't buy anything frivolous.* How could I ask my parents for more money? And to stay near two guys we had just met?

"It would be an insult to us if you paid," Wasim said. "It would be wrong. An insult to our culture. My family insists." The way he said the word "insult" and "family" was intense, like a strong wind. I stepped back from the front desk. The concierge handed us four keys.

In our room on the second floor, Jaclyn and I both lay down on our twin beds for a short nap before we showered. Heavy red curtains draped across the windows, shutting out most of the sky. I could still see a slice of the darkness splattered with stars. Even though this was some country place in Morocco, far from everything I knew—the hotel felt generic. Tissues by the bed. A small clock on one of the end tables. A rug. A bathmat. Tiny soaps wrapped in thin paper by the bathtub. The rooms were adjoining and only separated by a door. I was heartened by how polite the young men had seemed on the drive up. "Come talk for a little while," Ali called out. It was only 9 p.m., so we thought why not? Their two beds were on opposite sides of the room.

"I'm not interested in either of them. Are you?" I had said softly to Jaclyn just minutes before. She was brushing her long brown hair in the bathroom, until it glistened. I had just looked at myself in the full-length mirror after my shower. After swearing off sugar, my face was more angular, my arms thinner and even my thighs were less flabby. I liked my body now, a little closer to the skinny models on the pages of Vogue. The ones with ironing board flat breasts and tiny butts. Women who looked like children. I stood taller.

"Oh *no*," Jaclyn said, emphasizing the "no." "I'm not interested in either of them. Not Wasim, not Ali. Not at all. Not at all." She turned to face me and looked me in the eyes when she said this. All the nervousness about this night went away, leaked out my toes and pooled on the floor. We would be together, one force, a united front and say "No," even if one of them made a move. I was relieved.

I sat down on Ali's bed while Jaclyn and Wasim were on the other bed.

Wasim put his hand on her arm, moving his fingers back and forth. I looked at her from my opposite perch. She didn't push his hand away or say anything. I could see their bodies merging, Wasim's leg over her leg. Their breathing got louder, panting faster and faster. She didn't look over at me, not once. The conversation we had was now meaningless. My heart raced. Meanwhile, Ali, did the same thing, put his hand on my arm and tried to move it up and down, opening his fingers and put them on my arm as if he were stroking the keys of a piano.

"No," I said rather loudly. "I want to go to sleep."

Ali tried to follow me. He looked like a sad puppy.

"I'm going to sleep," I said.

"Please," he said. "You're so pretty and nice."

"No. No!" I slammed the door in his face, left him in the room with Wasim and Jaclyn, who were now beginning to undress each other in front of Ali. I locked the door so Ali wouldn't come in and took another shower to drown out the noises. Jaclyn could come in the other way when she wanted to. Ali could go outside. I knew Jaclyn had a key. As the water splashed over my body, tears stung my eyes. I didn't want to be in this hotel room. I didn't want to be with Jaclyn. I thought the trip would just be a happy one, a great adventure—I remembered the afternoon in the main square in Aix surrounded by the bustling market—when we spread our maps across the table at the café and then did a circle dance, holding hands. I thought that we might become great friends.

All I wanted to do now was get away from her.

The next morning when I woke up my pillow was wet. I cried in my sleep. I hadn't been raped or hurt. Ali left me alone. Jaclyn wasn't hurt either. She had consensual sex. Even though she promised to be with me—one force, united, sex with Hasim was what she wanted, and who was I to tell her what to do?

But why had she told me she had no interest in him? I felt betrayed. The breaking of trust. When I was ten years old, four years after the accident, I waited for my mother to pick me up on the corner near St. George's church, after girl scouts. I had a watch that I kept checking. A few minutes before she came, butterflies flooded my stomach. Could I trust my mother to be there for me? To not disappear again. She was never late.

Jaclyn's betrayal hurt, like a punch in my gut. How could I feel safe here, so far away from everyone I knew? How could I feel safe with her? I grabbed a tissue and dabbed my eyes and then looked over at the clock, 7:30 a.m. Jaclyn wasn't in the room. When I got up and went to the bathroom to brush my teeth, she came in through the side door. We didn't look at each other or say anything. The air in the hotel room felt sour. On the car ride back we both edged as close as we could to our opposite windows. The men dropped us at a bus stop. I hardly looked at the wildflowers on the way back to Fez. We didn't go back to the compound to say goodbye.

A few hours later, after walking through the labyrinthine streets of Fez, passing Berber women with tattooed faces, we were still not talking much; we climbed the steep stairs to the bus, taking us to Beni-Mellal. She never even said, *I'm sorry about last night. I know we made a pact.* I stared out the window, wishing she would go away. But then I'd be alone. Though it felt like there was not much difference.

Outside the city, hunched-over women washed their clothes in small streams and rivers and laid the colorful garments over the slate-gray rocks. The world passing by was eons away from what I knew, the sanitized apartment that I grew up in, washers and dryers in the basement. Such hard work, I thought, to wash all the clothes by hand. I wished I could leap off the bus onto those rocks and help the women wash their clothes.

Why was my life easier? My mother had a daily house-cleaner who did all the laundry. We always had extra rolls of toilet paper, extra shampoo and toothpaste in the linen closet. Evelyn, our housecleaner, even made my bed with crisp white sheets and hospital corners. Why did I deserve that kind of help? Why were some people so terribly poor? The accident that burned my parents didn't prevent them from going back to work, and my mother was determined to have the life they had had before. We moved to a beautiful, spacious Greenwich Village apartment with a doorman when I was 12. The building had Persian rugs on the wall and a courtyard filled with tulips in the spring. My mother's disfigured face would not take that away.

My father always wished he could have done more for his parents who worked eighteen-hour days and sent him to Yale, then died early, at 57 and 59. He wished, with a desperate sadness, that he could have saved his brother who died of kidney failure at twenty-four. He especially wished he could have stopped the accident that disfigured my mother's face and hands. He had nightmares of my mother riding a bicycle in front of him, her long skirt billowing in the wind. "Dorothy, stop," he told me years later that he cried out in his sleep. "Dorothy, stop!" He tried to catch her but couldn't. To stop her from lighting the match.

Perhaps all his guilt and regrets seeped into my soul.

The bus kept going down windy roads. The women washing their clothes by hand disappeared like small dots of color into the landscape.

CHAPTER SIX

The heat was excruciating; beads of sweat clustered on my forehead. We were so happy to be off the crowded bus and in a small village, the *real* Morocco. Where *would* we sleep? "I'm Omar," a young man said, politely extending his hand. Tall, with deep-set brown eyes, he stood at a comfortable distance and spoke to us in English.

"The hotel here is not good, very dirty with bugs. You can sleep at my mother's apartment. She doesn't live there. No charge! I'd be happy to show you around." *Bugs, dirty*, the words swirled around my brain. I imagined black dots burying into my skin. My eczema would flare up, my fingers scratching uncontrollably at night. I might wake up with hundreds of specks of blood all over my body. No, we couldn't stay at a hotel with bugs.

Jaclyn, I could tell, was thinking the same thing. Her eyebrows arched again, and she started scratching her arm, then stopped. Omar looked at us with a wide smile. "Really, no problem at all," he said. "Then you're right near where the bus stops tomorrow. You're going to Marrakesh, right?" Welcoming guests was part of the culture. We were being welcomed and cared for. Should I trust him?

Of course, I didn't realize every tourist from Beni-Mellal goes to Marrakesh. I just thought how smart he was—to know where we were going. Though I had grown up in a huge city and seen so much on the streets and in the subways, I was soft around the edges. Why not give everyone the benefit of the doubt. I was privileged. Being turned away from Morocco the first time was the only time in my life I had been labeled as a "hippie" troublemaker. I didn't grow up with the sound of gunshots. My parents had more than enough money. I never saw people fighting or taken away from their homes, drunk or on drugs. I had the best medical care in the world. *People are good at heart.*

"Okay," we mouthed and followed him down the road to his mother's apartment—a small rectangular one-bedroom with a kitchen, bathroom with a shower. Nothing fancy. But very neat as he promised. A wooden kitchen table. Twin beds on opposite sides of the room. Light brown cotton curtains. Windows only at the front of the house by the driveway. The apartment was walking distance from the bus and the road. The road to Marrakesh. *Wouldn't you know we're riding on the Marrakesh Express.* So close now.

He handed us the keys. "I'll be back later to show you around and take you to a beautiful village in the mountains. Only local people know this place. It's special."

Years later, I can look back at my twenty-year old self and say that was stupid, so stupid. Travelling in Morocco or anywhere in the world without a man at that time was stupid. We were easy targets. But with all the strength I could muster up inside of me, I longed to feel safe without my parents, without their privilege, accomplishments, and perfectly manicured home. That I, Louise, Weezie, that little girl who lost her parents for nine months and became terrified of the dark, that little Weezie could make it in the world.

In the shower the water tumbled over my body. I put cortisone cream on my rash, little sample packets my father had given me before the trip, and washed my hair and dried it with a big fluffy striped towel that hung neatly on a rod. Jaclyn showered after me while I sat on one of the beds and pulled out some postcards I got in Fez. I chose one with an image of huge pots of colored dyes to write to my sister in Montreal. I knew she'd like all the vibrant colors. She had moved to Montreal for college and ended up staying there for over ten years. I told her about the mosaics, about the crazy guys—but nothing *really* bad happened and about the women washing their clothes by the rocks. I didn't say anything about Jaclyn because I was afraid she'd read it. I wanted to say, *I'm lonely. I'm scared. I can't trust her. I don't know much about the culture.* I ended with "I miss you." I'd mail it from Marrakesh.

Omar knocked on the door after our showers. "It's me," he said. "We'll drive. To see my professor, to the mountains. An emerald lake. And to show you the sights. Very, very beautiful, like nothing you've seen in America." We'd see the real Morocco, escorted by someone who lived here! We'd have an adventure. I hated being confined just because I was a woman. But there was a cost to putting myself out there. Men still ruled.

"We need about 15 minutes," I said, "to get ready." I liked that he had a professor. It eased my nerves.

I finished my postcard. Jaclyn brushed her hair, lots of

brushing so it looked shiny. There was a full-length mirror. We both spent more time than usual checking ourselves out. We had similar looks, about the same height, long brown hair, brown eyes, Semitic looking (she was all Jewish). Front view, side view. My shorts practically fell off me. My stomach was flat. We had both lost at least five pounds on our no-sugar diet—at least I had had no sugar. Cold turkey.

"I'm still losing as much weight as you. But I have an ice cream every day," Jaclyn had said the other day. I didn't know what to say back to her. I was annoyed she could "go off the diet" and not go crazy. If I tasted sugar, I couldn't stop myself.

Once on a ski trip in Vermont, Joe and I bought jelly donuts with thick sugar sprinkled on top and a surprise burst of raspberry jam inside. I couldn't stop eating them, two or three donuts at a time. Why? Was it Joe? What was wrong with me?

We skied every day. We made love every night. We listened to the Beatles sing *Michelle Ma Belle*. It snowed outside and coated the world in a wondrous white blanket. Such a mixture of sadness and joy.

Did I stuff myself because of all the things I couldn't say?

Omar knocked again, a bit too aggressively for comfort. "Coming," I said. "Just a few more minutes."

We grabbed our money belts and passports, hid them under our t-shirts and walked out the door. We walked together, the three of us, not saying anything. Jaclyn and I slid into the back seat of an old, rusty-red car. The car made clanking noises.

Just minutes after we got into the back seat, after driving only a few blocks, he pulled into the main strip of town—a few blocks with some food stores and a Laundromat. Suddenly, three guys piled into the car. They tried not to sit too near to us and talked with Omar—one of them sitting up front and two others in the back. Jaclyn and I scrunched closer to each other. I put my right hand in my left hand and squeezed them together. The young men were laughing and friendly. One was quite tall and thin and the other stocky. For a minute I panicked before the car ascended the mountain. *Men just want one thing.* I could hear my father's voice. *Stupid, stupid. What a stupid thing to do*, my mother would be saying. *We didn't bring you up to ride to the mountains with strangers.* Demand that Omar drives us back to the apartment?

The two guys tried to be polite and held their arms close to their bodies and not touch us, but there was no way—they were now squashing Jaclyn and me so much—four people in the back seat—I had my legs on top of her legs. "What do you want to do?" Jaclyn whispered to me.

Before I could answer, Omar said, "My school friends. We all studied with the same professor. He lives high up in the mountains by the green lake." The car made a quick turn and climbed up a mountain road.

My breaths had been shallow for the past few minutes. When I heard the word "professor" again, I took a deep breath and my body loosened into the car seat.

Dry brown earth moistened into greenery as we rose higher. The four guys all talked in Arabic; occasionally, a French word stuck in there that I tried to listen for, decoding their lives and what we were about to do.

Where was Ken? Bopping around New York City now. So far away. I missed a real best friend. A guy for protection. Jaclyn stared out the window. The guys in the back seat relaxed, their bodies stretched out, so all the sweaty smells mixed with the exhaust fumes. I started to feel sick.

The car ascended into the mountains, hairpin turns with steep cliffs. I clutched my stomach, gazed out the window. *Please God,* I whispered, *let us stay securely on the road. Keep us safe.*

"Forty hairpin turns!" That's what the ad said for a bus my mother took years ago in Switzerland when she went to a nursing conference. The bus in front of hers catapulted down the cliff, a mess of metal and screams. No one survived. My grandmother saw it in the newspaper and thought it was my mother's bus that went down, that my mother didn't escape that time. But she did.

The lake suddenly emerged as the car climbed the mountain. "Très vert, très vert, very green, very green," the boys said and then stopped talking. If a color could rule the world, if you could bow down to the God of green, this emerald green was deeper and purer than anything I had ever seen, even more beautiful than the emerald ring in my mother's jewelry box that she said would be mine someday. Emerald was my mother's birthstone. I wanted that ring encircling my finger now. For protection.

The car rapidly turned into the mountains, and for a minute I thought we were driving directly into granite. We clattered down a dirt road for what seemed like forever, the suspension making clanking noises.

"We're at the professor's house," Omar said. A small wooden house loomed in front of us, a little abode sunk into the side of the mountain.

Jaclyn had fallen asleep, and my leg was numb under her leg. I nearly collapsed on the ground when we got out of the car.

"Let me help you," Omar said as I steadied myself with his arm. Jaclyn rubbed her eyes and heaved herself out of the car. She stood close to me as we all walked into a huge room with a massive wooden table. A small toothless man laughed as we entered. We sat on one side of the huge table and the professor on the other. He looked like a little boy with his missing teeth and spectacles half falling off. He could have been a guru, the way he said each of the young men's names. When Omar introduced us, the professor said our names very slowly, "Lou-ise and Jac-lyn." Then repeated, "Lou-ise, Jac-lyn," and burst out laughing. I found it odd that he didn't speak any French. He was a professor? Most people with an education in Morocco spoke French and some both French and English. Jaclyn looked at me and giggled, and I started laughing too.

"Food, food," he called out in English. A rotund woman appeared, carrying plates of chicken and couscous. The young men wolfed down their food like ravenous animals.

Two of them sat on each side of the professor like the lions at the New York Public Library.

"Hungry, hungry," the professor said, and pointed to Jaclyn and me. "You, eat, you eat!"

My stomach settled down. Here we were down a dirt road by an emerald lake in the Atlas Mountains—with Moroccans who lived here. Another home we had entered, crossing borders. I ate my whole plate of food. "Thank you for the food," I said. Jaclyn moved closer to me, her right arm touching my left arm.

Where would we go next? Through the huge window I could see that the sun was going down. "Let's ask them to take us home soon," she whispered to me, in a high-pitched whisper. Hairpin turns. In the dark. Everything is fine, I wanted to say.

Things blow up very quickly.

"OK," I said to Jaclyn a little too loudly. The boys and the professor spoke in Arabic. Two of them glanced our way for a minute, eyes darting from us to their food and back to the professor. The woman bustled back in, smiled at us and took our plates. "Thank you," we both said again. "Thank you."

"We're getting tired," I said to all the boys. At first they didn't hear me or didn't want to hear me. "Sorry but we're getting a little tired," I repeated. I put my head in my arms and faked sleep. Omar picked up his head for a second and nodded.

They were on the other side of the huge table. A gulf between us.

Home. Tonight, our home was a small apartment by the bus stop *in the middle of nowhere.*

Across the table, now empty of plates, the professor talked with his "students"—and then the boys rose. "Goodbye, goodbye," the professor said as we walked over and took his damp hand. "Nice girls," he said, looking at us with his broad toothless smile. "Nice girls."

When we squeezed inside the car again, four of us, Jaclyn, me, and two boys in the back seat, the space seemed smaller. "I'm squashed," I wanted to whine, like I'd say when my sister gravitated to my side of the back seat. "Annie, Weezie," my childhood nickname, "now behave," my mother would say in her firm voice. I missed that firm voice.

"We're going back to the apartment, right?" I said to Omar. The air was saturated with a wild silence. Too many men. A musky, masculine smell. It had been a very hot day. The green lake had turned black, all the exquisite color sucked away.

"One stop," Omar said. "One stop at a village. A Berber village. You meet Berber women." Berbers—my eyes widened and so did Jaclyn's. The Berbers were from an ancient culture. That's all I knew. I never dreamed I would meet Berbers on this trip. "We just stop for a little while and then back to the apartment."

Jaclyn and I had to stoop to enter the arched doorway of the brown mud hut, an igloo made of dirt packed together—where four Berber women lived, rain, shine, heat, cold. They laughed as we all entered a small room. The boys stood to one side. Three women swooped toward us wearing long brown dresses and flowing yellow scarves and took our hands. Their eyes, heavily painted with kohl, glowed like minerals in the earth. They spoke little English or French, so we just followed their gestures and entered a tiny alcove with a mirror. Two women carefully brushed kohl into our bottom eyelids and then told us to look. "Pretty, very pretty, look, pretty." We both had dark brown eyes and the kohl made them glisten, too, just like the Berber women. Then they put yellow scarves around our necks. They giggled when they looked at us with kohl and flowing scarves and gestured for us to follow them back out to the room. One woman smoked a cigarette, which I thought was odd. I had hardly seen any woman in Morocco with a cigarette in her mouth. The men still stood on the periphery, expressionless.

The Berber women gestured for us to sit around a small fire pit where one woman put water in a kettle for mint tea. Another woman offered us small candies dusted with sugar and then offered the candies to the men.

"Sing," one of the women said and giggled, "sing!" The first song that came to me was from the Beatles, "Michelle Ma Belle," and Jaclyn and I sang very softly at first and one of the women gestured to make it louder and we sang it again, louder. "Michelle, Ma Belle, ...these are words that go together well, my Michelle..." The three women clapped their hands. Then one of the older women served us mint tea, the leaves floating in the hot water. I thought of my

grandmother, my mother's mother, who read my fortune
when I didn't see my parents for so many months. We were
sitting outside in a garden. I was four years old. She poured
a cup of tea. "Look closely inside the cup at the tealeaves,"
she said. I saw funny black shapes floating at the bottom of
the cup.

"A package is coming," Grandma said. "A package is
coming, and a letter," and she was often right. How did she
know? The letters from my mother didn't have her handwriting, my sister said. "They might be dead," she said to
me one night, her bottom lip curling down. Tears welled in
my eyes.

Here in the house of the Berber women, I wondered
what my fortune would be. Would it be good?

Then we sang, *"All you need is love, All you need is love,*
all you need is love,

All you need is love, love. Love is all you need.

Love, love, love, love, love, love, love, love, love."

The men were smiling now, standing apart from the
women. I felt close to Jaclyn then. We were sharing something precious, crossing these borders that many never
cross. In a mud hut way up in the mountains. The yellow
scarf wrapped around my neck made me feel regal, like a
queen. How generous these women were, sharing their sugary treats which probably cost a lot of money, these women
who lived in a dirt hut and cooked in a pit in the middle
of the floor. Suddenly, I saw them move in towards each
other, three of them like the points of a star, and they sang

to us, their voices rising way up and falling way down into a grief-like wail, the minor key sounds that now seemed to rise out of the mud hut, their faces turned slightly upward.

I took a sip of warm tea, and we were in a circle now, all the women, and we held hands rocking to the songs as the hot water boiled in the pit. The men still stood far away on the periphery, as if this was a place they could never enter, perhaps mesmerized for a minute by the strength of so many women singing together. Sisters from two continents, so many light years between us. We all stopped holding hands and gazed at the fire pit for a moment. The fire was now embers. The songs had ended. I felt cold and just wanted to get back to our apartment. Our home for the night. The place with no bugs where we could rest our tired heads and bodies.

I put my head on my hands and yawned, gesturing to the men that we were tired. The women took us back into the alcove where we gave them back their flowing yellow scarves and hugged each of them. The men simply raised their hands to say goodbye.

When we left the small arched doorway and then looked back, the three of them were standing outside in the cold, shivering and waving. They looked like young innocent girls then, with yearning on their faces, as if they wanted to go with us, perhaps go with us to another life. One of the women, the youngest and shortest of the three, looked at me and sang, "Michelle ma belle." Tears sprang to my eyes.

Many years later I realized that because they wore not

only kohl but also lipstick and one of them smoked a cigarette, they were probably prostitutes. At the time, I just
thought they were friends of Omar's. The "professor" might
have found men for their "business." Here we were, finished
with our third year of university, eating their sugar-dusted
treats.

They would never get an education or have a chance at a
career they loved. They might not ever marry or have children. They might die early of disease. Their families probably abandoned them.

They would probably get very cold at night.

We slid out the door into another world.

The road was pitch black when we drove down the
mountains. Omar was driving too fast. The air felt stale,
so many people breathing in a small space. Jaclyn had fall-
en asleep on one side of the back seat. She was breathing
heavily with her mouth open. The guys started talking in
Arabic. Talking extremely fast. They didn't seem to notice
that I was awake. Omar seemed distracted and there were
hairpin turns. My stomach hurt, sharp, gassy pains. Did
something in the food make me sick? I didn't want to get
sick in Morocco, with only Jaclyn in a small town. Where
was a hospital?

Panic crept into my body again, as if someone had in-
jected icy-cold water into my veins that spread from head
to toe. A global loneliness took over. Who could I talk to?
Was there even a doctor in this town?

I imagined myself careening off the road in the middle

of North Africa, plummeting, crashing down the huge cliffs below. My life ending faster than birth. Suddenly the roads flattened. We entered the town. I breathed deeply. Omar deposited us at his mother's house and said an abrupt goodnight. His eyes moved back and forth as he talked in Arabic to his friends.

"Thank you for everything," I said. Jaclyn almost fell out of her side of the car, she was so sleepy, and I walked to the front door of the house and turned the key in the lock. The car left the driveway. "Hope to see you tomorrow!" I called out. "We'll be leaving early." We went in and double-locked the door. "Let's leave them some money," I said to Jaclyn. "They were so generous!" We changed into our nightgowns and got into our beds, our twin beds across from each other.

About ten minutes later we heard a knock at the door. One, two three knocks. Hard knocks. Knocks pounded with a fist. My body shook.

"Go away," I said. I could hear my voice catch, as if I might cry.

"Go away," Jaclyn said. Her voice was strong now. In charge. Different.

"We're going to sleep," I said, my voice trembling. Someone walked away.

We got down low on our beds. And then another knock, a loud, sinister knock, this time on the window. Jaclyn crept over to my bed, and we lay down next to each other. We could hear each other breathe in and out, in and out.

As a little girl I had trouble sleeping. Shadows on my wall turned into evil monsters or hairy spiders. When my sister came to bed, a half hour later because she was older and had older sister privileges, I finally relaxed into sleep.

Jaclyn pulled out a razor blade from her razor, the one she had used that afternoon to shave her legs. I got a small knife, one I used to cut fruit. We placed our weapons under our pillows.

"Go away. We're going to sleep. Don't come back!"

We're calling the police. We'll call 911, I wanted to yell. We weren't in a city. Were there even police around here? Who would protect us? Our parents, who had protected us for all those years, taken us to doctor's appointments, gotten us medicine when we had fevers, provided food and shelter, could do nothing. *Stupid, stupid thing to do.* I could see my mother and father shaking their fingers at me. I heard the sound of a car's engine running outside the house. *God,* I prayed, *make that sound go away.*

I looked at the stripes on the bedspread and counted them, one, two, three, four, five, yellow and brown, like the dust of Morocco, yellow and brown. Dust. Dust to dust. *You can stay at my mom's place.* I could hear his voice, so educated. So polite. So much like a gentleman. How he stood far apart from us. *Men just want one thing.*

How could he do this to us? Was it he and his "boys"? The car buzzed like a giant insect, circling and circling the driveway for the next interminably long twenty minutes. Another knock on the window. Even louder. We silently clutched our weapons. The headlights glared through the window. I imagined the worst—a break-in—and rape. *Our father who art in heaven...*Take me back home. *Hallowed be thy name.* Take me home. *Thy Kingdom come. Mama, Mama,* I whispered. *Daddy, come get me. Make it all right. Take me home.* Where was my doll, her soft fabric against my face, to look at her serene, unchangeable face?

My doll had been misplaced somewhere in Aix. I thought I didn't need her anymore.

Finally, the car drove away. We tossed and turned all night, terrified, listening for the buzzing of the car, or the chilling knock, knock, knocking on the window, one pane of glass, a thin membrane that separated us from danger.

Jaclyn sighed all night in her sleep, and I tried to drift into some other realm, but I couldn't sleep at all. The next morning, as soon as the sun rose, we quickly packed and left a note. "Thank you so much for offering us this place. We left early." We didn't leave any money.

Who knocked on the window? Probably Omar and his friends. We'd never know for sure. That's why we thanked them.

We left the key on top of the note, strapped our backpacks on our backs, opened the door, and marched to the open highway.

CHAPTER SEVEN

It was 6:30 a.m. We walked past small boxy houses like the one we stayed in, past one grocery store, shuttered and closed, and past a few cars moving slowly through the one-strip town. We walked briskly, looking backwards to see if anyone was shadowing us.

"It's hot already," Jaclyn said, putting on her hat. I did the same. We had a couple of bottles of water but no food. Gandhi lived on only water for 21 days. We could make it for quite a while.

Please don't look for us. Please don't follow us, I prayed as we made our way to the road.

In another hour or so, the heat would swell to over 100 degrees. We couldn't stand out on the highway for too long, hot and hungry. Jaclyn wiped small pearls of sweat off her forehead. The road looked desolate, except for mirages of water, little oases of nothing. We stuck out our thumbs.

Only five minutes later we saw it: a big car with a couple in front, and they stopped! A woman threw open the back door as air-conditioned air bathed our bodies with a piece of heaven. We threw ourselves and our backpacks into the back seat and shut the door.

"Please, make yourselves comfortable. I'm Jenny and this is Michael. We're happy to help out! Where are you going?"

"Marrakesh," I said, "we're going to Marrakesh." I loved the taste and feel of the word Marrakesh in my mouth.

"Well, you're lucky because that's where we're going. You've got a ride all the way. We just got married and are taking a trip in Morocco!"

I almost kissed the back of the car seat I was so happy. All the way to Marrakesh.

Jenny was short with a wide-open smile. Michael was tall and wore spectacles, a professorial type. He spoke little except to ask us about ourselves. "A trip after junior year abroad," Jaclyn said. When I told them I went to the University of Wisconsin, Michael relaxed more. It turned out they were both from Milwaukee. Maybe he thought we were carrying drugs. Jenny's lap was piled with guidebooks and maps. Just like my parents would have done, maps and schedules.

All familiar and safe, even though I didn't really want familiar on this trip, to be rescued from what I already knew.

Jaclyn and I were so beat we fell right asleep in the back seat. We had hardly slept the night before. I cradled my head in my hands on the window, breathing in the cool air, and woke up occasionally to see deep gorges, verdant hills and dry earth all at the same time.

The landscape shifted, more desert-like, dryer, browner. We stopped for lunch. "One of the best places in this area," Jenny said. "They have sandwiches American style. Our treat." The place was set up like an American diner. Cool air relaxed us into the red vinyl booths.

We had been eating no sweets and only small plates of food for the past week. Our clothes hung off our bodies, which we loved as we wanted to return skinny and tan. That was what the magazines told us to look like. Now we ordered buttery grilled cheese sandwiches and large Cokes. As I finished the last sip of my large sugary soft drink I panicked. Would my thighs suddenly balloon out again? My stomach bulge? Glossy pictures of perfect models with perfect-looking bodies slammed into my consciousness until I made them disappear.

Tomorrow's another day. But could I control myself? Would this be a slippery slope, from grilled cheese to rich pies? I remembered climbing on a stepstool to reach the marshmallow fluff my mother hid from my sister and me, and I chased after it like it was the holy grail. Jaclyn didn't seem to care. "I'll eat better tomorrow," she whispered to me.

Michael generously paid the bill and we slid into the backseat of the air-conditioned car and drove for another hour.

"Here, right here," Jenny said to Michael. He took a sharp right and we drove down a long driveway to a huge rug factory. As we entered, beautiful gold, red, and green-patterned rugs were being woven on large looms which filled the huge factory. Shockingly, many of the workers were small children, six or seven years old, their tiny hands pulling thread. I stared at the small children who never looked up from their looms. Jaclyn stood near me and had trouble keeping her eyes open. She always seemed to zone out.

Jenny and Michael walked back and forth in the huge

loom-filled room, puffed up like strutting birds with their determination to buy something. They picked a rug from one of the huge piles next to the looms, red and blue. They filled out papers, which took over fifteen minutes, to have it shipped back to Wisconsin where it would be exotic in their suburban house.

I wanted that, too, exotic things to bring back, but if that rug was in my house, I would only see the tiny hands on the loom, the small, fleshy palms of the children laboring for hours each day. But what other choices did the families have to eat and have shelter? Easy for me to say they shouldn't be working. But would that mean—starvation? For them and their families? Why couldn't they go to school like children in America? New outfits in September. Carrying lunchboxes with their favorite princesses and superheroes splashed on the front. Why were they so poor? Could we help them?

As we left the factory, Jenny stuffed the papers into her purse, and she and Michael excitedly talked about where to put the rug. "The living room, of course," Jenny said. "Or maybe the foyer, when you first come in?"

I suddenly didn't want to be with them, as I didn't want to be with my parents who had created a beautiful home with exotic things. But my parents, especially my dad, would have been upset by the child labor. How could Jenny and Michael just gloss over the child labor?

"But the rug will get too dirty in the foyer."

"Yes, sweetie, you're right. The living room it is." They

held hands and leaned into each other, hips and thighs touching. I missed having a boyfriend, interlacing my fingers with the fingers of the person I loved.

Would I meet someone when I got back to New York? "I have a new boyfriend. I'm happy," Ken wrote to me before I left Aix. "I have a friend I think you'll like. My best friend from summer camp. A filmmaker. I miss you. I love you." I carried the letter in my backpack.

We followed Jenny and Michael outside into the blinding sunlight. They didn't talk to us about the rug. They saw me staring at the children.

I learned later that these factories relied on the "nimble" fingers of children to help with the complicated designs. They also relied on their good eyes—so they didn't have to spend a lot of money on lighting. These children were as young as six or seven and later were often ill or died early from lung diseases. Their lives were spent breathing in dust and fluff from the wool. Some of the children were kidnapped and sold to the "loom masters." Other kids that I saw on the streets of Fez—beggars—crippled and blind— haunted me. What chance did the children have for a safe childhood?

I was in university. I would probably go on to graduate school, have a job I liked, "follow my passion," maybe be a writer and a professor. I had enough food to eat and clothes to wear. My parents could always bail me out.

When I worked in the Yakima Valley with the American Friends, the summer before I left for Aix, I saw children pick apples and faint on ladders, their bodies unable to bear the suffocating heat. One afternoon, little Julia fainted. Her mother moved her into the shade, worry creasing her face as she smeared water over her tiny daughter's parched lips and then tried to get her to sit up and take little sips, one after the other as she sang to her a lullaby in Spanish, words I couldn't understand. She sang and sang until her daughter moved and threw her arms around her mother's neck.

Would I ever have children? Would I really love someone?

We pushed on to Marrakesh, "the apex of cool."

Jenny and Michael dropped us off at the youth hostel on the Arabic side of town and they drove to their fancy European hotel. We thanked them profusely. Jenny and I hugged. For a minute, I wished I could go with them, to luxury and comfort, beds with crisp sheets and hospital corners, airconditioned air, fancy meals with linen napkins. But I was glad they were gone. The youth hostel was where I wanted to be, on the side of town where the people lived. Jaclyn decided to take a nap. I threw my backpack on my top cot and made a beeline for the souk, the main square. I craved time alone.

Walking through the labyrinthine streets, I soon realized only mad dogs and Englishmen would be out in the brutal heat of the summer afternoon. Beads of sweat pearled on my forehead. I missed the air-conditioned car.

I strode across the square and into the honeycomb maze of shops—store owners selling jewelry, rugs, food, mint tea, many calling out to me as I passed. "Psst, psst, discount, big discount." Wooden slats covered the souk. Those slats would protect me from collapsing in the over 100-degree heat.

Stray cats languished in shaded areas by big wooden doors. Clothes, scarves, pots and pans hung up high by the many vendors. The covered wood ceilings let me walk, at least a little without getting too hot, the striped shadows from the wooden slats' dark spots on the concrete and tiled floors. Young children sped by selling beaded necklaces. I bought six necklaces for my friends and sister and continued on my walk, past old men in long robes sitting quietly in the shadows. The sun beat down, scorching my body where the slats had broken off. I desperately needed a drink.

As soon as I sat down at a small table a young and quite handsome man approached me. Tall, brown hair, chiseled features and a kind smile. He was well dressed and spoke beautiful French. He said he was a university student. Of course, I had heard this line before. Was it true? University. Student. Professor. All the right words to pull me into the familiar. What I grew up with, education as King.

"May I sit with you?" he said. And we started a conversation. He asked me about myself and told me about his studies—a philosophy major. Perhaps he would be a professor. I was drawn to him more than to any other man I had met in Morocco. It had been so long since I had been with anyone, so long since I felt a man's arms around me.

"Do you want to buy something? Perhaps I can help you.

The Arabic price is the cheapest." He seemed sincere, so I gave him money for a long white shirt—told him my size, and he was off. I ordered a mint tea and sat back and rested, sipping the sugary liquid. Every once in a while, I looked at the clock and heard the monotonous tick tock, tick tock. At least 15 minutes had gone by. How far did he have to go? Fatigue flooded my body. The heat, the drive.

It was stupid to be out in this heat. *Stupid. Stupid.* I could hear my dad's voice. Sweat formed on my arms and so many flies landed there I stopped brushing them off. No one had warned me about the flies. Did they carry diseases? I looked at their small black bodies swimming in my sweat. I wanted to leave, but I didn't want to leave. I wanted my shirt. I wanted my change, as I had given him, as he said, more than he thought he needed. "You have to make do with your money," my mother said.

I wanted to be back at the youth hostel taking a nap inside where it was cool with three fans blowing in front of an open window in the women's dormitory. Plus, tons of stores were just a few footsteps away, and they *all* sold white shirts like I wanted. V-neck, thin cotton with embroidery around the neckline. A cool shirt from Marrakesh that I could wear in New York.

I stared at the clock. *What a stupid, stupid thing to do. Giving a stranger your money!*

I started to give up. Tears formed at the sides of my eyes. That was a lot of money to just give away. How humiliating to ask my parents for more money, money I might need before the trip ended. As I was about to pay the bill—wipe the flies off my sweaty arm and walk back to the youth hostel, he came back, smiling, his beautiful brown eyes glistening, my white shirt in his hand.

"Voici votre change," he said, handing me some coins, "and here is your shirt. I hope it is what you want."

"Parfait! It's perfect!" Tears still rested on the sides of my eyes. I hoped he hadn't noticed. We talked for a few more minutes—and he invited me to meet him the next day at noon.

"I can take you on a camel ride in the Atlas Mountains. Wear long pants, though! The camels are easy to ride." Many years later I can see how naïve I was, even thinking I would just go ride a camel with a stranger. But I wanted to believe so badly that people are kind—that they were simply welcoming me into their culture. Plus, he was attractive, and I was 20 years old.

Ever since the day at the beach when I saw the camel train, just before the Sirocco wind fiercely blew on the beach at Tetouan, I had wanted to ride a camel. To sit up so high! He would show me the countryside. I wrote down the information and said I'd be there—but I wasn't so sure. There had been too many near misses before with men. I didn't know him. Would he really take me on a camel ride? Maybe he picked up my thoughts. "You'll be there, won't you? Won't you?" I just nodded yes. I craved being with him, with a man. Feeling liberated to do what I wanted. Even have sex with a semi-stranger. My mind was racing ahead.

To ride a camel, finally. But I didn't know him at all.

That night, Jaclyn and I walked into the main square, our senses accosted by smells of spices—turmeric and curries—and the sight of monkey trainers, acrobats, and snake charmers. I recoiled from the ones who came near me, the snakes with their long tongues lashing out at the air from their captive state. Tourists had snakes coiled around their necks, reptilian scarves. One woman made an attempt to smile but looked terrified as her husband snapped a photo. Then the snake uncoiled from her neck and into the hands of the snake charmer, looking for his next victim.

Clots of people stood in circles listening to drummers; drumbeats that resonated from deep in the earth, ancient sounds. People swayed their bodies to the drumbeats, couples leaning into each other and rocking to the rhythms. Joe and I both loved to dance, and I wished he were with me, on that night, dancing to the drumbeats.

Wealthy tourists, student hitchhikers and poor children all mingled together—the children selling necklaces—which I bought—and cigarettes—that I wouldn't buy from the children. My dad was a lung doctor. I worked for him one summer. His waiting room was filled with patients with oxygen tanks strapped to their bodies. I had stopped smoking for a while, but I still craved a cigarette. I knew as soon as I left Morocco, I'd start again.

I ordered chicken and salad at an outdoor restaurant, and we talked with others at a long wooden table and listened to the musicians wandering from table to table playing the drums. North Africa flooded me with sights and sounds I had never seen before. I dreamed of traveling deeper into the continent—farther away from everything I knew. Schedules, school, a career, all the expectations of an "accomplished" life, whatever that was. But for now, my parents were paying the bill. Deep down, I wanted them to be proud of me. I knew I'd return to college.

That night I bought a square drum, made from animal skin with brown hieroglyphic designs, more necklaces from the children and a silver necklace with small purple stones for myself. I also bought some jewelry for my mother and sister and a book of poems translated from the Arabic for my father. I was glad to have these gifts as I had only a few small things to give them from the South of France.

The next morning, I glared at the walls from my top dormitory bunk, alone, hallucinating bright colors—mainly oranges and reds—colors that looked like sunrises. "The Marrakesh Express" still played in my brain but the needle was stuck on the record player. *Don't you know we're riding? Don't you know we're riding?* My fantasies of travel and new places were erased. Marrakesh. I had finally made it to Marrakesh.

I vaguely remember trying to drink water, but everything went through me. I was sick, seriously sick. Everyone in the hostel was gone, Jaclyn too.

I didn't think of going to the European side of town, to a European doctor. *Make do with what money you have.* Plus,

I was not a rich American—I was a student and one of the *real* people. That's what I still believed even as I got sicker and sicker.

The next afternoon, though, I asked Jaclyn to take me to a doctor near the hostel; someone told us about this clinic. We walked through the brutal heat for what felt like forever. I leaned on her, weak and dehydrated, my throat dry and parched. Jaclyn looked worried and also pissed off. This was not the vacation she wanted. My legs buckled as we walked up a huge flight of stairs to the waiting room. I wanted to lie down and sleep forever in one of the shadowy places under the wooden slatted ceilings, terrified that if I didn't get medicine soon, I could collapse. I had one bottle of water, but it was almost gone. Just a few warm sips left. I wanted Jaclyn to get some more water, but I didn't want her to leave me. She was quiet, her lips pursed as if she were angry.

When we went through the door to the waiting room, around forty people, many who looked extremely sick, from the very old to the very young, sat in chairs and waited. The room smelled of desperation and sweat. We luckily found two seats and I collapsed into one. A tiny sick boy lay in his mother's arms next to me. I immediately had to go to the bathroom that was mercifully empty. I came back and sat in the stiff wooden chairs. I clutched my stomach as if that would stop the churning. I waited. I needed medicine. I wanted my daddy. Jaclyn read a book next to me. An old school clock ticked loudly. What was time? My mother taught me to tell time and how proud I was when I finally learned, just like my sister. I loved the big clock on the wall in my room as a child, round as a moon. This clock ticked too loudly. Sounds hurt my ears. One small fan blew some hot air across the room. Some adults, even, had tears dripping down their creased faces. Sick children with glazed eyes tried to sleep in their parents' arms. I began to feel my eyes, too, were glazing over.

"Here you go, here you go," my dad would say and hand me a prescription or better yet, if I were this sick, he would bring the medicine to me. Or my mother would bring it to me. It would work in six hours or so. Always six hours. Half a waking day. I would have enough liquids, soup, and juice. My mother might brush the hair away from my forehead, take my temperature. "Sweetie, call if you need me." In high school and when both my parents were at work, I'd watch quiz shows or *Lassie* on T.V. in my parents' bed. In one episode, Timmy and Lassie leapt through small brush fires that threatened to devour the forest. *Run, run, run—escape the fire*, I whispered out loud when I saw the show. *Make it out. Don't get burned.*

Years later I realized I was always running away from fire.

Fire and love got meshed together.

My mother would call two or three times to make sure my temperature was going down.

I was an unlucky girl because of the accident, but I was also a lucky girl.

But not now. I wasn't a lucky girl; I had to wait so long. What was luck? What made you lucky? My mother's mother, my grandmother, Fanny, always wanted to bless me. She always wore a big cross around her neck and prayed silently before eating. "Grandpa and I pray for you every night," she said. But Grandpa had died. Could he still bless me and pray for me from heaven? Call me his little buttercup?

I had also done something stupid. I was told not to eat salad in Morocco. I didn't want to be like my parents, to follow an itinerary, to follow all the rules. "In the world of mules there are no rules." I loved that Ogden Nash poem but not following rules could be deadly. I had been distracted, like skiing off trail and getting lost in a snowstorm.

Jaclyn sat beside me, on the stiff wooden chair. The suffocating heat gripped my body. My stomach did flip-flops. I ran to the bathroom, praying that I wouldn't have to wait in line, but there were three people in front of me, one coughing so hard it sounded like her lungs would rupture. I came back and sat down. I tried to sleep, resting my head on the back of the wooden chair and then in my palms. Nothing felt comfortable. Plus, what if the doctor called my name and I missed my turn? I was number 45 on the sign-in sheet. I counted all the people who went in front of me, 19, 20, 21, one after the other while I waited, trying not to nod off. When I went to the restroom again, I hoped Jaclyn would listen carefully for NAYER. It might be mispronounced. Would she hear it? Could I trust her to hear my name? To listen so hard?

So many sick people. An avalanche of sick people. I always had "professional courtesy" growing up if I needed to see a doctor. Huge rooms with diplomas from Ivy League schools on the wall. Tastefully colored walls. Leafy green plants in the corner, a friendly receptionist. "Oh, you're Louise, Dr. Nayer's daughter! The doctor will be with you soon. Have a seat." I'd look through magazines, maybe *The New Yorker* or *Vogue*, and the doctor would come out with a friendly smile. "How nice to see you, Louise," he would say. "How are your parents?"

I had no professional courtesy here and was swept into the sad reality of poverty and not enough medical care. One doctor and a room overflowing with terribly sick people. I wondered if some of them might even die waiting. I wondered, for a quick, terrifying second, if I could die waiting.

My dad had helped start one of the first HMOs in America. He sometimes took paintings or food instead of money. His parents taught him to take care of the poor, not just himself. To give back. So many poor people in this waiting room and just one doctor.

"NAYER. NAYER," the doctor called out.

My legs and hands quivered as I lifted myself out of the chair and walked with great hope into the doctor's office. I sat down in a chair. He looked haggard. His white coat hung loosely over a thin frame. He wore spectacles and looked down at me. "I can't treat you," he said in English. Tears flooded my eyes.

"Why not? I need medicine. I'm very sick." Now my tears gushed down my face.

"I can't treat you," he said again and then whisked me out of his office, coming close to pulling me up from the chair and physically throwing me out of the room. "Look at all these people I need to see. My people. Look at all these people! Go away."

I could hardly talk as Jaclyn and I descended the stairs. I was a middle-class girl from America. A doctor's daughter. Why wasn't I at the European side of town, near Jenny and Michael? So many poor Moroccans sat in that waiting room, many with sick children on their laps, waiting and waiting for their medicine, and then a rich American comes in and takes one of their spots? I wanted to think of myself as a poor student, but I wasn't.

Now, too much time had elapsed to think, ruminate, cogitate, deliberate. You had to be deliberate to think, and I was losing that ability. Thoughts left my head and turned into blue, red, and yellow balloons that vanished in the sky. My parents could always wire me money, but I couldn't make that happen now or make anything happen. I was too sick, descending into hell when the hot air of the street hit me. People went by walking too fast. Why wasn't Jaclyn taking me to the European side of town?

I imagined what I wanted her to do. If she had been a real best friend, like Ken, this is what she would do. *I'll take care of you. Just relax. We're going to get help from a doctor who will treat you. Who cares about the money? I'll wire my parents and then you can pay me back. You're going to get better.* She'd hug me, say, "It will be okay." She'd whisk me into a cab, rush me somewhere, near where Jenny and Michael were staying—help me get better. Take charge. Red alert. 911. Flashing buttons. Screeching sirens. Ambulances.

In Malaga, at the very beginning of our trip when we jumped out of the crazy driver's car, I got ice for her, making sure she was okay. Where was she now? A buddy. I needed a buddy. These wretched thoughts drifted in and out of my consciousness. I was back in the dormitory.

Jaclyn walked back with me, but now she was gone.

I think she went shopping.

I managed to climb to the top bunk again, but my legs shook on each rung of the ladder. I wondered if my hands would hold me. I collapsed onto the thin mattress, smelling of my sickly, fetid, feverish sweat. A few words spun around and around, but it was a grinding sound I was hearing. My mind felt separated from itself, like puzzle pieces that don't fit. A round piece shoved into a square hole; all the edges ragged like a rip in my stocking. "Put nail polish on the rip," I could hear my mother's voice, bossy, comforting. "Don't throw them out. We've become too much of a throw-away society." I reached for my water bottle, thin, clear water. A bottle like a baby but no one held me. I was in a tunnel of animal hides. I could hear drums like at the souk the night before. People came and went, in and out of the room. No one noticed me. Then the room was empty.

Even moving my arms up was difficult. I saw my daddy standing in the doorway of my bedroom where I grew up, then heard him recite Shakespeare: "Good night, sweet princess. Let flights of angels sing thee to thy rest." But angels signified a darkness I didn't want to go through. I'm just 20, I thought to myself. Just two decades. Two sets of ten. Four sets of fingers on my hand.

Then I was Tinker Bell, the tiny fairy from *Peter Pan*, who held a mirror near her, lit by a lamp. She was always surrounded by light. In *Peter Pan* when Tinker Bell's light was dying, all who loved her clapped for her and her light returned like an epiphany. At first it flickered then died. But then suddenly, like a heart that starts beating again, the light surrounded her, and she could soar. My sister and I watched *Peter Pan* on T.V. and would clap and clap for Tinker Bell. How could such a sweet being die? Why did anyone die? I shivered and prayed I could keep some water in me. I lay still like a rock and tried not to move. Maybe if I stopped moving, I'd get better. My breaths were thready and shallow.

Had I been bad? I ate salad at the souk. I shouldn't have had salad at the souk. That was bad. Why did my parents return with burns all over their bodies? Did I whine the day they were burned? Not take a nap? Refuse to tie my shoes myself, one little stringy shoelace over the next? Count to ten wrong?

My eyes drowned with tears as shadows raged across the walls. My sister, Annie, and I played flashlight tag at night when we couldn't sleep. But these shadows came from the dark and not from the light and my mouth tasted metallic. I couldn't even spit.

"Help me, help me," my parents screamed when they rolled out their burns on the lawn in front of our Cape Cod cottage. The neighbor heard their shrieks. My sister and I heard nothing.

I couldn't even say the words "Help me." The dorm had emptied of people, only scattered knapsacks covering the five other bunk beds.

I conjured up all the people who loved me, even my dead grandparents I'd never met—my Jewish grandparents on my dad's side who came from Vilnius and died before I was born: *Lena, David, Uncle Philip,* who died when he was 22 of a kidney infection—*such a loss—such a waste,* everyone said. And then the ones I knew in this life—*Rev. Joseph and Fanny Daubert,* my mother's parents. My mother's father who called me his "little buttercup" and bought me books about animals at the 8th Street bookstore. *Mom, Dad, Annie,* and then names of best friends, *Nancy,* my next-door neighbor growing up, *Ken.* Lights still flickered chaotically on the wall above me. "Clap louder," I whispered to myself, "clap louder," as I thought of each new name. I heard the claps, quiet and then thunderous claps, like the drumbeats in the souk. Then I heard the door open. A tall woman entered, long red hair and blue eyes like my Aunt Rusty, who cared for me when my parents were burned. Aunt Rusty must have sent her. Perhaps she rode here on wisps of Aunt Rusty's red hair. She put her things on her bed and then saw me. I lifted myself up for a minute and stared at her warm blue eyes. She plopped her stuff on a free bed then came over to me.

"You're very, very sick. This is serious. I'm a nurse. Is it dysentery?" She had an English accent.

"Yes," I said, my lips parched, slightly bloody and so cracked that it hurt to talk.

She rummaged in her purse and found charcoal tablets.

"These will stop the diarrhea, but you need fluids."

I don't remember much more about that day. Bowls of chicken soup and bottled water emerged from out of nowhere. For the first time in three nights, I didn't get up in the dark to use the bathroom, my legs shaking each time, trying so hard to steady myself. I rested all through the next day; the colors that had danced across the wall, now turning white again. I took the charcoal tablets, slept for hours, and drank fluids. Little by little getting my strength returned.

My angel, my nurse, my miracle.

CHAPTER EIGHT

Jaclyn and I needed to get back on the road, our next stop Essaouira, and wend our way out of Morocco, back up the coast of Spain and finally to Paris, to catch our flight back to New York City. New York City. I could taste it, roll those three words in my mouth, and smell the musky odors from the heat vents, the restaurants, and in the hallway between apartments. I even missed the steaming concrete in the sweaty summer, the sickly-sweet smell of cotton candy and peanuts in the humid heat at the 14th Street subway station and the urine-coated concrete, where so tragically, homeless men and women lay slumped in doorways in the land of liberty.

I just wanted to go home.

That day when I was in bed and recovering, now eating cooked chicken and rice, Jaclyn wandered in Marrakesh with some of the other hostel guests, buying presents. I was glad we had a day apart. I felt like I had become a burden to her, and I didn't want to collapse or die with only her to take care of me. I had gotten so thin, but I wasn't trying anymore to get Twiggy skinny, to look like the glossy pages of *Vogue*; weight just slipped off of me. I could see my hip bones. My stomach was flat as a board. I felt she was looking at me with envy, her eyes scanning my body. I had gotten thinner than her. Perhaps boys would like me more.

Sex was the last thing on my mind. I would never meet the philosophy major for a camel ride. I never mailed the postcard to my sister.

The next morning, we left for Essaouira. As I walked through the main square, a little girl of four or five raced up to me holding beaded necklaces. I had already bought five or six of the necklaces. "No thank you," I said politely.

"Fuck you Americano," she screamed after me as more children appeared, surrounding me, this time trying to sell cigarettes. "Fuck you Americano." I walked away.

"Fuck you Americano," one of the little boys screamed again.

Jaclyn and I got on the road again. My backpack felt rock-heavy and my arms weak as a frail old woman's. We caught a ride to Essaouira. The driver dropped us off at the purple-painted "hippie" hotel, the cheapest in town. We staked out our places in the room, two single beds on opposite ends. I flopped onto the mattress and dreamed of sweet sleep. As soon as I put my head on the pillow, water dripped down from my forehead to my mouth even with a fan blowing right into my face. My stomach turned over, like an engine that had been temporarily stopped but was now rumbling again. I panicked. I ran to the bathroom, devastated. Tears exploded out of my eyes. I heard Jaclyn let out a sigh from her bed. "Are you okay?" she said, her voice flat.

"I'll be fine," I lied. Tears now streamed down my face, but I didn't want her to see and quickly wiped them away with a Kleenex and came out of the bathroom. I could hard-

ly stand up. I missed my father so much at that very moment, inside the brightly painted purple hippie hotel with
its longhaired men and groovy women, either on acid or
about to take acid or stoned. I didn't want to die here.

Jaclyn decided to do some shopping for her new and
thinner body while I slowly got up and walked out of the
hotel and down the main street, desperately searching for
a doctor. Then I saw it: A big sign on the second floor of a
building. Médecin. He was French. He must have studied
at a French University. I could talk with him. I climbed the
13 steps up to the office, no easy task even though I was 20
years old. I huffed and puffed in my weakened state. When
I entered the office, I asked a tall man to use the bathroom
(s'il vous plaît —la toilette?). I assumed he was the doctor
or maybe the doctor's assistant. There was no nurse or receptionist—perhaps away on a break? The doctor had a full
beard and politely pointed me to the right door. The small
bathroom was painted a bright white. The wall was covered
with photos of Essaouira, the main street, and the beaches,
black and white photos in silver frames. There weren't over
eighty terribly sick people waiting in the waiting room to
see him like at the clinic where I had been turned away. I
was the only one. I was so relieved. I had some traveler's
checks in my pocket. This would all just be a bad dream,
this awful pain, the weakness, and the vertigo. It would be
wiped out. Erased.

I washed my hands and face, took out a brush from my
purse and brushed my hair. When I glimpsed my face in

the mirror, I gasped. My face was always thin compared to my heaver (zaftig) thighs and "rear end" as my mother called my backside. Now I looked angular and a little like a Modigliani face on a long neck, but my skin was colorless and waxy, not filled with the pinks and reds of the women by the great painter. I looked extremely sick.

As I stepped out of the bathroom the doctor was right there. "Follow me," he said, now in English. His voice was kind, tender. Father tender. He would take care of me. I took a deep breath and my whole body unwound.

He led me to his office. I saw his prescription pad on his desk and wondered what his handwriting would look like when he handed me the prescription. I glanced at the diplomas on the wall, one from a French University. Montpelier. I breathed more deeply. I told him about my history in French and sank into a comfortable leather chair. "I ate lettuce at the souk in Marrakesh," I said. "I have been sick for almost a week. I've never felt this sick before. I hallucinated at the youth hostel. My mind feels strange as if I can't hold on to thoughts very well. I've lost a lot of weight. I feel shaky. My lips are parched. Even a bit bloody. Sometimes I have trouble peeing."

He sat behind his desk, nodding, while I said all of this and then got up and came towards me. I wasn't sure why? Suddenly he was awfully close to me, and his breathing was labored. Then he pulled a chair right in front of me and sat down and put his hand on my thigh and tried to move it up under my thin green skirt. I had put on a skirt and a white button-down shirt. I had dressed more formally to see the doctor. His breaths were shorter now, and he tried to rub himself against me, his penis erect through his light beige cotton pants. I can hardly remember even running down the stairs, my insides churning even more, feeling like I was running but probably just walking slowly I was so depleted, each step an obstacle to overcome, every limb so weak, and it was so hot outside and now no hope except hoping I could make it back to the hotel to the bathroom and just make it through the night. Just make it through and wake up again.

If only I could drink and keep the fluids down. The room had a teakettle, and I boiled water and drank one cup of tea and then another and another. I was feverish. My white shirt was soaked with sweat, and I rarely perspired. I must have fallen into a deep sleep, thank God. In the middle of the night, I woke up, still in my clothes, surprised it was dark outside as it was light when I lay down, the sheets soaking wet from perspiration. Something shifted in my body. The sickness had broken open.

Jaclyn slept on the twin bed across from me, her new clothes spilling out of bags on the floor, her breathing labored. She restlessly moved her head and arms back and forth as if comfort eluded her. For the first time on the trip, I felt an overwhelming sense of compassion for her—for us—for all we had gone through together—for all the danger and the illness. This was supposed to be a wonderful adventure. But it had been laced with terror. And Jaclyn, more than me, had grown up in a protected, suburban community. And she wanted to look good. To attract guys. Was that so terrible? We were both so young and knew so little. I had wanted to take risks, not be the little girl who looked out the window waiting for my mother to return from her 37 operations, terrified she wouldn't come home. With Ken, walking the streets of Aix, I felt strong, inside and outside, in charge of my own life. But I wasn't so sure that feeling would last. A terror, buried deep down, deflated me, kept me a scared little girl.

I got up early, pulled open the curtains a little and peeked out the window. I could see the sea outside, the long and blue sea.

"I just can't hitchhike anymore," I said to Jaclyn, when she woke up. "I'm just too tired."

Jaclyn was running out of money, too, but I think she was relieved we would take busses. We both counted what we had left and boarded the bus for Casablanca. I had trouble even climbing the six stairs to get on the bus, but we found seats in the front. I scrunched up my sweatshirt again, just like I did on the ride to Fez and lay my head against the window and fell asleep for hours. I missed all the landscape, but I was so tired and weak I didn't care.

We reached Casablanca, a crowded city where I bought a black-and-white-striped jillaba that I wore for years. A year later, my mother, though she didn't like the long "hippie" robe, actually put a zipper in it so I could easily take it on and off. Humphrey Bogart's sexy, throaty voice was drowned out by the crazy Casablanca drivers and my still weakened state. The next day, we made it back to Tangier. We showed our passports to the officials under huge signs that screamed down in black bold writing: *IF YOU HAVE ANY DRUGS, YOU WILL BE ARRESTED IMMEDIATELY AND SENT TO PRISON.* I thought of the American in prison for 17 years, still living right next to the beautiful mosaics of the Kasbah. I shivered. I wished I could pray him home.

With the same determination that I wanted to get into Morocco, I wanted to leave.

At the upscale campground near Malaga, Jaclyn and I walked in over gray cobblestones, sweaty and exhausted. We passed SUVs and mega tents with four rooms as we walked to our spot on the ground, put down our sleeping bags to save our place, then went to the air-conditioned restaurant. Europe. *I made it back.*

"Long and Winding Road" by the Beatles played on the sound system. What did my road lead back to? After feeling almost giddy to be back in Europe, I felt a sudden emptiness. *You left me standing here a long, long time ago.* As I sipped my coke, sugar flooding my system, the hollow feeling vanished. I thought of all that could be new in my life and that soon I would see Ken. I sipped my Coke, cool, sugary Coke. My mother only let us drink soda for special occasions. This was a special occasion.

When we got to Paris, the honking horns hurt my ears and the haunting sounds of sirens brought back terrifying images of the movie of one of my heroes, Anne Frank, a budding writer who got mowed down by evil. At least I could speak French. Some nights, I dreamed in French and woke up reciting French poems.

At the hostel I told Jaclyn I wanted the lower bunk this time. I was too frail to climb up and down and thought I might tumble if I had to get up in the middle of the night.

That night, we took the Metro and went to the top of a hotel and saw the whole city lit up below. The Eiffel Tower loomed in front of us. We both ordered banana splits, three scoops of ice cream, a banana, butterscotch sauce, and whipped cream topped with maraschino cherries. The sundae rose up so high it could have competed for the highest whipped cream sundae in the world. I spooned more and more luscious whipped cream into my waiting mouth. Jaclyn and I didn't talk much as usual, but we both gazed out the picture window to the shimmering lights of Paris below. I hadn't had sugar for over twelve days, except for one Coke. When I finished eating the sundae, I wanted to sleep so badly, my head almost crashed on the table.

When we got back to the hostel, I rolled my clothes into little balls two and three times and stuffed them into crevices in the knapsack. On top, tied with my bungee cord, were my precious black-and-white jillaba and my sleeping bag. I pulled out a small purse and inserted my passport and student visa papers. I noticed all the stamps: stamped in and out of places and remembered the slow walk through no-man's land with Ken between Spain and North Africa, a place between borders.

CHAPTER NINE

When Jaclyn and I arrived in New York City, we exchanged phone numbers and hugged briefly. Her body felt stiff. The airport smelled of plastic, sweat, and the acid, thick smell of coffee. The linoleum floors shone too brightly. America overwhelmed me, and for a moment, all I wanted was to go back to Aix to my little apartment, to the bakeries that opened in the early morning where Ken and I got square pieces of chocolate that tucked into the warm bread and melted. I wanted to go to Mt. St. Victoire again, to climb to the top of Cezanne's colorful cubist mountain where I had picnics among the wildflowers.

Sometimes, Ken and I recited lines from our favorite poets or snatches of songs.

In the chilly hours and minutes
of uncertainty I want to be in the warm hold of your
loving mind...
Ah, but I may as well try and catch the wind.

Donovan

I was back in Aix in my mind, momentarily dreaming of the past and waiting for my weathered backpack to appear down the chute and enter the circle of spinning luggage, lives stuffed into small spaces. Finally, I saw it and grabbed it to me, when two huge male police officers came up to me. "This way, young lady," one of them said. They shuffled me into a small room, sat me down in a cold metal chair. They stood looming above me. "Have you been to Morocco? What did you buy there? Do you have any drugs on you?" They rifled through my knapsack, their gloved hands touching my underwear. They held my Moroccan drum up to the light. I hated the cops and their questions. I had no drugs on me. I didn't even smoke pot that much. I had only smoked that one time in Morocco.

What was happening? This was my country, finally, America. I was home. I had been aching to go home for so long. If I hadn't been white and sounded so educated, I might have ended up in airport jail even with nothing on me but dirty underwear and gifts for my family. The jillaba was probably their tip-off to someone carrying drugs. I had no drugs on me.

"You can go now," one of the officers said, gentleness creeping into his voice, especially when he saw how upset I looked.

Jaclyn was still at the carousel, waiting for her backpack. It was a huge airplane. We didn't look much at each other. Her parents came to pick her up and were in a rush—said hello and goodbye and she vanished from my life.

I left JFK airport with the hefty weight of my backpack securely on my tired shoulders. I emerged from the air-conditioned terminal into the humid summer city air, hot even at 10 p.m. I lugged my body up the steep steps onto the bus to Port Authority. My sleeping bag, perched on top of the pack, smelled of dirt, sand and sweat. I wished someone had come to pick me up: my parents, a friend, or a boy-friend.

My parents picked me up once, my freshman year of college, when I came home for the holidays, but the drive took too long in bumper-to-bumper traffic. "Never again," my mother said. I had taken public transportation my whole life; I knew where to go. Though rationally I knew they were right—what crazy person would drive to any New York City airport, it still hurt to go home alone. I had been gone an entire year.

As the bus pulled out of the terminal, I pressed my face to the dirt-smudged window, assaulted by the urban sprawl, the darkness, and all the city lights. I was exhausted and restless at the same time. I couldn't sleep on the bus, even though others around me were sleeping, some even snoring. I stared out the window. So many lights and so much darkness.

"Port Authority," the driver called out 40 minutes later with a familiar New York accent. My arms ached from the simple effort of grabbing my knapsack off the luggage rack.

The cab ride was quick. I relaxed into the familiar concrete city, watching the numbered streets descend towards Greenwich Village. Friday night, summertime—people lolling outside of restaurants, lovers with hands intertwined.

Ah, New York. I was glad to be back. Soon I would see my parents, and then soon I would see Ken. It was 11 p.m. when the driver deposited me in front of Butterfield House, my apartment building on 12th Street.

When I entered my building, Frank, the doorman, stood up. "Louise, you're back!" he said and looked at me a bit strangely. I looked different, very tan and very thin.

The backpack dragged me down, but I was so happy to see Frank. He had sung to me every morning when I left for high school, *Every little breeze seems to whisper Louise.*

When I rang the bell, my parents were up but ready for bed. My mother was wearing a pink polyester nightgown and a pink quilted jacket. My father was in his striped pajamas and robe. So predictable. The house as always was OCD neat, a combination of my mother's need for constant order and the fact that she had household help every single day. I liked the predictability, at least for the moment. My mother couldn't help glancing at my dirty knapsack.

"You're so tan," my father said. He looked happy to see me, but tired.

"And you look too thin," my mother said while scanning my body, which was a first since they were always egging me on to be thin. "Have you been sick?"

"A little in Morocco. I'm okay now." There was so much I didn't tell her.

My mother showed me my red towels, the shampoo. No-nonsense and practical as usual. "I didn't get conditioner. If you want some, you can get it tomorrow. Put all your laundry in the hamper. You'll be looking for a job soon? Good night, sweetie." She just wanted to get back to bed, I could tell. I knew she would put some Vaseline on a white patch and then put it over her right eye with a piece of tape. That eye never closed after the burns.

I had been away so long I forgot what she looked like at night, the silly putty face, how you could see where the skin grafts were sewn on, red lines that she covered with make-up in the morning. When I walked into the living room, two unseen photos perched on the coffee table, both of her before she was burned—peachy skin and dark jewel eyes. She was wearing a white shirt with a collar that looked like huge petals. I didn't remember her face then. I didn't remember her face at all before the accident.

Now, looking at the photographs, I could see all that she had lost, and perhaps what we all had lost.

I could see all that I was trying so hard not to remember.

Completely worn out because I hadn't slept at all on the plane, I undressed quickly, brushed my teeth, put on a clean nightgown that I found in my dresser and got into my old twin bed. I wanted to sleep late and hoped my mother wouldn't barge into the room like she did when I was a teenager. "That's enough sleep," she'd say even though I was still groggy.

I was 20. I wanted to be left alone.

The stiff sheets were tucked in too tightly. The room smelled of antiseptic cleaning fluid. Everything had looked perfect, pristine, until I'd entered with my dirty backpack and soiled clothes, already strewn on the floor. My blue and yellow flowered curtains were shut over the bay window, the curtains I looked at all through high school. My poster I made in high school with Frost's poem still hung on the door. "And miles to go before I sleep."

I had gone so many miles in the last year.

"I am always tying up and deciding to depart." Frank O'Hara's words found me, even now, at home in New York. But was this home? I would depart again before too long.

I curled up into a little ball. I could hear ambulance sirens. I could hear a dog barking from an apartment across the courtyard. I looked over at my knapsack. My drum had fallen to the floor on top of some of my dirty clothes, my drum in all its glory, deep brown hide filled with hieroglyphics and sounds from an ancient world.

When I woke up, saliva dripped out of my mouth onto my pillow. I had slept on my arm, and it ached. The digital clock flashed 10:30 in bright red, like an emergency. Thank God my mother let me sleep. Then I remembered it was Thursday. She was working at The American Journal of Nursing. A cigarette. I wanted one. I wanted one badly. Desperately. To puff in the smoke, inhale into my lungs and blow it out, feel it coursing through my system. The Virginia Slims pack—white with gold stripes—meant liberation, independence—the cigarettes longer and thinner—what every woman wanted. Oh, to be long and thin and inhale toxic smoke. I was hooked again. I had stopped for a few months while abroad, but the lure was too much. The pack was stuffed way down in my purse. I bought it at the airport and smoked one on the cab ride home then doused my mouth with mint spray.

What was I doing filling my lungs with smoke and toxic chemicals? A few years ago, I would have turned up my nose at smokers. I was the virtuous one about to go ice-skating or skiing, wearing my white parka splattered with blue snowflakes. But smoking felt so good.

My father, an ex-smoker and a lung doctor, had "Smoking Causes Lung Cancer" buttons all over the house. We thought he had stopped years ago, but one afternoon when he was teaching me how to drive, I lost control of the car uptown on Fifth Avenue and almost ran down a man selling hot dogs at a Sabrett stand. My dad started coughing uncontrollably. Fresh red blood splattered on his white handkerchief. "I need to stop smoking," he said, his brows furrowed and his hands gently shaking. And he did, forever—no more bumming cigarettes from nurses, which my mother had suspected for years.

Both his daughters puffed nicotine now, my sister since she was 16. And neither of us was about to quit.

When I got out of bed, almost tripping over my dirty clothes, the musty smell was in sharp contrast with the antiseptic sprayed on every inch of my room. I hated that my parents were so neat. It just underscored my messiness. When I was in high school, I wanted to break things in the house. Everything was too formal. That morning, the predictability that I had loved the night before felt suffocating, round in an angular world. I didn't want to be in my twin bed anymore with the stiff, clean sheets.

I had to get a job, fast, so I could make money to move out. A sublet for the summer. More rested, though, than I had been in a month, I didn't have to think about where I would sleep that night, or where I would eat. Or be worried about men. I *was* looking for sex, but I wanted a bona fide boyfriend.

I was relieved, also, that I didn't have to deal with Jaclyn. She was waking up, as well, in a parallel universe in her parents' home in New Jersey, just over the bridge. Part of me always longed to make everything right. To call her, talk it out. Still be friends. "Hey, Jaclyn, sorry the trip wasn't as good as we planned. But we made it through! We saw a Berber village. And we lost weight!" I would giggle when I said that. Or "How's your diet going—me, I can't wait to get another banana split! I'm trying just to imagine it and not really eat it!" I read about that in *Redbook. Pretend you're having a piece of chocolate cake; imagine the frosting in your mouth and little bits of it on the fork. Really eat it in your mind until nothing is left on the fork, and you feel satisfied.*

Maybe Jaclyn and I could smooth it over. No bad feelings. Bad feelings suffocated me, like cement blocks all over my body. Crushed me. But I didn't call her. And she didn't call me.

My mind raced.

Call Kelly Girls. You need a job ASAP. I was a fast typist, 90 words a minute. It helped that I'd played piano for years. I should have no problem getting temp jobs. I had had many of them before and a good track record. My mother always made it clear: *Either you're in school or you're working.* So, I had always worked—babysitting, mother's helper before college and then temp jobs during school breaks. I always felt deficient in practical skills compared to my cousins who "worked their way through school." My mother often reminded me of that

I had one traveler's check left—$5.00. Just enough for subway fare and to bring over a bottle of wine to Ken's tonight after dinner and to buy cigarettes and breath- mints.

Meet Ken's friend. "Good-looking, smart, and artistic!" Ken had said in his letter. "You're both adorable. I think you'll like each other."

When I went to the bathroom to brush my teeth and run the bathwater, I looked at my thin, tan face in the mirror, unusual for me as I usually burned and peeled. My face always got super thin before the rest of my body when I went on crazy diets. Stillman diet—no carbs or sugar. My skin rashes and allergies always cleared up, though. My face was now too angular. Not how I looked when I left on the *Aurelia*, thick thighs bursting out of my jeans, my stomach hanging over my belt. I liked being thin, but my struggle and obsession with food wasn't over.

Being in my parents' house, old memories surfaced: my mother hiding M&Ms in the bottom drawer of her desk, opened packages closed with two rubber bands—tempting to sneak some. In the heat the M&M colored dyes would come off on my hands, and I would have to wash them repeatedly to hide the evidence. My mother also put the Marshmallow fluff jar up so high my sister and I practically broke our arms falling off the kitchen stool trying to get to it when our parents were out. My mother had a "sweet tooth" so she might have been hiding it from herself as well, but then I just thought it was mean. It made me want sugar even more.

Evelyn, our house cleaner, came in around 11 a.m. and changed into her white dress and sturdy shoes. We hugged and then talked for a few minutes—about her daughter who was finishing high school—and a little about my trip, and then she got busy cleaning. She was a quiet, sweet woman. She couldn't understand why my sister and I had such trouble with my mom. She once even said that to me very softly. "Your mom's a good person." Her allegiance had to be with her employer. Plus, she must have thought that my sister and I were just ungrateful. Spoiled. She was right in terms of money and opportunity. But I didn't feel it. To me, spoiled was how I felt when a woman in a small town in Spain picked a rose for me. I was with a group of friends in a big van, and we had just bought warm bread and honey. Suddenly an older woman urged me up some steep stairs, and I followed her. She gazed into my eyes and hugged me and said, "You are pretty" and then handed me a beautiful red rose She was a stranger, but her arms felt so warm that I basked in the aftermath of that hug for days.

Spoiled to me also felt like the words, "poor baby," the words my mother couldn't say when tears poured out of me after I ate, when I came home from the playground, my key on a lanyard around my neck, and especially at night waiting for my older sister to come to bed in our room." Crybaby," she called me. "Crybaby."

It would take me many miles and many years of going away, far away from home, and going far inside myself to understand the depth of my mother's sorrow. *Poor baby* were words she would never say.

Evelyn took my dirty clothes downstairs and washed and dried them. How different from the women washing clothes on the slate-gray rocks in the unbearable heat in Beni-Mellal. How different from the children lining the streets of Marrakesh, their eyes filled with pus, blind or crippled, their crutches beside them.

Sometimes I wanted to rush to Evelyn, take the clothes out of her hands and say, "I'll do it myself." The same way I felt when we were having dinner and my mother rang the "dinner bell." "I'll tell Evelyn we're through eating," I'd say, and quickly get up and go into the kitchen. Maybe I had been born into the wrong family. I didn't like the formality. I didn't like being served. I didn't like that we called her Evelyn, and she called my parents Dr. and Mrs. Nayer.

"Don't do that." My mother's voice was firm then. "Evelyn knows to come when she hears the bell. It makes it easier for her. This is her job." I knew my parents were good to her and her daughter. But it felt all wrong. Why should some have more than others? I had never been to Evelyn's apartment in Harlem, but I knew her only son had died of a drug overdose. I could only imagine the long subway ride at 6:30 p.m. worried about the hours her daughter had been alone in the house, leaving one world for another.

Evelyn was going to make sure her daughter finished

school and make something of herself. Kim was a beautiful and smart girl. I hoped she'd make it through what James Baldwin then called "the killing streets" of Harlem.

I was happy, though, to see that all of my clothes would get cleaned. I was spoiled beyond belief in that way. My backpack was another story. It could never be cleaned. It felt like a person to me, a person I was deeply attached to, the house I carried on my back. My mother would have gladly thrown it out, but I loved all its dirt and smells, its crusty zippers and memories of the open road.

That night, we were having dinner together. A reunion. I had spent the day sorting through my backpack, taking out the dirty clothes and putting them in the laundry, sleeping again in the afternoon and luxuriating in the bathtub.

"Whoa," my parents both said in unison as I grabbed another half of a jelly donut. "One half is enough." She parceled out sugar. I had put on a Mexican dress from my closet, red cotton with a black brocade across the bodice. My hair was washed, silky sleek like in the ads. For dessert my mother bought jelly donuts sprinkled with thick sugar, my favorite, and cut them in half. My crime was I reached for a second half and then ate it.

"So, tell us more about Morocco," my mother said, trying to change the subject. She was wiping the sugar off of her face. She couldn't feel her face because of the surgeries, so would just dab it two or three times with a napkin every time she ate. "Is everything off?" Sometimes it wasn't. A big piece of food, even a piece of steak with the fat dripping off would be stuck to her lip and she wouldn't feel it at all. I would touch my lip lightly and look over at her to let her know.

"What about the towns you went to—and Marrakesh."

My voice had grown flat after the jelly donut incident. Their "no" made me feel like I was bad girl. I hated eating dinner with them when they grilled me or told me what to do. I just reported a few things without any feeling or detail.

"Women washed their clothes on rocks. There were snake charmers at the souk in Marrakesh. Casablanca is too busy and filled with cars that honk day and night. I saw a camel train." They looked annoyed at my tone of voice. After all, they had given me money for this trip, and I was ungrateful in reporting back. Why couldn't I tell them what I was feeling? To back off over the jelly donut? Was it a crime to have a whole donut?

"Well, that's good," my mother said. "Quite an adventure." Her voice belied her words, though. I was sure she just wanted to move on.

"All 109 died," my mother said, of the Air Canada flight that had crashed near Toronto the day before. "Terrible, just terrible." Underneath I knew she was relieved I had come home—safely. My flight hadn't crashed. Somewhere deep down I knew that that was all that counted.

This talk about the plane crash underscored that we were a family that could have easily exploded as well. That's what the fire captain said after the explosion in the basement, that the automatic action from the gas buildup would have blown the whole house up the next day. My parents took the brunt.

We were a family that had narrowly escaped death, and each time something happened in the world, but it didn't happen to us was another notch in our survival. The scars, visible and invisible that remained, were not up for discussion. *We really didn't escape*, I thought, but kept my mouth shut.

My mother folded her napkin neatly, placed it on the table and stood up. "Let's get the dishes." Evelyn had left to go home. I carted plates, bowls, silverware and the butter dish to the kitchen, making three trips and placing the dirty dishes and cups on the counter near the dishwasher and the butter back in the refrigerator. I was aware of how small the kitchen seemed or perhaps how big my mother seemed, as if she took up all the room.

My dad was in the living room, reading *The New York Times*.

"You certainly had quite a trip," my mother said as she began loading the dishwasher. She opened the refrigerator to put away the salad dressing. I began to take over the loading to help her.

"Don't put the dishes in *that* way," she said, pushing me aside. "They'll never get clean." I slunk away to the corner of the kitchen, paralyzed by her sharp tone of voice. I just wanted to get out of the house. But I stood there, my eyes glazed, watching her sigh, rearranging the dishes I had put in already.

She picked her head up from the dishwasher, maybe trying to apologize. "Do you have some pictures?"

She wasn't one to say, "I'm sorry for snapping at you." Years later I found out she was the one who insisted she and my dad go downstairs to the cellar of the Cape Cod cottage when there was no hot water at 2 in the morning. She wanted to wash her face. She was the one to light the match.

How do you say "I'm sorry" about that?

"A few pictures," I said. "I'll get them developed. The Moroccans don't like to have their pictures taken. It's like stealing their souls. I have some pictures of the landscape. I'll see if anything came out." I wanted her to know that I knew about the *real* Moroccans, that I didn't want them to think I was stealing their souls.

Since she paid for the trip, I felt I owed her something, but all I wanted to do was get away now. She kept loading the dishwasher and didn't look up at all. My mouth had an invisible seal on it. I didn't want to talk anymore. Talking would hurt. Soon we would go to our separate rooms or areas of the house. Even then, at 20 years old, I felt the sadness of all that separation.

I heard my father fold the paper in the living room and heard him walk down the hallway to his room. He probably wanted to "deal" with the mail, a term he often used. Later they would watch *Columbo* on T.V.

Before I left that night, I peeked into the room and said goodnight. "Don't come back too late and be careful," my father said. "Say hi to Ken." They liked Ken, a lot. They saw how he made me feel happy. He could even tease my mother, something very few people could ever do.

"Yes, sweetie," my mother said. "Don't stay out too late." Sometimes the "sweetie," the way it slipped off her tongue so easily, helped bridge what felt like a wall between us. But it was temporary. I couldn't wait to leave the house.

I climbed down the stairs instead of taking the elevator, already worried about how the second half of the jelly donut might stick to my thighs. Would this be the beginning of a downward slide? I walked out on 12th Street. It was still warm outside. New York City summer when even the pavement sweats.

I crossed Fifth Avenue, where dog walkers were taking their pooches around the block one or two times before bed. I kept going toward 8th Street, passing by the small graveyard in front of the church on Fifth Avenue. A harried mother, smoking a cigarette, pushed a baby stroller. I immediately lit up a Virginia Slim and inhaled deeply. It was late for a mother to be out with a baby. Where was she going? She looked lost.

As I walked, passing a small 24-hour deli, and a pharmacy, I thought about all the things I didn't tell my parents. I hadn't gotten my period in five months. I knew I wasn't pregnant.

Tears rimmed my eyes. The light changed, red to green. I walked towards the East Village, the new real estate market named for anything below 14th Street and east of Fifth Avenue. The apartments looked shabbier than in the West Village but more alive. More young people lined the streets.

In Aix six months earlier, I had taken a nap and had woken up with pulsating pain in my head, like a knife stabbing into my brain. Most of it was on the right side and throbbed so much I felt like vomiting. I got up from bed and put on my pink terry cloth robe and limped to the medicine cabinet praying there was aspirin. Mercifully, the little white pills sat like saviors on a shelf. I popped three of them and drank three cups of water. That would make the pain go away.

Maybe it was an aneurism that would burst. A silent bomb that was set to go off. No one was home. Light, even a small, tiny slant of light from the window after I closed all the shades, stabbed me in the eyes, and now the throbbing continued on the right side of my head.

At a science fair in my high school, I saw a human brain, sliced, yellow and green and mushy. This was the center of all our thoughts? I imagined my brain exploding. No more neurons would fire. Terrified, I called Ken, who rushed over but couldn't even make me laugh. Ken could always make me laugh. We thought of going to an emergency clinic, but the pain subsided. Before I had left for Aix, I saw an OBGYN who told me migraines could be an effect of the pill. That day I threw my pills into the garbage can. But my period hadn't come back.

Now, I had only five more blocks to walk to Ken's house down Eighth Street. Tons of people swarmed the streets of the Village, going to restaurants or movies or going home. I didn't want to think any more about that horrible headache, but I knew I'd have to tell "my history" to my father's friend and let my parents know my period had stopped.

I looked up momentarily to see if the light had changed to green before I stepped off the curb. Cab drivers drove so fast that it was easy to get hit.

After the migraine and no period for months in Aix I went to a French doctor who said this could be "grave." Very, very serious not to get my period. He told me to see someone when I returned to New York City. I felt icy cold when he said that and held my hands together, shivering with fear all the way back to my apartment.

Now I was almost at Ken's house. I was also only about a half an hour away from meeting Ken's friend, Michael, who was coming over that night. "I have a best friend. I think you'll like him," he said in the letter I carried with me through Morocco.

How could I even imagine starting a new relationship until I figured out what was wrong with me? I had always wanted to have children. The summer I was a mother's helper on Fire Island, little Martha ran to me, crying, "Mama, Mama," when she got hurt instead of to her mother, who was standing right next to me and whose face looked like crushed velvet when I held her little daughter and said, "It's all right, Martha. It's all right." How could they spend the summer going to cocktail parties while I took Martha to the beach?

Joe and I had even talked about having children. Maybe they would have his blue eyes and my dark hair.

I walked up the five flights to Ken's East Village apartment with a new lightness in my step. Finally, I could talk about how I felt. About my mother's tone of voice, and how she pushed me aside when I didn't put the dishes in the dishwasher the right way; how that made me feel small; about the scary airport cop who looked at my drum trying to find drugs inside; about the terror in Morocco and what I felt about Jaclyn, that I couldn't trust her.

Ken could say "poor baby" and not be afraid to say it. He could also make me laugh as he often did about meals at my house. "Did you have a fistful of tuna on some iceberg lettuce? And maybe one lady finger for dessert?" He often said he was hungry when he left my parents' house after dinner. He would love the jelly donut incident. "You're a skinny minny now," he'd say, "I think you can have two halves of a measly jelly donut!" Ken was the one who helped me shed all the beer weight from the Yakima Valley. He never put me down, and I lost the 20 pounds learning to eat more salads and yogurt, to savor good food.

When I knocked on the door, and he opened it, we hugged for a long time. He looked great: sparkling eyes, curly hair, thin and bubbling with energy but also grounded. He could bring me back to earth.

After we hugged, he looked at me for a long second. "Louise! You're skinny and so tan. You shrank! I would hardly have recognized you. As beautiful as ever." Tears filled my eyes. I was so happy to see him. So relieved to be back in New York City.

"I have some cake. You want some?"

After the jelly donut incident, I felt like I could devour a whole cake.

"Yes! I'd love a piece."

He went into the kitchen and sliced a generous portion of a white cake with chocolate frosting. Sugary frosting coated my mouth. I wanted more though I stopped myself from asking for a second piece.

"Michael should be here any minute."

Butterflies flooded my stomach. The doorbell rang, and Ken buzzed him in. Would I like him? Would Michael be the one? *You're just meeting him—not marrying him*, I said to myself and took a last scrumptious bite.

When Michael came through the door, he and Ken hugged briefly. Ken was right. He was *really* good-look-ing—black curly hair, bright blue eyes, and an athletic body. He buzzed with energy and talked fast.

"Louise, Michael. Michael, Louise."

I had gotten up from the table and made sure no frosting stuck to my lips though I wasn't sure I got all the crumbs off. Michael looked directly at me. It felt disarming but also sexy. He had full lips. For a moment, I felt dizzy, maybe from the sugar or the heat in the apartment, as there was no air conditioning.

Michael and I started to hug each other but both backed off and shook hands. An awkward moment. His hand was warm. Mine were cold from nerves. I had a few cake crumbs on my lip. I turned away and brushed them off.

We squished together around the small kitchen table, near the only window, wide open and mercifully blowing in some cool air. "So Morocco," Ken said. "You actually made it in. I'm jealous!" He quickly explained to Michael how we had gotten turned away at the border during spring break. "You had a lot of guts trying to get in again—and to go with another woman!"

I drank the first glass of wine too fast. "The kef was so strong," I said, "you just needed one puff. We went to a rug factory where children worked with looms." I told them about the snake charmers in Marrakesh, and then how I got sick, extremely sick, so sick I wondered if I would make it out of there. I told them about Tinker Bell, that I had called up all the people who loved me.

"That's partly why you're so very thin," Ken said. "Wow! What an ordeal. Poor baby!" He got up and gave me another hug and tears rimmed my eyes. I really had wondered if I would make it back to New York City, and here I was. I didn't want to go into all the stuff with Jaclyn or the things with men. Michael sat there silently. He hadn't taken his eyes off me, and though I didn't look directly back at him I could feel his presence sweeping over my body. He moved his chair closer to me when tears filled my eyes. Our knees touched. I felt a surge of energy.

"What about you," Michael, I asked. What have you been doing? I know Ken said you're a filmmaker."

"I just saw *Window Water Baby Moving*," Michael said, leaning back in his chair, "by Brakhage. Brakhage is so experimental. He just threw the film on the ground and stepped on it. That's how he edited the film. The birth of his child. Can you imagine that? Music by Cage—haunting music." He seemed to want to say more but stopped. Instinctively, I put my hand across my belly. For the next few hours, Ken talked about art and art history. He would be studying now at NYU. Michael talked more about film, and I pulled out my black journal that I carried in my purse and showed them a few of my poems. I felt at home now, with Ken and Michel, a glass of wine and the world of art, film, and poetry.

Michael saw me yawning. "How about I walk you home?" Jet lag had taken over, and it was almost midnight.

A smile spread over Ken's face. Ken and I hugged goodbye.

"Aren't the lights amazing?" Michael said, when we got out to the street, his eyes moving from the streetlights to the Empire State Building lit up and then to the 24-hour stores. His eyes even rested on the lights from my Indian bracelets, five of them, with tiny fake diamonds that jangled as I walked.

"Yes, lights are everywhere," I said. Even his eyes were like lighthouses, searching. He was filled with energy, like Ken. But Ken came down to earth. Michael seemed to always buzz. He moved closer to me as we crossed Fifth Avenue, our shoulders brushing as we walked down 12th Street, where my parents lived.

"This is my house," I said. We turned to each other.

"I'd like to see you again. May I call you?" Light from the streetlamp shone on his black curls.

"Yes, I'd like that too." I fished through my messy purse and found a piece of paper and pen and jotted down my number.

"Maybe this weekend. We can do something?"

"Yes, great!"

Then we hugged. In the distance, I could see Frank rising from his chair.

As I walked into the building, Frank opened the door for me, and we both smiled. I passed the Oriental carpets on the wall, a huge glassed-in patio, and the hallway to the back apartments. We had moved here when I was 12, a move up in class. At first I hated it, too fancy, too formal. I missed Peter Cooper Village, my middle-class housing development with three playgrounds filled with noisy kids, my key dangling from a homemade red-and-white lanyard around my neck. I wondered why anyone would put rugs on the wall! I liked all the dogs, though, who morphed to look like their owners. We couldn't have dogs in Peter Cooper. My sister and I wanted one badly, but my mother said, "Evelyn and I will have to do all the work and I'm not going to burden her." That was the end of the discussion.

When I turned the key in the lock, footsteps pattered through the house. My mother always seemed to be up or get up when I returned. I always hated that and never understood it until many years later when I, too, became a parent.

She had the white patch Scotch-taped to her eye, the eye that never closed. We pecked each other on the cheek, and she returned to her room. I brushed my teeth, put on a thin white nightgown and got into bed, imagining Michael's sensuous lips on mine, his body on top of mine, my fingers running through his thick, black curls.

CHAPTER TEN

Two days after coming home, I got a Kelly Girls job. Still jet lagged, I trudged in the heat to the IRT subway and uptown to a mercifully air-conditioned office. A few days later a sublet popped up in the want ads, 9th Street in the East Village, a cute one-bedroom. Five-floor walkup but all mine for eight weeks. No air conditioning but two fans that I put near the windows. My mother gave me the money for the first month's rent. I had my own place for the first time.

At work I sat in a dark back office where I typed address labels all day and imagined I lived all over America on streets like "Spruce" or "Maple," cute streets with leafy trees. The boss was thrilled with my typing speed, 90 words a minute. I typed names of people like Eric Johnson, Mary McDevin, Rita Goldin. I gave them faces and histories. What were their lives like? What did they think about? A long-lost love? Whether or not their kid would get on the baseball team? Get married? My mind wandered during the eight hours I was there every day. So much was going on in America this past year and now. The Kent State killings. Four students shot dead. The protests in Madison. The teargas. Could we really stop the Vietnam War?

Imagining ordinary lives all over America helped me keep my mind off the violence. What would it be like to return to college? Could we be shot if we protested? The Dow Chemical demonstration my sophomore year haunted me. I could still feel my eyes burning as my friend Joanne and I desperately raced toward Lake Mendota to wash them out. Which of our friends had gotten their heads cracked? Who was in the hospital?

A few days later, after work, I came up out of the IRT to 90-degree humid heat, my armpits sweaty, and perspiration beads sprinkled across my forehead. I stopped in the East Village bookstore, down one short flight of stairs. I loved bookstores, the musty smells. I loved vanishing between the rows into a million worlds of words. When I was in high school, I'd leave my apartment after dinner, relieved to leave my parents perfectly ordered domain, sometimes meeting friends. We would go to the penny candy store where I would buy malt balls, candy corn and Tootsie Roll pops and pop the sweet sugar into my mouth. Then Sara or Suze and I would make our way to the 8th Street Bookstore. We'd talk about books, poetry, boys, friends—a respite from home.

Today, at the bookstore, one small fan whirred near the entrance. I scanned titles of books I wanted to read: *Slaughterhouse Five* by Vonnegut, *The Promise* by Potok, and then I turned a corner to the health section and was assaulted by the title: *The Pill Causes Infertility*. I suddenly felt nauseated. An arctic chill hit my hands even in the extreme heat. The chill spread all over my body. I grabbed the book off the shelf and looked at the table of contents. Mostly names of women: Margaret, Jennifer, and Sandra—case histories of women who became infertile. I began to read—and tears streamed down my cheeks. Women who took the pill for a year could not get their period again.

I never found this exact book again, and all the studies now disprove its claim.

When I was little, I would pick out names of my future children: Cassandra, Penelope, Joan, David, Carl, Alan, three boys' names and three girls' names.

I thought of how Michael had used his hands when he talked about the film *Window Water Baby Moving*. I imagined his hands on my breasts and then his mouth kissing my body and my hands touching all of him. I wanted children, made out of love. But I hardly knew Michael.

An acid taste rose to my mouth.

I closed the book and put it back on the shelf and walked slowly up the stairs to Eighth Street. I just wanted to get home. Michael was coming for dinner. I walked up the five flights to my apartment; my hands still felt clammy, my stomach unsettled. Tomorrow, I'd call my parents about an OBGYN appointment.

I peeled off my sticky clothes and got in the shower. The warm water cascaded over me, cleansing my body and mind, but the book's title: *The Pill Causes Infertility*, kept flashing like a hallucination before my eyes, or like the sign of the bar in the movie *The Days of Wine and Roses*.

You are no longer able to produce offspring. No spinoffs.

I heard the voice of the doctor in France, the doctor I saw after my periods stopped, a constant whisper in my ear. "The situation could be grave." I remember how he said "grave." I thought of graves, baby graves I had seen when I visited cemeteries, the years so thin, 1880-1881. Little short lives. Sometimes there would be a baby shoe coated in bronze, a shoe a foot never slipped into. How quickly life slipped in or out.

I turned off the water and dried myself. I wanted to feel light. Michael light. This was to be our time alone, together. I remembered his knees touching mine as he leaned toward me, the first time I met him. I wanted to put my fingers through his black curls. I wanted him to put his lips on my lips.

So what if I couldn't have children? The world was populated enough. I walked into my bedroom and opened the dresser and put on my bra and a red silk shirt with a V-neck. I found clean jeans. What if my life were to stop here? I looked at my face in the mirror, and its strange asymmetry. There would be no more "me" in the world. None of my DNA would spill across the continent. I could always adopt. It was stupid to even have kids when so many children lay helplessly malnourished on small cots in orphanages across the world. But right now, all I should be thinking about was Michael and getting dinner ready in time. He was coming over at 7 p.m.

I chopped the vegetables, onions, garlic, mushrooms and zucchini, put some olive oil in a pan and cooked the onions first and then the rest of the vegetables, rich smells and colors all mixing together. Then I poured in some Ragu sauce. Would Michael like spaghetti? Who didn't like spaghetti?

My body tingled as I imagined us twirling the long

spaghetti noodles smothered in sauce. It had been so long since I had cooked for someone. The heady smells of the vegetables and sauce permeated the room. Then I put on the hot water for spaghetti and made sure I had enough lettuce and tomatoes for a salad. I wondered if I should have gotten meat? Maybe the meal wouldn't be enough for him? I shaved enough parmesan cheese so that it filled the small bowl I put out on the table, which was now neatly set with violet flowered placemats and napkins to match (part of the package deal of my sublet). I put out wine glasses as Michael said he'd bring wine and dessert. I turned on the fan, something, anything to circulate the humid New York summery air.

The knock on the door was exactly right. Not too loud and aggressive, not too light. Confident. Happy. A good knock. When I opened the door, Michael, handsome Michael stood on the other side, wearing jeans and a light blue shirt, a broad smile spreading across his boyish face, his eyes so electric blue. He handed me a bottle of wine and a chocolate cheesecake for dessert. The last time we met, we awkwardly put out our hands. This time we hugged. I secretly hoped we'd have sex that night, even though we hardly knew each other. It was the 1970's, women's lib. My parents wouldn't approve. But he was Ken's good friend.

The words: drought, barren, desolate, grave, grave, grave, flashed in front of me again. I pushed them away. My possible sterility wasn't something I was going to bring up on our first real date. He asked me more about poetry and I talked about Sylvia Plath, her searing images of life and death. "I shut my eyes and all the world drops dead; I lift my lids, and all is born again," I recited from Mad Girl's Song. That's the way I often felt, my moods shifting as if I were simply blown by the wind. Just a few days ago I wrote in my little black journal. *When I am ready to root myself in some earthbound place, it's not geography that stops love from growing.*

It's the wind.

"I want to capture the clouds," Michael said. "Not just what they look like but how they move, how they're three dimensional, almost breathing." I envied him that most of his classes in the fall would all be film. All I wanted to do was write, to capture the breathing world that Michael talked about. Sometimes he ran his fingers through his thick hair to ground his thoughts.

That night, after dinner, we made love on the rug in the living room with Cat Stevens's song "Peace Train" playing on the record player, a song for our generation, a song of peace. *Oh, I've been smiling lately, dreaming about the world as one.* No wars. Wouldn't that be wonderful! The windows to the apartment were thrown open. Sweet summer air mingled with our kisses and the smells from our bodies, learning each other as twilight descended and then night fell. Our lovemaking was passionate and gentle. It had been so long. It brought back memories of Joe. I felt safe and on the earth with Joe. That he could hold me. I was still getting used to being without him. I had known his body for so long. Solid as a tree I could latch on to.

I wasn't sure how safe I felt with Michael, but I didn't want him to leave.

"Stay over," I said. He smiled and kissed me again.

"Sure. I'd love to." We both sat up and lit cigarettes, our naked bodies pressed against the red woolen couch, smoke swirling through the room, our arms touching. I put on Cat Stevens, again, *How can I tell you that I love you*…and we sat for what felt like a long time, smoking and listening to the music. He told me a little about the film he was making and then got up to use the bathroom. "I'll be right back, baby," he said. No one had called me "baby" before. My parents called each other "dear" or "darling." I wondered if my parents would like him?

I seemed to measure every man against my father, Ivy League graduate, a doctor.

All night we kept waking up, startled to be with each other. We made love two more times as ambulance sirens screamed down First Avenue. We could hear people leaving the Indian restaurants when they closed.

I'd have to get up early for work and once glanced over at the red flashing clock. Six hours of typing up names and addresses.

When I woke up and looked over at Michael, who was still sleeping, I let myself imagine the children we might have together and then I had no idea why, but I felt something catch in my throat like a small wishbone.

"I haven't gotten my period in six months," I said to my mother. "I know I'm not pregnant."

My parents made an appointment for me with their OBGYN friend.

"Remember, sex is not like a cocktail," the doctor, my father's friend, said to me, for the second time. I sat on the examining table wearing one of the crinkly paper robes and shivered as the air conditioner was on full blast. He had said that before—that sex is not like a cocktail—before I left for Aix. He examined me and said he didn't find anything unusual. I got dressed and met him at his office.

"Sometimes the birth control pill can cause your period to stop. Here are some hormones. Take them for three days. Your period should start by Friday." He seemed rushed and annoyed as he led me toward the door. Sex before marriage was still considered a bit risqué in many circles. He knew my father.

I had always hated the cramps, the mood swings, the cravings for sugar, associated with menstruation, and I certainly filled myself with cakes, donuts, anything I could grab. I first got my period at Camp Mudjekeewis in Maine. It was pitch black when I picked up my flashlight and headed towards the restroom. I was twelve. We slept in wooden platform tents. I never woke up in the middle of the night except the first week of camp when the crickets sounded so loud, so different from the blaring sirens in New York City. I heard rustling, a small animal, maybe? I glanced back at my tent, one of many, for a moment petrified I'd walk back to the wrong tent, to the wrong bed.

I heard rustling in the bushes, again, and then nothing.

The dampness between my legs was new. For a moment I felt embarrassed. Did I wet myself? But then I knew. I was twelve. I was waiting to get my period because then I would be like Susan and Nancy and Jane in my class at school. Though the light was dim, I saw the mysterious rush of red on the toilet paper. A thick smell like nothing I had ever smelled on my body before.

After I peed that night at camp, I washed myself with toilet paper and soap and when I walked back to my tent, I stood up taller.

"Now you're a woman," my mother wrote to me.

"You're in the club, now," my friend, Nancy, wrote to me. "It's pretty awful, though, don't you think—all that blood!" The blood didn't revolt me. It all mixed in with that moment in the woods, alone with my flashlight as I walked through the trees on pine needles that smelled like heaven.

The first set of hormones never worked. Every morning, afternoon and especially in the evening when I wasn't at work and busy with typing names and addresses, I kept neurotically checking for even a tiny speck of blood, something red.

On Friday morning when the alarm buzzed and I got up, I headed straight for the bathroom even though I really didn't have to pee. Nothing red. When Michael came up the stairs to my East Village apartment that night, I told him. We had only been together three times, but he and Ken were best friends. That helped me skip some of the formalities.

"I haven't gotten my period in months. The doctor gave me hormones and said they would work by today." I turned my face away from Michael's face. "But nothing happened!"

He tried not to look sad. But his bright blue eyes under the long thick lashes faded for a minute. He held my hands a little too tightly and then let go, and walked around the apartment in circles, fast moving like how he talked. I was sitting down. I wanted him to say, "It's you I'm interested in, not whether you can make babies," or "we can always adopt," but we didn't even know each other well. Who knew if we would stay together? It all felt awkward, so confusing, making love so soon after meeting someone. The sixties accelerated that.

I wished I hadn't even told him.

"Oh, I'm sure it'll work out," he said, going toward the window and not looking at me. I felt like I might be damaged, like the Hibakusha of Hiroshima, women near the killing flash after the bomb dropped, women who had gotten radiation poisoning but survived and now had potentially bad DNA. They would never marry.

"The doctor said he'll give me another five days of hormones if this doesn't work. I go in after work on Monday. Then I don't know." My voice grew faint as a whisper. I wanted him to hug me.

I didn't know bodies could shut down and then would have to be jump-started. Maybe it was the effect of the pill? Maybe it was all the weight I lost in Morocco?

When Michael and I made love that night, a thin membrane, a wall, came between us. We were lying on the rug in the living room. B. B. King was singing "The Thrill Is Gone." *The thrill is gone. The thrill is gone away.*

The Beatles split up that summer. Their last song together, "Long and Winding Road," played across the airwaves. Race riots exploded in Hartford, Connecticut. I just wanted to feel safe, but the violence outside continued. Inside, fear and panic took hold of me. One morning, five days later, I went to pee and saw blood. My body had returned to normal. When I washed up and looked at myself in the mirror, my eyes were shining.

One afternoon, Joe visited. I don't remember how we got in touch but when he came to the door his blue eyes sparkled and I could smell his Old Spice perfume, the same smell when I used to sink into his body like you sink into a bed of moss. Michael was there—so awkward—and insisted on coming with us to a lunch place in the East Village which had swings. Joe swung alone on a swing in his long legs and kind eyes while Michael sat close to me on a wooden bench talking too fast. Joe didn't walk back to the apartment, and we hugged when he left. I could hardly look at him. I had hurt him again. I didn't know what I wanted, yet I still longed for him as if he was still solid earth that could keep me from cracking up. Years later I wrote *I am going to meet you in the Fall. Our hands have aged eleven years.* But we never met again. That day after lunch I knew it was over forever.

Years later, I went to an Al-Anon meeting, to support an

alcoholic friend and learned about amends. I wrote Joe that the kind of love he gave me was what I hoped to find again. That I didn't know how to love. That I was sorry. That I was a poet. That I had too much grief. That I was learning. That I hoped that he was happy. I heard through a friend he got the letter. He married soon after.

On August 24th—just a week before I returned to school, Vietnam War protesters blew up Sterling Hall in Madison, which housed the Army Math Research Center funded by an army think tank. They used 2000 pounds of ammonia nitrate. A lone student, Robert Fassnacht, father of three small children, was working late into the night, not for the army and was killed. The protesters said they had scoped out the building two and three times and only wanted to blow up property.

How could his wife explain this to his children? I could only imagine the tears and the grief. Their father was doing his work late at night in his lab, an innocent, and was blown up by other students protesting innocents blown up in a war, thousands and thousands of miles away. Mr. Fassnacht, 33, was, his family said afterward, against the war.

When I heard the news of the bombing, I was in New York City and saw the headline in the *New York Times*: MAN DIES AS BOMB RIPS MATH CENTER

Just a few minutes before the bomb decimated the building and killed Fassnacht, the Madison police got a call: "Hey, pig," the caller said, "there's a bomb in the math research center."

The war had come home. I shivered at the thought of being near the epicenter of the explosion.

Two nights before I left New York City for Madison, Michael and I went out to see a film and then went back to the apartment. The lights in the city seemed dimmer than they had that first time he walked me back to my parents' house.

I felt queasy as Michael kept talking about a filmmaker he'd be working with. A new project, a new camera. I imagined him up all night, throwing himself into his film as I opened my black diary every day, words spilling out of me. *If you lose your fear, do you lose your life?* How could we continue to love each other through such distance?

My parents had married in 1942 just before the war and for four years my father kept a picture of my mother on his desk as he treated the troops in Persia, mostly for heat exhaustion. My mother worked as a nurse and waited for his return. They were committed to loving each other through thick and thin, through sickness and till death do them part.

Michael and I weren't married. I didn't know if we would stay together. I hadn't even said, "I love you."

We walked past the Indian restaurants to my apartment. Michael's arm draped over my shoulder, but the weight was too much. As usual he was talking fast about the independent film we had just seen at a huge warehouse. A child was swinging and swinging and swinging. No words. Lots of trees surrounding a long white house. The swinging mesmerized me. The look of joy on the girl's face pulled me into her pure joy, as if she was the swing and the trees and the air. Michael's eyes were a zoom lens, talking about one image after. Anthology Film Archives would open that fall, and all the well-known independent film makers would finally have a place to show their masterpieces. We talked about going there together.

When we climbed the five flights and went in the door to my apartment, all the air had been sucked out of the summer. The apartment was filled with boxes, mostly books, records, my typewriter and clothes. I would cart it all, with help, to my parents' house the last night before I left and would sleep in my old twin bed. Though my parents had met Michael once, there was no great love between them.

When my father asked what he was majoring in one night when he came for dinner, Michael said, "film." My father retorted, "That's what we did for pleasure at Yale, went to films after classes." The tone was not good. I knew I should have defended Michael then. Defended film as an art form. A few minutes of silent eating followed. Maybe I didn't love him enough? Or I was still a child inside and didn't want to displease my parents? The silence was thick.

When we returned that night, we lay down on the rug in the living room and put B.B. King on the record player, again. We groped for each other in a passionate and desperate kind of way, my cotton blouse quickly unbuttoned by his nimble fingers, my fingers loosening his belt, our kisses deeper than they had been for a while. Afterwards, we both lit up a cigarette, but hardly untangled at all from the ways

our limbs intersected, my blouse, his jeans all mingled together in a pile in front of us. Neither of us wanted to move.
I put BB King on the record player, again.

The thrill is gone
The thrill is gone away
The thrill is gone baby
The thrill is gone away

I made the first movement away and turned my face to
the right. The rug felt scratchy on my skin. At that moment,
he got up and went to the bathroom. The thin membrane,
that fragile wall, had reconstructed itself, again. I always
seemed to create walls.

When Michael came out of the bathroom, he said he was
tired. I needed to continue packing. It was dark outside. I
gathered the remnants of my "stuff" in three packing boxes while Michael fell asleep in the bedroom. With a black,
permanent marker I wrote my new address in Madison on
top of each box. I had spent the summer typing names and
addresses through my Kelly Girl jobs and created stories for
names like Mr. and Mrs. Larsen who lived on Maple Street.
They must have children, I thought, maybe a boy who col-
lects stamps and a girl who sings. Maybe they had nothing
bad that ever happened to them. Was that even possible?

When I saw my address—Louise Nayer, Mifflin Street—I
tried to make up a story about who I would be —living
on that street in Madison. I tried to get excited about my
classes. But what I really wanted was to squat in this apartment forever, plant my feet somewhere solid. I didn't want

to leave Michael. I didn't want to leave Ken and my other friends. I didn't want to leave New York.

And perhaps, though I didn't admit it then, maybe I didn't want to leave my parents.

An hour later, exhausted, I spilled into bed, a mixture of water and blood circulating through my veins, millions of tiny molecules vibrating in the air that was our combined bodies. I hugged my body to his, smelled his smell. How do you loosen yourself from that cocoon?

The alarm sounded like a siren. "I'll call you tomorrow," Michael said. He got up right away when the alarm rang. He was putting on his clothes already and seemed to want to rush out of the apartment. He brushed his fingers through his thick hair. "I need to go over my notes—and think I'll go out and get some breakfast and look over them there." I knew he had a meeting about a film he was doing at 10 a.m. I loved how he threw himself into his films; I loved that he was always seeing beauty in tree branches, lights on skyscrapers, the wings of sparrows. He had the eyes of a filmmaker, scanning the world, transforming the world.

"Good luck! I'll keep my fingers crossed for you!"

He came over to me and gave me a deep kiss.

"This is hard. I need to leave." His voice caught in his throat. A few tears coursed down his face. My eyes flooded with tears. "Call when you get to Madison. Baby, remember, I'm visiting as soon as I can."

I listened to every step until all traces of him vanished into the concrete below.

CHAPTER ELEVEN

It was 90 degrees in Chicago when my plane landed. I sweated as I raced through the airport to a small propeller plane that terrified me when snow and ice covered the runway and dark clouds menaced the sky. "There might be turbulence," the pilot would say, especially over Christmas vacation. I hated the loud sounds. I'd clutch the side of the seat, not even realizing I was tensing my fingers and holding my breath—until the plane landed.

When I got off the plane, I grabbed my suitcase, got a cab and rode to my address on Mifflin Street. The streets were empty. Madison seemed bleak. The electricity of "the movement"—throngs of us fighting for civil rights and against the war in Vietnam—had been deflated by the explosion at the chemistry building and the killing of an innocent father of three. The house was empty as I carted in my suitcase and found my room, right off the kitchen.

Patrick Quinn, a working-class kid from Wisconsin who became a campus activist, said, "The blowing up of Sterling Hall cast a pall over the entire radical movement in Madison from which, arguably, it never fully recovered." He also said that after the explosion, Madison felt like a "morgue."

No one would find out until years later, but Nixon had ordered 1000 new agents to go undercover on college campuses. Madison was one of the three most radical campuses in America.

Blowing up buildings terrified me. I lived with the sounds of explosions in my brain, quick lightning flashes.

I didn't see the explosion that burned my parents in that dank moldy cellar; I didn't hear them rolling out their flaming bodies on the lawn, but what I imagined was almost too much to bear. My father supported the anti-war movement and Civil Rights, my mother, too, but they were worried about the danger. "Be careful at these protests!" my dad said, especially after Kent State.

I started to unpack my bag, got out my toothbrush, toothpaste and cosmetics. Then I looked over my class schedule again, memorizing where I would go each day. Exhausted, I fell into a deep sleep.

With my roommates Betsy and Nancy, our communal house was filled with pots of spaghetti always bubbling on the stove and visitors wandering in and out. We shopped at food co-ops, recycled, knowing then that we all needed to do something to preserve the planet. We were considered crazy hippies for recycling. It was 1970. I got a beautiful gray cat with dark black stripes that I named Apu, from *The World of Apu*, an Indian movie about love and child-parent separation that mesmerized me when I was eleven years old and studying India at school.

I painted my walls purple and white and got a tree stump, a la Frank Lloyd Wright, that I put in one corner of the room and placed a huge jade plant on top. With my precious Apu, my purple and pink Indian bedspread, incense, photo of Michael on my bulletin board, my record player and my books, my room became a sensual haven. Michael visited a few times from New York, and we ate organic granola for breakfast, held hands at a small movie theater, the Green Lantern, and made love, saying too many hellos and goodbyes.

Apu was my rock. In the morning he ate from a small white bowl and drank water, his pink tongue lapping up the water so fast it was as if he had been stranded for days in the desert. He slept with me in my bed, his warm, striped furry body protecting me from bad dreams where I was either drowning or running away from a wall of fire. He sometimes roamed through the house but more often than not waited for me on my bed when I came home from class each afternoon. I kept him inside—always—as I didn't want him to get in catfights or get hit by a car.

Though I took a full load of classes, it was only my poetry workshop and graduate poetry seminar that I loved. I managed to get an A in that class. I didn't do as well in my major, comparative literature, chosen quite late in the game. I even got a C- on one comparative literature paper. When I saw the grade, tears sprang to my eyes. I could hear my mother's voice, "What happened??" and could see the disappointment on my father's face and tried to push that voice away that bored into my soul. I got a B- for the class but that was the lowest grade I got and in my major. *I can never measure up to them.*

When I was six years old, I had scarlet fever and missed a whole week of first grade at Public School 40. I stayed in my pajamas, listened to Peter and the Wolf on the record player, listening for the flute, Peter's light voice. I ate toast and jam and watched the strange red spots grow bigger all over my body. I was lucky to get antibiotics. Scarlet fever was serious. It led to one of my heroes, Helen Keller, becoming deaf and blind. When I returned to school, I was put in the "average" reading group and kept glancing at the "high" group, ashamed, until I was moved up.

In my graduate poetry seminar, Professor Rehder, who dressed in tweed suits and white shirts and always wore a tie, let me read poems out loud in French, since I spoke French fluently then, and had an ear for language and music. That small class, which I felt honored to be in as an undergrad, became a cocoon of sorts. Images, line breaks, similes and metaphors spun around my brain. I loved the sound and the taste of words. I went home and secretly drafted poems of my own. *Father/ Your hand/rests on a window/inside the house. Outside, I press my nose against the pane, wrapped in scarves/a peasant/before the palace. /It's not that you're rich/or hold treasures/I cannot receive;/but all these silences form a curtain of glass.* So much I couldn't talk about except in my poetry.

In Rehder's class we also read *The Doors of Perception* by Aldous Huxley. I was drawn into Huxley's description of taking mescaline and the quote by Blake. "If the doors of perception were cleansed, everything would appear to man as it is, infinite. For man has closed himself up, till he sees all things through narrow chinks of his cavern." I still remembered how the old world shimmered one after-

noon and evening on the island of Ibiza, after Ken and I
were turned away from Morocco. All the stars were shooting, thousands of bolts of light speeding through the firma-
ment. The world had more to it than we would ever know.

Later, Professor Rehder was asked to leave campus because he supported the student anti-war protests. He knew
I had been part of the protests and asked me for a letter of
reference. I wrote him a reference and years later, he would
help me get into an MFA program in poetry. Sadly, he was
refused tenure, probably fall-out from his politics as happened to so many during that time. I looked him up years
later; he taught in Europe and had become a poet.

The other class I loved was a creative writing class with
the poet Ruth Stone, a sweet and fragile woman who taught
at her house and made dinner for all of us, usually a big
pot of spaghetti and a salad. Eight of us huddled in a circle
around Ruth and read our poems aloud. She never made
me feel inadequate and said I looked like her daughter. A
few times she cupped my face in her hands. "Sweet, sweet."
My poems were anything but sweet: about disconnections,
a terrible loneliness, war and loss. *When the clock strikes the
hour/a bomb drops/when the land is/burning, nothing left/but
jewelry/artifacts/we are the cruelest animals.*

I don't remember the moment it leaked out, but Ruth
Stone's husband had committed suicide in 1959, and she
was always reeling from a terrible, terrible grief. "I am always writing love poems to a dead man," she said.

With her porcelain skin and dyed red hair, she looked

like a good witch, especially in front of her blazing fireplace, where she could have easily placed a cauldron. We were the special ones, hand-picked to be with her that year. Perhaps I could be a poet? I could also teach.

But that route of the heart, to be a poet, would not be easy.

The temperatures dropped way, way down by October of that year and I liked clustering with the others in front of the fire while brilliant, fragile Ruth Stone held court and carefully pulled apart our poems, line by line, feeling by feeling.

On the next school break in late October, Michael and I drove upstate in his old car. I didn't even tell my parents I was flying back to New York City. I waitressed part time at a Jewish deli and saved my money for the flight. The first night in New York City, I was afraid I might run into my parents and kept looking over my shoulder as Michael and I walked in the Village.

The next day, Michael and I drove upstate listening to Dylan's "The Chimes of Freedom" on the radio.

> *Tolling for the rebel, tolling for the rake*
> *Tolling for the luckless, the abandoned an' forsakened*
> *Tolling for the outcast, burnin' constantly at stake*
> *An' we gazed upon the chimes of freedom flashing*

I sang the song, a deep sadness coursing through me. I didn't realize it then, but I was hoping that the chimes would play for my mother, facially disfigured and stared at every day.

The cityscape turned to country on the New York Thruway. I rolled cigarettes for Michael and me and became quite proficient with the tiny rolling machine. Yellow stains covered my hands. I felt moments of guilt about smoking.

The trees were shedding their leaves and soon would be just branches like old crones dancing on the fields that were covered in light snow.

Right after my parents were burned, my uncle appeared in our apartment one morning, and we rode in the back seat of his car up the New York State Thruway on this same road to live on his farm in Sherburne, New York. We stopped at Howard Johnson's and got hot dogs and malts. It was late July, and the trees were lush with leaves.

The night before, my sister cried all night walking in and out of our parent's bedroom. The beds were neatly made, no indentations of their bodies. She sobbed, "Why can't I talk to them?" I put my hands over my ears.

"They're too hurt to talk," our Aunt Peggy said.

Now, many years later on the same road, the trees were shedding leaves.

The next day, around 8 a.m., Michael and I woke up early at his dorm room, our arms around each other on a twin-sized bed. We ate some crunchy granola and milk at the cafeteria, walked out into a sunshiny day and popped two tabs of mescaline. The drive was gorgeous, down a country road with towering trees towards a lake. Yellow, red and green leaves formed a huge curtain of color over the long, winding road. Fallen leaves covered the ground. Yellow leaves, the color of banana peels, were dotted with black specks. Hand in hand, we walked towards the lake and then it came on, poof, a jolt of energy. Dizzy, I leaned into Michael. He put his arm around me, held me close and then we gazed directly into each other's eyes. My pupils grew bigger and bigger as if to take in more of the world. His blue eyes exploded with all the colors of the sea.

Still hand in hand and leaning into each other, we ambled over to the lake, a swirl of green, blue, and black, like a huge multi-colored lollipop. Then we saw it, a turtle out of the water, on the sand. An enormous and gorgeous turtle, a turtle in all its glory, perfect shell, its armor against the world. Front feet solid flippers so it could glide through water. But it looked so desolate—one huge turtle without its turtle family. Michael and I were together. The turtle was all alone. Waves lapped, making a strange twinkling sound at the shore, but the waves never reached the turtle. We believed, in our mescaline heart of hearts, that the turtle needed to be back in the water, to do its turtle thing and swim. Something was terribly wrong.

"Do you think we should try and move it?"

"I don't know," I said. "I don't want to hurt it." My voice was soft and loving. I loved caring about the turtle with Michael, love from both of us pouring like a silky raiment towards the same thing.

Just then the turtle lifted its tiny head. "I'm scared we'll crack its back and once that happens then a turtle dies." I didn't know if there were turtle vets, or anyone who could uncrack a cracked shell. If I cracked its shell, I would have to live with that for the rest of my life. I was trying to access all my turtle information from the World Book Encyclopedia, the beautiful set of books with green covers my parents bought when my sister was in junior high school. I could see pages flip in front of my brain, pages about turtles from every book I had read. My grandpa bought me so many animal books from the 8th Street bookshop. There had to be turtle information inside my brain, a line or two that would save this turtle.

Our feet were planted at the edge of the water, our hands still intertwined, watching the turtle move its head up and down as if it knew we were there and contemplating its future. Suddenly, and he seemed to just drift into the scene like a piece of dust drifts across the road, a man in a very official uniform walked by. The khaki uniform, so neat and pressed, looked hilarious, and we giggled softly. Under the canopy of leafy trees and by the glistening water, uniforms seemed so unnecessary. Uniforms reminded me of war.

"We have to tell him about the turtle," I whispered to Michael, who then marched right up to the ranger. "We think the turtle needs to go back into the water. We're very worried about it."

The ranger looked directly at us, his eyes square cubes against our rounded mescaline brains. "That's what turtles do," he said flatly. "They come up on shore. Nothing's wrong with that turtle."

"Oh, thank God," I said a bit too loudly. "Thank God." Michael put his arm around me, and we started laughing uncontrollably. By then I'm sure the ranger knew we were high on a hallucinogen. He drifted away like tumbleweed again—just like he had come into view. As we left the lake, we glanced back at the turtle, and both were sure that he picked his tiny head up from inside that huge encasing—as if to say goodbye. "He said goodbye to us, I'm sure he did," I said to Michael.

"I'm sure he did too." Michael and I moved away from the lake back toward the car.

We found a clearing and sat down on the grass, leaning into each other as we ate peanut butter and jelly sandwiches I had made that morning and peach yogurts. We rolled a couple of cigarettes, puffed away, and contemplated the leaves, mesmerized by the colors and the silence. Our arms and legs touched gently, as if we were one person.

Michael then rose from our grassy picnic spot and did some filming. I remember the cool autumn wind, Michael excitedly holding his camera up to the sky mumbling something about the cirrus clouds.

I took our litter to a nearby garbage can. I began to feel unsteady on my feet and unsteady in my heart. I was glad the turtle didn't need to be rescued, but I didn't like that it was alone. I didn't want to be alone either, but the loneliness I felt inside never really seemed to go away, only for moments when I was held.

Michael had classes the next day; I had to go back to school in Madison, so I took the bus back to NYC, sleeping the whole way except for writing a poem.

I'm all wrong up here/and knotted in my chest. I have nowhere to go but a white page.

I didn't want to let anyone climb over the wall I constructed, like an iron curtain, and find out the truth: that I lived inside a lake of sadness.

CHAPTER TWELVE

Three months later, my plane touched down at JFK airport. Winter break. I wished my sister was coming home, but she wasn't. The first Christmas without her. Sometimes we'd talk for hours in her room that was far away from my parents' bedroom. We'd play Edith Piaf records and sing in French to the songs "La Vie en Rose" and "Non, Je ne Regrette Rien." Or she would read to me from *The Little Prince*. Then we'd sing together. Two little sparrows, like Piaf, singing our hearts out.

The bus to Port Authority sped through the dark highway going nearer and nearer to New York City, my dazzling city filled with electric lights. I folded my yellow turtleneck sweater into a pillow on the window, but I couldn't sleep.

When I rang the bell as I couldn't find my key in my purse, my father answered in his brown-and-white-striped cotton pajamas and my mother in a pink nylon negligee and a white quilted jacket over it—the same nightclothes they often wore. At that moment, I liked the predictability. As soon as they saw that I was perfectly whole, in the flesh, just like you do when a baby is born—ten toes and ten fingers—we kissed each other on the cheeks, and all went to our rooms. At that moment, I loved that my bed was made so perfectly, and the room so clean.

My room was a disaster when I left Madison, tangled sheets filled with crumbs and cat fur. Drafts of papers that hadn't made it to the trash lay strewn on the floor, clothes spilling off of the hamper. Splinters from my decaying tree stump with my only plant covered one section of the floor. I hadn't vacuumed in two weeks, and Apu's cat fur was matted to my purple rug and to the floor. *Keep your room clean!* I could hear my mother's scolding voice.

All the order in the world couldn't stop terrible things from happening.

"You have an appointment with Dr. Kittay tomorrow morning at 10 a.m.," my mother called out from her bedroom as I was brushing my teeth that night. I was annoyed. I didn't want to get up early.

"Okay. I'll be up by 8:30." I should have been grateful, but I wasn't.

"Set your alarm. Grandma and Grandpa will probably be up by then." They were visiting for the holidays. "Goodnight, sweetie." She came towards my room, and I walked towards her as she put out her cheek for me to kiss again. She never leaned over to kiss me. Her lips were often wet from the way the grafts were sewn on.

I opened my closet door and hung up my winter coat by the Frost poem, blue marker on white poster board: *I have miles to go before I sleep.*

That winter night it was a relief to not think about food or laundry—because I was lucky, a girl from an upper-middle-class family. We had help for laundry and food stored for a couple of weeks; extra tubes of toothpaste, Crest and Colgate, extra bars of Dove soap, extra shampoo all neatly tucked into the closet.

The heater blew warm air from underneath the bay window that looked onto the courtyard. I liked that our apartment building had a courtyard with a gardener who planted flowers in the spring— red and yellow tulips. I could see color from my fifth-story window when I was in high school.

That night when I came into the building, I gave a hug to our neighbor's daughter Stephanie who lived next door. She was sixteen. Her parents were both deaf and when they fought with her (she was not deaf) the grunting sounds were difficult to hear. When I waited for the elevator during high school, I could hear the noises coming from their apartment. I got used to the noises, though, and knew her parents loved her deeply.

I don't know why, so many years later, I remember running into Stephanie in the hallway that night; only that it was so ordinary, like the tight sheets on my bed, my Frost poem, the blue walls, the heater blowing warm air across my thick dark blue carpet.

When a home coming is ordinary, how do you reconstruct it to make it extraordinary? The extraordinary and frightening part would come later.

The morning was ordinary as well, except I was more tired than I had been in days. All the end-of-the-semester papers, the tests, the getting things ready before I left, the goodbye to my roommates, Betsy and Nancy, and to my cat, Apu, and to making sure he was cared for—all that was still heavy in my body. It was like swimming against a raging current to wake up to go to the dentist. I bolted upright when the alarm went off, though it was like walking through molasses as I got dressed and pulled out my coat from the closet. I didn't have time for breakfast. My mother and father had left for work. My grandmother was reading in the living room. I gave her a big hug. My grandfather was taking a shower. "He'll be so excited to see you," she said. "You're his little buttercup." I couldn't wait to feel his huge arms around me.

"Tell him I'll see him after the dentist."

My grandparents were deeply religious, my grandpa a minister, so it was awkward having them around when I was smoking cigarettes, popping birth control pills, having sex before marriage and sometimes smoking grass. I had a stash of breath mints in my purse.

My new boots that I had gotten in Madison over the Thanksgiving break felt good on my legs. My calves had always been big, and I never fit into sleek-looking boots, but these boots had ties that I could open. My legs now looked sleek, too. My jeans were tucked into the boots so I could show them off and my warm brown ultra-suede coat with fur and delicate pink flowers down the front went down to my knees. It was cold outside, so I put on the mink hat my mother brought me from a trip to Moscow and, of course, mittens.

I looked like a Russian girl then, a Jewish Russian girl from my father's side of the family, from Vilnius, the side of the family that all died, collapsed within five years of each other, mother, father and brother, and often seemed lost to me. My mother always wanted a picture of me in my beautiful brown coat, mink hat and new boots.

I'm not sure why I never took the photograph for her. I've wished over the years since her death that I had done that for her.

I carefully double locked the door and walked to the elevator, pushed the button like I had done all through high school and went across the glassed-in courtyard past the walls with the Oriental rugs on them and right by Frank. "Hi Frank. I hope you're well! I'm back from college."

"I can see you are, dear. You look nice and snug and warm in your coat and hat!"

My Virginia Slims were tucked snuggly into the bottom of my purse. I'd have to wait until after Dr. Kittay to light up. I didn't want him to know I smoked. I made my way to the corner.

It was lightly snowing that morning. I loved the snow flurries. The word flurry was dazzling. Snow flurries dusting the concrete like thousands of tiny angels floating down from the sky. The one block I walked that I could remember, I felt very safe and warm in all my clothes; underneath my coat I wore a white turtleneck and a yellow sweater with beautiful red buttons in the shape of stars. I was going to the dentist, finally taking care of my teeth, As I looked at the snow flurries, I thought about nothing except the fatigue in my body and lighting up a cigarette after my teeth were cleaned. I had to push through an enormous weariness to walk the 15 blocks to Dr. Kittay.

I slipped as my feet left the curb on Fifth Avenue and 12th Street. A short man reached out his left arm to my right arm and steadied me. My new boots didn't have good treads, and the tiny snow flurries felt like the street had been oiled underneath. I was grateful for his arm, so gentlemanly. We moved in tandem to the other side of the street, the side where a restaurant had an outdoor area that was of course empty in the winter. The gentlemanly man who helped me suddenly grabbed my arm tighter. My arm was in a vise, trapped.

As he grabbed me tighter, his small hands now aimed— ready, set, go—at taking me down to the horrible concrete, now no longer beautiful even though it was dusted with snow flurries from the angels. I pulled with all my strength to release myself from him. But release was impossible. To my right, a bright gray metal truck parked at the curb glared at me.

He swung me against the truck with a brutal force and my head crashed on that cold gray metal. Then he threw me down on the ground right behind the outside area of the restaurant, which was filled with delighted customers during the New York City summer. I don't remember the snow flurries or the air or anything except an inhuman shrieking sound exploding out of my throat, a sound like the keening of an elephant who has lost its mate. A sound that could shatter glass.

He had me pinned down, his suffocating body weight trapping me as he kept trying to undress me.

All I had to survive was my voice.

I was in a cul-de-sac, and if he had planned it, which I'm not sure he had, he couldn't have planned it better. No one walking down Fifth Avenue could have seen me. No one. Not Frank the doorman who was only one block away. Not my grandmother or grandfather. Not my parents who were at work. Not Ken. Not Betsy. Not Michael, my boyfriend. No one.

As I lay on the concrete and my attacker lay on top of me, frantically wrenching at the buttons of the beautiful warm coat my mother had bought me, my mink hat now blown off my head somewhere, like helmets of soldiers blown off in war, my legs and arms pinned down even though I kept trying to move them, using all my muscles, all I remember was that I realized he might have a weapon, and there was no one on the street, and I would probably die.

Out of the corner of my desperate eyes and amid my keening sounds, an older man suddenly stood near the cul-de-sac. He stopped and watched. For a minute, I thought he, too, was an attacker and that the whole world had schemed against me at this very moment—a perfect storm—that my upper-middle-class, spoiled existence would again be destroyed as it had been in the fire, and for a very sad moment I wondered what I had done as I tried always, perhaps too hard at times, to be a good child. My grandparents might have thought I had gone off course. I smoked cigarettes. I had had sex before marriage, and I had even tried drugs. But I tried to be kind and nice and polite and all the things great religions say you should be in this world. My heart was beating so rapidly I feared it would just give up and stop. I knew then I would not make it to the dentist and see kind Dr. Kittay.

What happened next was a miracle; the snow flurries really were angels, glistening white protectors. *Your time has not come yet* they murmured into my frozen ears.

In that paralyzed air of the cul-de-sac, my memory shut down and those moments have never returned.

"Where do you live," the man who saved me said, and I must have pointed us both in the right direction, only a half a block from home. I don't remember my attacker fleeing; I don't remember how my mink hat now covered my head or returning to Butterfield House, on 12th Street. The man who saved my life, as my attacker must have run off when he came by, disappeared.

I never even thanked him.

I'm not sure what I looked like or what I felt like because that is the nature of such a horrible shock. But I do remember saying hello to Frank, who had a startled look on his face, his eyes not looking right at me as if that would be an intrusion. He must have been alarmed to see a strange man release me to my house, and that I had left and come back so quickly.

I walked back through the glassed-in courtyard. My limbs leaden. My head throbbed. I cupped my hand over the top of my head as if my palm could take the pain away. Everything was desolate, dried, brown and cracked in the courtyard garden because it was winter.

"You're back so early?" Grandma said.

Grandpa had gone down to the bookstore, probably to buy a book for my sister and me.

I told my grandma what happened, but it was an extremely hard thing to do, so I don't remember the exact words, but I used the words "attack," "the ground," and my "head." I don't think I told her that he lay on top of me trying to rape me. She didn't hug me or look in my eyes. She called my mother at work, which was a big deal. I do remember an ice pack on my head. The cold stung.

I felt embarrassed that this had happened to me.

"Are you tired?" Grandma said, as I'm sure that would be a sign of a concussion, and I think I knew even then what she was asking.

"I'd like to lie down." I walked slowly toward my room.

"Keep the ice pack on your head." I wanted to shut the door, but my grandmother said she would come in and see me, soon. "Leave the door open." She didn't say "darling."

I must have called Ken because I vaguely remember his voice then. I called Michael. He sounded frantic as if this had been done to him and not to me. I called my sister, too, in Canada, even though it was expensive, but I don't remember any of these calls really, just that I dialed their numbers.

Grandma came into my room. "Just stay put. That's what your mother says." Her voice was a flat line.

My mother came home first. I don't remember the door opening or her hugging me or calling me sweetie, but maybe she did.

When my father came home, he shined a light in my eyes and asked me to walk in a straight line. I felt like a specimen. My mother called the police. When the police officer came through the door, I noticed he was tall with red hair and freckles, a round face and very white teeth. I was sitting on the left side of our couch, a white couch with gold brocade that my mother got when I was twelve, and we moved "up" in class from Peter Cooper Village. Newsprint made marks on the couch, and my mother constantly chided me. "Don't read the newspaper on the couch." Now, years later, I can sympathize with her desire for a clean and beautiful couch in our fancy apartment near 5th Avenue, but back then I didn't want "fancy" or to have to be so careful. Once I said to her, "If it's a museum then put up those red velvet ropes so no one will go in there." I'm sure my words stung, and perhaps she chalked it up to the move or teenage angst, but when the officer came into our living room, I pressed my body into the couch and hugged the armrest as if I, too, wanted to be expensive, beautiful and untainted.

He had a wide, friendly smile. If he had said "Top of the morning" with the Irish lilt that he had, I wouldn't have been surprised. Under any other circumstance I would have smiled back at him.

"Sorry to hear about what happened," he said with too

much earnestness. He moved side to side as if he couldn't stand long on one leg. With my mother's disfigured face, the fancy apartment and a 20-year-old woman from an upper-middle-class neighborhood clutching the side of the couch and not wanting to talk, I'm sure he just wanted to get out of there.

"Can you tell me what he looked like?" I was still sitting, and he was standing like a monument in front of me. My father stood next to him, silently, his eyes probing the threads of the Oriental carpet. My mother sat across from me on a rocking chair. I had no arms around me. I wanted the police officer to go. I wanted to go to sleep for a long time, but I wasn't allowed to sleep, not just yet.

"He was short," I said. I lifted my head up momentarily and loosened my grip on the armrest. "I think he was Hispanic. Brown hair. Brown eyes." My voice felt flat. It hurt my lips to talk. I wanted to leave my body and float above the pristine gold brocade couch, above the blue and beige oriental rug, above my parents' thick silence, above my mother's disfigured face, above the police officer's wide smile which didn't belong here and above his pressed blue uniform.

"It's rare we can catch these guys, sorry to say." He bent his head down for a minute. I wondered if he had a daughter, a toddler, and he just wanted to go home and hold her. His breezy smile vanished.

I don't know why I felt this way—and maybe it was because I wanted to leave my body and exist on another plane where bad things never happened, where there was no racism or poverty, or prisons—but with all my heart I didn't want this man who attacked me to go to prison. I almost felt relieved he wouldn't be caught, though I also knew in my heart he could attack someone else. Maybe I was embarrassed that I had given him my arm when I crossed the street. Maybe I thought he could be helped, differently.

"I doubt he'll ever be near here again," the officer said as if to assure me that that this was a good neighborhood and getting attacked here, near 5th Avenue—that this was not anything ordinary. This was extraordinary.

I was relieved when the officer left. I stopped clutching the couch. I had never seen a police officer in my building.

My grandparents remained in their room, probably praying together. I was glad they were tucked away because a sexual assault took the wind out of everything. I also, even then, saw the irony. Nothing this bad had ever happened to me in Morocco, or in all my crazy hitchhiking days when I was so far away from home.

I took a bath that night, the warm water like the amniotic fluid I imagined floating in before the abrupt suddenness of birth. I dried myself and put on pajamas. It was only 8:30 p.m.

"I need to sleep," I said going into my parents' room. They were watching T.V.

"It's okay now," my father said. "It's not a concussion." He got up and got me a glass of water and two aspirin. "This will help with the pain."

I walked into my blue room. I noticed my hands shook slightly, but my body was exhausted. My mother followed me in. "I'm so relieved it's not a concussion, sweetie," she said.

I didn't feel relieved.

She pushed my hair back from my forehead like she used to do when I was very small. At the feel of someone touching me, I stifled some tears. She left the room. My father came into my room then and stood near my bed. He seemed smaller and didn't stand right next to me. He didn't take my hand or bend down to kiss me.

"You can't be scared to go outside," he said as if it was a line he had rehearsed, or something that my mother had told him to say.

"Good night, Weezie," he said, his voice softening. "Try and sleep well." I didn't know if he meant him or me. I was so exhausted, but even with the two aspirin, which I hoped would soon work, my head still throbbed, and I turned my face to the wall.

"Good night, Daddy," I whispered back to him.

I couldn't sleep on my right side as I usually did because of the lump on my head. I reached up my hand to feel it, a huge lump the size of an egg.

I said the 23rd Psalm silently to myself. *The Lord is my shepherd; I shall not want…*imagining I was lying down in green pastures filled with soft moss and sunlight on my back. I had to push away the darkness.

CHAPTER THIRTEEN

The next day at Horn and Hardart's automat, Michael sat on one of the bright chrome chairs with red seats. As a little girl, I loved Horn and Hardart's because I could put nickels in the slots in the windows all by myself and out would come a small round piece of cake covered by orange icing. The icing, which had hardened, would sometimes slip off the cake. I would eat it forkful by forkful until only the little round cake was left. The automats were popular and bustling in the fifties, a miracle that all these tiny windows lined up on one big wall would magically have food inside them, windows that would get refilled again and again, like Santa bringing presents. I planned on skipping lunch and going right for the little orange cake. Maybe I'd have two or three. Sugar would ease the pain.

Michael's head was bowed behind a psychedelic poster of Janis Joplin. The clientele had changed: no smartly dressed couples with little girls wearing wool coats with velvet collars. It had become a hangout for the homeless who cobbled together enough nickels for macaroni and cheese.

When I walked inside, Michael didn't get up to greet me or hug me.

"I'm here," I said and slid down on a chair next to him.

"Oh, baby," he said, "I could have lost you yesterday." He stifled a sob. I was the one who was supposed to sob, but I put my arms around him. All I wanted was my little round sugary orange cake.

"Well, I didn't *die*," I said, my voice rising on the word "die," trying to interject some humor, but when I looked around at the automat—at the men in torn coats, no teeth, and a few women who were obviously on speed as they kept getting up and walking around in small circles—I felt like maybe I *had* died, or at the very least that this was one of the circles of hell. I had signed up to study Dante's Inferno for my last semester at college, and sadly felt like I was doing research.

"Do you want anything?" I said to Michael as I opened my purse and counted my nickels.

"Coffee would be great. I'm not hungry. I haven't eaten since I heard the news." I got him coffee and me a little cake with icing.

We sat there, talking little, the inner circle of hell mirroring our moods.

We hugged goodbye on 14th Street, stores lit up with red and green pulsating Christmas lights and shoppers frantically going in and out of stores holding huge bags of presents. Michael put his head on my shoulder and cried for a minute. My body stiffened, but I don't think he noticed. Why did *he* get to cry? Sometimes he seemed too wrapped up in himself and his own problems. That he didn't *see* me. Or maybe I needed too much.

"The lump on your head will take about two weeks to go away," my dad said matter-of-factly the morning after the assault. I wanted to erase all the evidence of what happened, but I couldn't.

That night I stopped by Ken's house. The five flights up to the apartment took me a long time. I wasn't tired from jet lag, or final exams. This was different.

"Oh Louise, Weezie, sweetie, what an awful thing to go through!" Ken gave me a big hug and I cried for the first time since it happened. I rested my head on his shoulder.

"Let me get you a tissue. And how about some hot tea? Or something to eat?"

"I'm not hungry much, but tea sounds good."

"You need to eat something!" He got a yogurt out of the fridge and gave me a spoon. It actually felt good to eat yogurt, like baby food, something that slid down easily.

A few minutes later, a hot cup of chamomile appeared in front of me. I watched the water turn from clear to yellow as the teabag did its thing.

After the evening with Ken, I never talked about the assault. It would take me twenty-five years to talk about that morning when the snow flurries looked so beautiful. And I lived a nightmare, lucky to be alive. I buried it like an amputated limb, six feet deep.

On the plane ride back to school, all I could think about was Apu, his soft fur, his warm body, his vacuum cleaner purring sound, how he would cuddle up next to me on my purple-and-pink bedspread. "Keep your seatbelts on, there's turbulence," the pilot said, and I noticed my hands shook more than usual. The man next to me had his legs spread out so they leaked into my space, and he didn't seem to care. I didn't want to die next to him.

The thought of cuddly Apu next to me calmed me. At four years old when my parents disappeared, every day I played out in the fields with Shep, the farm dog. My aunt snapped a picture of me and Shep right by the house, under a white wooden awning, my arms around him. Only animals *really* understood me. I loved their heartbeats next to mine, their furry bodies and long tails.

I grabbed the flight magazine from the pocket of the seat in front of me. A photo of a perfect-looking thin stewardess with blonde hair graced the cover. Inside were articles about how to fly with children, the kind of snacks mothers should pack, and island travel destinations. I forgot I was in a metal bird plummeting through the sky.

When I walked into my house, Betsy's brow was furrowed. "Where's Apu?" I said. He hadn't bounded from my room to greet me.

"Oh Louise, he ran away just yesterday! He must have gotten out the door." She looked down at the ground, her fingers twisted together.

"Ran away? Apu? What time? Did you look for him?"

I didn't even go to my room to put my suitcase down, my suitcase filled with brand-new jeans and thick sweaters my mother bought me that now I wanted to throw away. My mother had given me extra money to go to the dentist since I never made it to Dr. Kittay. New clothes. Dental cleaning! I didn't care about anything but Apu.

"I walked up and down the street calling his name. I left food on the steps," she said. "He didn't come back last night."

It was 10 degrees outside. I imagined him frozen, a small furry slab on someone's door, crying for me, crying to be inside, disoriented. Sweet, precious Apu must have searched for me for days and thought I was never going to return.

It was 9 p.m. but I didn't care. I'd find him. He'd hear my voice and come running. He was my cat. He even sat on the edge of the bathtub when I took baths. He purred in my ear at night, and we helped each other sleep peacefully.

I almost slipped down the front steps like I slipped as my feet left the curb on Fifth Avenue that horrible day.

"Apu, Apu," I called out, cried out. Tears drowned my cheeks. I couldn't see much of anything in the dark, but I believed with all my heart Apu would run to me. He had to. He knew his name. "Apu, Apu," I called out repeatedly, for the next 45 minutes. I didn't even have on gloves, and my finger that would turn white because it had once gotten frostbitten lost feeling, but I didn't care if I lost a finger. I thought I saw a cat, like Apu, a small shadow with a tail, run through a neighbor's yard, but it couldn't have been Apu because he would have run to me, leapt into my arms and started purring into my ear.

After the flight and all that had happened in New York I was finally too cold and exhausted to keep calling out for him. He had a collar on with my phone number. Someone would find him. He couldn't be lost forever. He had to come back. I came back to the house, defeated.

I ate a few bites of spaghetti and sauce. Betsy and I said little to each other. Milton, Betsy's cat, was snuggled up on her lap.

I plastered posters all over the neighborhood, but the phone didn't ring with news of Apu that night, the next night or the next week. Every afternoon after school I'd look on the sidewalk, in backyards and behind stairs, believing he would come home, but he never did.

For about a month, I reached for Apu in the dark before I fell asleep and smelled his wet cat-food breath and even heard his purring. Over time, the sounds and smells began to dissipate. I changed my sheets, vacuumed my floor and dusted my room. Apu's fur, beautiful gray-and-black stripe markings, trusting brown eyes, and his sweet cat scent were all lost to me.

In April, 500,000 descended on Washington, D.C. Friends who had dropped out, young men whose lottery numbers came up, were either figuring out ways to make it to Montreal, tripping on acid when they went to induction centers, so they were hallucinating, or fasting for days so they were exhausted and underweight and therefore not army material. I heard of some people who even amputated toes. Some got notes from doctors (my dad wrote a number of notes for his asthmatic, young male patients). Students for a Democratic Society began to unravel, too, as FBI informants infiltrated, and a small group of activists began planning violent acts.

Just as the external world seemed to be unraveling, I was unraveling too, like a ball of yarn that had been too tightly wound and was now seeking release.

I trudged up Bascom Hill to my classes, plagued with senioritis and a system on high alert after the assault, and after losing my precious Apu. My mother couldn't understand why I didn't write one honors paper, so I could graduate with honors. Little did she know what was happening inside my mind. Writing in my black journals helped.

Houses are alive with thunder
Each day survives the next.
Houses rise out of mouths
Like meals
to break down.

Something was breaking down inside me.

When I entered my English classroom after about a month of studying Dante's Inferno, I felt dizzy. Gorgeous pink flowers exploded all over campus. Some friends walked to school in t-shirts, yet I was freezing to death, the opposite of the burning fires of hell.

"What's going on in the Seventh Circle of Hell?" the professor asked. I knew the answer, but my voice caught in my throat. Another student said, "You have to get through the gate guarded by the Minotaur and then you'll reach Phlegethon, a boiling river of blood and fire."

Yes, the professor said, but what does that represent? One of the students started to talk about guilt and violence to oneself and others. I vaguely remembered the reading, but my mind started to separate from itself, like skin peeling off a burned hand, like a glove just slipping off, something thin and white. The fluorescent lights hanging from the ceiling blinked on and off, warning signals about something I couldn't quite grasp. The voices of the professor and the other students drifted from millions of miles away and had no pitch like the voices of humans. The sound was droning, and robotic.

The worst of it was I was starting to have memories I wanted to erase.

High school. My mother was ironing in our small kitchen. She wasn't paying attention and the iron rested on her arm for a minute. She had no feeling in that arm because of all the scars. My mother's skin on her arm, the arm that held me as a little baby, started to bubble up like the boiling river in the inferno. I came into the kitchen, and she looked startled. I remember her flat voice: "I didn't feel it at all." She walked to the bathroom and put a huge gauze pad on the burn. A burn on top of a burn. I wanted to help her, but she shut the door.

As the professor continued to talk, a low murmur that skirted the edges of my ears, I tilted my head so I could look out the windows at the trees blossoming with light. But the memories invaded my mind. "Your mother's face looked like roast beef." That's what her friend told me, after visiting my mother in the hospital. It made me want to feel what my mother had felt, to put an iron on my face. It made me want to throw up. It made me want to run out of the room that seemed to be swirling in boiling water. Why did my mother's friend tell me that?

About twenty minutes into the next class, the walls closed in on me like they did at the jazz concert after the breakup with Joe. The fluorescent lights not only flashed incessantly, but the buzzing screamed into my ears. I was on fire and had to run out of the room to escape; all that blood and fire leaking into my eyes. I gathered my books, knapsack, and coat. I felt ashamed to walk out of a class and put my head down as I gently closed the door.

Outside, spring had sprung after a terribly long, frigid winter. The world was suddenly green, the trees filled with leaves, but I couldn't feel the joy of new life.

I knew I needed help.

"I'm just giving you ten pills," Dr. Mendenhall said at the student health center. "You can always come back if you need to." She was the "cool" doctor at the clinic who prescribed Valium to those of us with anxiety. The minute I walked into her office I knew I was in the right place. She was short and moved fast, but her eyes radiated warmth. She had a photo of a waterfall over her desk. I took my first deep breath in hours.

"Don't be afraid to go out into the world," my father had said to me the night of the assault. I remembered hearing my mother saying, "I didn't need a psychiatrist after the accident. I had my friends." If she could get through something so terrible, her face and hands a mass of third-degree burns, why couldn't I tough it out? I didn't want to tell my parents that my body was constantly trembling with fear.

Dr. Mendenhall prescribed the little bitter pills without making me feel like I was crazy. She solidly believed that with just a little help and encouragement, most of the students that came into her office would soon thrive. "It's a tough time—senior year," she'd say. Or, "Finals can take a lot out of you. This will help." I nodded. I wasn't much of a pill taker, though, and worried about the side effects. "You can break them in half," she said.

The first time I felt jittery right before the *Inferno* class, I took a whole pill, and when class ended, I didn't even get out of my seat for a few minutes.

"Are you okay?" the professor said. It was a small honors class, and I'm sure he knew something was up.

"Yes, thank you—I'm fine," I said, my face stretched taut into a fake smile as I walked as fast as I could out of class. He was trying to reach out, and even asked me to come see him, to talk about getting an A instead of a B+—"You have brilliant thoughts but need help with organization." I never went to see him.

The last thing I wanted to tell anyone was that I was having an anxiety attack, or that I had visions of my mother being burned.

CHAPTER FOURTEEN

Lake Michigan was coated with dead fish strewn across the water. Thousands of helpless eyes floated noiselessly through the waves. I had finished the semester, my last one in Madison. Michael and I were taking the boat to Canada and then hitchhiking to Montreal where my sister lived. My hands felt swollen. I remembered Dr. Mendenhall told me to breathe deeply into a brown paper bag. I didn't have a paper bag. *Now my veins are filled with carbon dioxide*, I thought. Michael was looking at the water when I disappeared into the bathroom. When I gazed at my face in the square bathroom mirror my eyes looked glazed, just like the dead fisheyes.

I took a deep breath and walked out of the bathroom tucking my turquoise-and-green Mexican peasant blouse into my jeans, trying to look put-together. Michael was sitting inside the boat, next to a window, hunched up as if his muscles had died. His jacket looked like it was swallowing him alive. I sat down next to him.

"It's rough water," he said searching my face. But my face was not registering anything.

"Yes, it's really rough and all the dead fish." I noticed how few people were on the boat, or maybe they were all upstairs.

"It's really a shame. This country is a mess. So much pollution."

I wanted to cry, but not in front of him.

"Are you cold?" he said, straightening up.

"A little. It is a bit chilly."

"Maybe you should put on your sweatshirt."

Maybe I should, I thought, but didn't do anything. My arms felt heavy as if I couldn't even lift them. Michael turned to look at the waves again, hunched over.

"Time to get off!" the crew member yelled, walking up and down the boat. He had a round Irish face like a European Santa. When I looked at him, I thought of advent calendars, doors opening to magical scenes. My mother had gotten one for my sister and me every year. We both wanted to open up the window on Christmas day with the baby Jesus. Sometimes the windows had tiny chocolates inside wrapped in gold foil. I devoured them before breakfast.

The crew member had fat, stubby fingers and was giving a couple of directions to a state park just over the border.

"We've got to be aggressive about finding a ride," Michael said, scanning the crowd. "I don't want to be stuck in this place forever." At the word "stuck" my breathing got worse. Veins swelled up on my hands, little blue worms peering up from under my pale skin. Michael confidently approached a Japanese businessperson on the customs line. He came back smiling.

"Hey, baby, we got a ride! He's going all the way to Montreal." I relaxed, imagining us in the back seat of an expensive car, air conditioning on, my head on Michael's shoulder.

It seemed so final, though, getting all the way to Montreal.

Sunlight splashed across my arms and face. We just had to get through the line and then our ride would be waiting. Michael put his arm around me. I liked the solid feel of his arm on my shoulders. I felt hungry for the first time that day. I had some cheese and apples in my backpack. After the line I'd eat something quickly. I didn't want to mess up the man's car.

"You two, come with me." The voice was loud and gruff. No one else was being pulled off the line. A uniformed border guard shuffled us through doors as the Japanese fellow waved a sympathetic goodbye, picking up his leather briefcase and disappearing to the other side of customs.

We entered a square room with square walls: no art or plants. The bulletin board to the left of the huge desk glared at me with all the WANTED signs. The first photo was someone I knew, Eric Bibb, the son of the folksinger Leon Bibb. Eric went to my progressive high school. I assumed he was now a draft dodger. He refused to go and kill in Vietnam. I turned my face away, but my body was shaking. Growing up with so many blacklisted teachers made me feel different. I learned about the Native Americans and how we took their land. I learned about the horrors of slavery in this country. That was great, to learn about the real history of the country, to fight for the oppressed and try and change the world. But right now, I felt like I was wanted, too, by association. Kathy Boudin was my "big sister" in high school. She showed me around my school as a new seventh grader. Years later she would be part of the Weather Underground, blow up a building a block from where we lived—one person dead—and end up in prison for over twenty years. She left prison clutching flowers she wanted to put on her mother's grave. My parents and her parents were friends. I wanted to change the world, too, but not through violence.

My heart pounded in my chest. I heard the voice of kind Dr. Mendenhall: "Stay out of stressful situations as much as you can. Baby yourself right now, as your body finds its equilibrium again." I wished I could see Dr. Mendenhall, have her hug the jitters out of my body.

"How long do you plan to stay in Canada? Show me your money and mister, show me your draft card." Michael handed him his draft card. We were sitting on cold metal chairs in front of a metal desk. The sun tried but failed to blare through the venetian blinds that covered the one small square window.

"We're on vacation for a week," Michael said. His voice quavered. He was a young man. There was a draft. Anything could happen, even though he had a school deferment. "We're camping out."

"Open your knapsacks." The official picked up the phone. A man and woman ushered us into another, smaller room with no window. They rifled through our knapsacks and hunted through our things. Some of my underwear had bloodstains from my period. My clothes were crumpled. They even opened my diaphragm case.

"Are you married?" the man said. His voice sounded taunting. We weren't wearing rings. *We're never going to get married,* I thought. *We're breaking up. That's what we're doing.* Over the past few months, when I felt panicky, Michael's phone calls never made me feel good. He talked endlessly about his films; there was no room for me. He didn't anchor me. Sometimes, if I was talking to someone else at a party, he looked over at me, as if I was doing something wrong. As if he possessed me. But it was so hard to let go.

Michael's father once walked in on us in the bedroom of his house. I was snuggling in Michael's arms, my face buried in his red flannel shirt. We were about to kiss, his thick lips reaching for my lips, our legs intertwined. His father barreled into the room. "Take her home," he said to Michael, "immediately! Not in my house!" as if we were doing something dirty. His father's belly hung out of his expensive blue-and-white bathrobe and his slippers made a grating noise on the wooden floor. Michael never said anything to his dad. He just got dressed, and we left the house. When Joe's dad walked in on us having full-blown sex, he felt so embarrassed. Joe's dad was coming to the room to check on his yellow budgie. "I'm so sorry, so sorry," he muttered as he left the room, head down, and walked down the stairs to the first floor.

"No, we're not married, sir," Michael said. He was trying so hard to be polite. Michael and I were both Jewish (at least for me, my dad, and I figured for the Nazis that would have counted). Thirty years ago, we could have been carted away to the camps if we lived in Europe. The official was writing something down and then kept glancing up at us. My nervousness unsettled him. I tried to calm down, but thoughts raced through my mind. I reached for Michael's hand but then remembered we were not married. What would they think when I reached for his hand? So, I pulled it back.

The man and the woman left all the insides of our knapsacks on the floor like a gutted animal and huddled for a few minutes to talk. My underwear was thrown on top of my poetry books.

"My sister lives in Montreal." My voice was soft and steady now though my hands shook.

"Where does she live?" The officer looked at me as if he didn't believe me.

My eyes disappeared for a minute, the irises like black holes with nothing inside them. I couldn't remember her address. I was forgetting everything, like how to breathe or where people lived.

"We can't let you into Canada until we know her address. And show me your money."

We pulled out our traveler's checks, some bills and loose change, $275 in all, plenty of money for camping and food and maybe one night at a cheap motel.

"That's not much. Where are you going after Montreal?"

"Back to New York City," Michael said.

I searched through my little black velvet pocketbook; the small purse stuffed into my knapsack. I looked through

it frantically. The green walls and the WANTED signs floated around me. I felt porous. Gravity whisked away. Then
my blood collided with my body. I felt my feet on the floor
and took a deep breath. My eyes came back, my ancestral
eyes.

I knew I had a letter from my sister, somewhere, a letter
on thin blue stationery. We wrote to each other all the time.
We rarely called. Too expensive.

"I found it," I sighed, and read the address. "2019 St.
Lawrence Boulevard. Montreal."

The inspector looked surprised and grabbed the letter
from my hand and began reading it. I knew what it said.
"I stayed over at Dan's house last night. I really like him."
Why did he keep reading? It was my letter, not his letter. He
finally handed the letter back to me and didn't look at me.

"You can go now," the officer said. We hurriedly put
back all the insides of our backpacks strewn on the cold
floor. He didn't look up from his desk. That was probably entertainment for him, I thought, humiliating us. We
walked out of the small office, into the bigger office and out
into the sunlight.

"What a bunch of assholes," Michael said, "going
through our packs like that!" He started laughing wildly
and put his arm around me.

"And reading my mail! There's got to be a law about
that."

*Maybe that's what we need. Something to fight against to-
gether. Maybe the relationship will work after all.* Stuck in a

room like that—being searched. That was real life.

The panic attacks were imaginary. That was what I wanted to believe. How could those terrible feelings that I might die, or stop breathing, be real?

"We're in Canada," Michael said, yawning. "It doesn't look any different than Michigan, except some of the signs are in Français." I laughed when he said "Français."

"At least we're off that dreadful boat with all the dead fish." I suddenly felt cold. So many dead things. I reached for Michael's hand, for something solid. He held my hand for a moment and then let go. I felt limp then. I wanted him to hold my hand for a long time. His mind always buzzed. *He won't be the one to bring me back to earth.* When he dropped my hand, I knew that.

We stood on Route 17 and put our thumbs out. The road was big and wide, filled with Canadian sunlight. Michael sang Dylan's "Blowing in the Wind" I began to sing with him, our voices mixing together on the open road.

A truck driver screeched to a halt in front of us.

"Where are you kids going?"

"To Montreal. Anything in that direction," Michael said.

"Hop in. I'll take you about 100 miles. Sault Ste. Marie."

I liked the sound of the words, the alliteration. So many Ss. I wanted to write a poem to Sault Ste. Marie.

"Where you kids from?"

I told him I just graduated from college and that Michael and I were going to see my sister in Montreal. The truck driver seemed so normal with his sturdy hands on the wheel. I liked talking to him, listening to his voice that didn't waver. My arms relaxed into the green upholstery of the back seat. A small picture of his little girl was pasted on to the dashboard. She had long pigtails and wore a sleeveless pink shirtwaist dress. She looked happy, as if she'd always be happy, even if things around her got bad.

"Well, there are a lot of kids on the road. But I'll tell you, I wouldn't let my kid ever hitchhike. You never know what might happen. You kids are college graduates, so you have some smarts, at least I hope you do." He laughed for a minute. "But be careful. I've been hauling pipes from the west to the eastern provinces for 10 years and I've run into some pretty strange drivers. You kids watch out." I turned to look at Michael. He was glaring at me. He didn't like me talking to the truck driver. Why not? I wasn't doing anything wrong. That had happened before—at parties—Michael's stares.

"Here you are. You kids take care." We got off near a hotel and one small grocery store but otherwise the land was flat and empty. "Thank you so much," I said. Michael mumbled something.

"So, he drops us off in the middle of nowhere. Some nice guy!" Michael said.

"He was giving us a ride—not door-to-door service! Plus, there's a motel. We're in Sault Ste. Marie."

Michael started counting his money, pulling the bills he had left in his wallet.

"I don't want to spend anything on some dumb little motel. Let's sleep outdoors. It's warm." He didn't seem to listen to what I wanted. I didn't say anything else.

It was beginning to get dark. Tall grasses blew in a light wind that kissed the flat land. I could see sky for miles. I wished I could fly away and never come back. But I didn't know where I would fly to. I leaned against a tree and felt the scratchy bark on my back.

"There are two trees. We can use one of the ground sheets as a tent," Michael said.

"It doesn't look like rain at all. Maybe we don't need a tent. We can sleep under the stars."

"I don't want to be in full view of people!"

A tent felt cramped again, suffocating. I didn't want to be inside something. But after we set it up, we both crawled in. We were both exhausted, but my body still hummed. I knew the stars were outside, and that they were beautiful.

Inside the tent, Michael reached for me habitually. I slid my head onto his chest.

"It's been a long day," I said, but Michael was already falling asleep. I listened to the crickets, wishing I could see the sky. Bits of light from the stars slid in through the roof of the tent. I buried my face in Michael's chest, wrapped my legs around his legs, like a small bug trying to lose myself in the soil. The sky was far away then. My eyes stayed open for a long time until I drifted into sleep.

The next morning, we stuck out our thumbs, hoping for a good ride.

"Hey, where you two going?" An old white dingy Chevrolet stopped in front of us.

"Montreal. Or anywhere nearby."

"Going that way." I didn't like the sound of his voice. It didn't have the ups and downs that voices are supposed to have. But we both jumped into the back seat.

The driver puffed anxiously on a cigar that stank up the whole back seat. He had thick hands that moved recklessly up and down the steering wheel. He was bald and the top of his head was oily. *Be careful. A lot of crazy drivers on the road.* I remembered the solid voice of our last driver. I doubted this driver had a daughter that he cared about.

Our new driver kept looking in the rearview mirror, his eyes darting around like they weren't connected.

"Hey, you two look awful cute. Are you going steady?"

I stiffened and threaded my left hand through Michael's. Again, we had a common enemy, something to fight against. That would bring us closer. That would take away my anxiety. The driver kept gazing in the rearview mirror and now he was smacking his lips. He took one of his hands off the steering wheel. He seemed to be jerking off. He made small moans. Disgusting. I held Michael's hand tighter, and his fingers answered back; our palms were yelling *help us.*

"Awful cute, yes. Both of you. Awful cute. See what I can do to help."

Michael looked nervous but paralyzed inside himself. If we were going to get through this and not end up on some dirt road in the middle of nowhere, raped or stabbed, we had to make a move. It started raining, everything out the window murky and muddy. Our lives inside metal. The driver kept touching himself, lightly moaning and looking in the back mirror. "Cute, awful cute. Both of you." And then he'd moan lightly. The one hand he had on the wheel kept slipping and it was pouring rain now. Just like down the coast of Spain when I told Jaclyn *we have to get out, we have to escape.*

"We have to escape," I whispered to Michael, who was now on high alert, his blue eyes lighthouses, looking out the window.

"Hey, what are you whispering about, lovebirds?" the driver said.

"Just about the weather," I said in a singsong voice. "The rain is really coming down!"

"I don't believe that's what you said, but I'll let it go, this time." A chill ran through me.

I thought of my parents puttering around their apartment. It was a Saturday. My father would have come home from hospital rounds. Perhaps they were both sitting in their tweed chairs in the back bedroom, reading, my dad the *Manchester Guardian* or maybe a medical journal. My mother might be editing a piece for the *American Journal of Nursing.* Nothing chaotic.

Nothing chilling like a psychopath's voice over the pounding rain.

"What are you two up to? What are you planning? Tell me. Tell me now." His voice was loud and gruff. His eyes, which I could see in the rearview mirror, didn't look angry or frightening. Worse—they looked empty. Dug-out sockets. The driver swerved for a minute and mercifully put both hands back on the wheel. I thought we might end up in a ditch, but he righted the car. "Hey lovebirds, what's the problem? I go to church. I call my mother twice a month. You want credentials? You're the weirdoes, don't you see that? Hitchhiking with strangers," and then he laughed hysterically. His head shook back and forth like it was attached to a spring. "Give me twenty bucks and I'll let you lovebirds fly away."

Michael fumbled for his wallet. The man sped up, faster and faster. It was noon and a warning siren signifying the sun's height blew all around us. I thought of ambulances. My parents carted away in the middle of the night. Ever since then, nights had beginnings, middles and ends.

Michael handed him $20.

"You think twenty bucks will do it? You lovebirds keep your goddamn twenty bucks. What I want—you come to my pad. Nothing kinky. Nothing I'm sure you've never done. I know what you're thinking." A red light loomed ahead. No town. Why was the light there? For us? I hoped and prayed the light would stay red. *Stay red*, I silently said to myself. *Stay red. Stay red.*

Michael sat up straighter and clutched my hand. *We're holding on to each other*, I thought, *holding on.*

"NOW." The car was stopped. I opened the left car door by ramming my body into it and Michael and I propelled our bodies onto the wet, muddy road. Our backpacks cushioned the terrifying fall to the ground. The driver sped away, thank God, tires screeching on the wet pavement. Lightning sliced through the sky. And then thunder, a terrible groaning sound. But we were out of the car.

An abandoned barn loomed in front of us, where we could go to get out of the rain. A barbed wire fence ran around the property, but a big hole had been cut through it. We slipped through and walked about a quarter of a mile through short grass. Our fingers wound together. My sneakers sunk deep into the mushy soil. With the squeaking sound of mud, and with the rain pouring on my face I felt suddenly and completely alive.

On the farm where I lived when my parents were in the hospital, recovering from their burns, my sweet and gentle cousin Robert, 13 years old, would lift up my four-year-old body to protect me from the holes the cows made in the mud. Sometimes my short legs would slide into the long holes, and I would get stuck and cry as my sister and cousin Jean kept running, running further away from me in places I was too small or too scared to jump over.

When Michael and I reached the barn, rain poured down, cascades of rain. My long brown hair molded to my face. Michael's face glistened with water.

"You look beautiful now," he said, "wet and glowing." We were in the middle of a huge field, as we made our way through short green grass,

"We're alive," I said, throwing my arms around him. Michael started crying.

I felt in control for the first time in months. No panic.

But it was short-lived.

I wished with all the life force bubbling up inside me that I could change the death I knew that was coming.

"Yeah. We escaped. We escaped," Michael kept repeating and then ran behind the barn. He re-appeared clutching wet daisies. "These are for you, my beautiful lady," he said, handing me four perfect flowers. I folded them to my breast, looking at the dainty geometry of the petals, then looked deeply and painfully into Michael's eyes.

"I guess this is the end," I said, my voice breaking.

"I guess it is," he said, tears running down his face.

I turned my face away, waiting to taste salt in the rain. My breathing got shallow. I was drifting molecules.

I looked at Michael again and brushed a few stray curls out of his wet eyes.

Images flashed before me: the lone tree he filmed, a gorgeous oak in the middle of a green field in Upstate New York; after the filming, we found a secluded spot and made love one autumn afternoon; the turtle we thought was stranded in our mescaline haze; how we wanted to take care of that turtle, help it live—Michael's films, my poems, two artists tangled together. But it wasn't enough.

"Let's go inside," Michael said. Tears still streamed down his cheeks. We strode to a ladder to a huge hayloft, and I climbed up first, feeling more sensual than I had in months, my backpack on my back, the four daisies in my hand, Michael's moist eyes following the movement of my hips. The ladder wobbled, but it held us in its antique rungs. When we got to the top, Michael put his arms around me and started kissing me.

"No, Michael, no," I said. If we were breaking up, this felt wrong. To connect again so deeply.

But as soon as we spread out our sleeping bags on the wooden floor, we moved towards each other, his hands gently caressing my breasts, moving in a soft, circular motion as I reached out to kiss him. We devoured each other in that abandoned barn, like we devoured each other the first night we made love with the sirens screaming down First Avenue. Rain still pounded on the roof. The next morning, we woke up in each other's arms and made love again, as a rooster crowed.

I pulled away then, remembering that this was the end. It could have been a beginning but a chasm too deep, a fear that I couldn't name, a fear that stuck in my chest like the terror I couldn't cross in the farm as a little girl, loomed darker and larger than the possibility of enduring love. My breath got short. Michael got up abruptly, angrily. *It's so easy to be in love,* I thought, *knowing it will soon be over.*

We landed in Montreal at noon, three rides later. My sister was at work and couldn't get the key to us until 4 p.m. Montreal was quieter now, like Madison had become.

The Front de Libération Nationale went underground after a bombing of a building owned by Brinks and Company on January 6th. Ninety-three bombs had been detonated in that city and the War Measures Act invoked, so military police paraded on the streets holding weapons. Premier

Lévesque denounced these measures as French Canadians fought for sovereignty. My sister, a student at McGill, had been whisked out of classes a number of times over the last two years when leftist activists threatened to blow up buildings, just like radicals had ended up blowing up the chemistry building in Madison, to protest the war. Peace and love had turned violent, though only by a small number of activists; now they were always the ones portrayed on the news media.

Landing in Montreal, a city that had recently been on the cusp of violence, my body felt like it was also on the cusp of violence inside and outside. Broken things lived inside me. That night Michael and I fell into our own corners of a blow-up mattress in my sister's house, an old sleeping bag on top of us.

The next morning Michael had to get the bus at 9 a.m. for New York City. He dressed quickly. I got up after him—I didn't change out of a long t-shirt I wore to bed and made coffee, which took forever to percolate. I heard Michael brush his teeth. I just wanted him gone. He must have felt the same way because he gulped down a few sips of coffee, said goodbye to my sister who was up as well and gave me a perfunctory hug and left. I couldn't even cry. I stared at my coffee, added more milk, and kept stirring it and stirring it as the clock ticked and my sister's cat, Petrushka, tunneled in and out of my legs.

CHAPTER FIFTEEN

One night after a chicken dinner, my parents were about to get up from the table. "I feel panicky," I said in a small, tinny voice. I had come back from Montreal a week ago. I tore up my paper napkin under the table and my feet rocked back and forth like a four-year-old's.

"Let's talk about it when the dishes are all in the dishwasher," my mother said. I got up to clear the dishes. My father looked sad for a minute like he had failed at something. He didn't get his doctor's bag out of the closet to fix me.

A few minutes later we were all sitting in the living room. This time I sat on a chair and didn't sink into the pristine couch.

"I feel like something's wrong with my heart. It's fluttering."

My dad got out his stethoscope and my mother sat on a chair across from me. She looked concerned in a scientific kind of way. I felt detached from the living room, my living room. The portraits of me and my sister in gold leaf frames on the wall looked like children of the damned, eyes too big, necks too long. My dad's voice sounded condescending as if he thought I was just faking it. All he wanted to do was probably have a martini and watch *Columbo* in the bedroom with my mother. He must have known I didn't have heart problems. What I did have, I don't think he wanted to face.

The stethoscope felt chilly on my chest. My dad was quiet, leaning towards me and listening. "Your heart sounds fine. Let me know if you still feel it."

That night I had trouble going to sleep. For what felt like hours, I kept counting backwards from 100 like I did as a little girl. I went from 100 to 1, two, three times before sleep overtook my body.

The next morning, I felt it again, the thump, thump, thump. Tears pooled in my eyes as I left for work. At work, typing for Kelly Girls, I felt it all the time, morning, noon, and night. I couldn't take a deep breath. Something was stuck in my chest and wouldn't move.

"I can't take deep breaths," I told my dad when I got home and even showed him how I tried but my breath would only go so far. "I don't know why. Why do you think?" My eyes were pleading. He dutifully got out his doctor bag from the closet and listened to my chest again. My mother came and sat on a chair near me.

"Everything sounds fine. Just try and relax." He got up and walked into the back room. My mother didn't seem convinced nothing was wrong, but she got up when my father got up. I was left sitting on the couch with my heart racing, hearing my father's voice in my head, "Nothing's wrong."

Their voices were hushed, but I heard them whispering in their bedroom. "She needs to see someone," my mother said.

"But nothing's wrong," my dad said.

"It doesn't matter, she'll feel better when she sees someone."

"We're making an appointment for you with a neurologist," my mother said, coming into the living room, where I was still sitting, staring at the bookshelf, wondering if I could just find the right book, the one perfect book to help me—"to get things checked out."

I had so much energy the day of the appointment that I walked all the way uptown, seventy blocks, even in the heat. I was trying to outrun the panic like people run away from fire, a determined invisible screaming pressing me on. I passed fancy stores, Saks Fifth Avenue, Lord and Taylor, and lunchtime crowds moving rapidly across the streets. I passed bronze, muscular Atlas holding up the world. For a minute I wanted to be a baby, cradled in his arms. Then I pulled myself up taller. I could be powerful, too. I could be Atlas, holding up the world.

My heart thumped, thumped, thumped so fast I feared it would jump out of my chest cavity, my fragile heart landing, like in a surreal painting, on a strip of Manhattan concrete.

I crossed one street after the next, red lights, green lights, the kind of pedestrian dance that people who grow up in New York City do every day. I was moving fast, rapid-fire uptown. I was always early for appointments.

My parents said I was seeing a neurologist, but when I entered the office I saw a big sign that said "psychiatrist/neurologist" and felt betrayed. My parents didn't tell me they were sending me to a shrink. My mother always said she didn't need a psychiatrist when she was burned. She was strong. Did they think I was weak?

"The doctor will be right with you," the receptionist said in a perky voice. Maybe the doctor had hired someone perky as an antidote to all the pain. There were only a few people in the enormous waiting room. I passed a mirror. My eyes looked strange, pupils too big, as if I were on LSD, taking in so much of the world. I could even see the furniture breathing, the walls sweating, and the fluorescent lights humming. Once my father had talked about a woman who didn't look in mirrors. She was schizophrenic. It was long ago, and a time when every woman looked in the mirror to put on her hat or see that she was "put together" before going in to see a doctor or out into the world.

"She didn't look in the mirror. That was a sign," he said.

Sometimes I didn't look at mirrors. Was I going crazy? Sometimes my eyes looked dull as stones. Maybe I was going to really lose it, to hear voices. Maybe my brain had fissures in it that I couldn't jump across. Maybe I would hear radio voices humming between my ears, my brain taken over by some alien force. I took a deep breath as the receptionist called my name; my hands shivery. *I'm not crazy.* I kept repeating it to myself like a mantra.

"Louise, please follow me." A young woman, perhaps a nurse, led me to the doctor's office. I stood up straighter, wanting to be strong like my mother. How come she was so strong?

I could ski on advanced slopes, black diamond slopes, which my parents never did; I jumped moguls. I won tennis trophies, climbed Mt. Washington, won water-skiing awards. I wrote poetry. My craft. Ancestral words floated to me from the cold winters of Vilnius, Russia. *In Russia, /our Father's dead parents/thread a needle that I hold. My fingers remember/interminable winters/and grow cold. Then I look at you, hoping and hoping.* I was also from the purple-heather moors of England, my words riding the backs of Shetland ponies. *Grandma/born under a thatched roof/in Thorverton, England, /One graveyard, one butcher shop, one stream/and the ghost of her 17 year old dreams/of a new world.* I was trying to figure out who I was and where I came from. Through words.

I wanted to teach, too. I loved the thought of having students. I knew what I wanted. Wasn't that enough? What more did my parents want? I had been assaulted, thrown down on concrete, but I was saved, and now I was fine. How could my parents think I was crazy? If they thought that, then everything I had done to please them my whole life would be meaningless.

Years later, I realized that my panic sprung from the accident, my panic sprung from the assault and sprung from losing my cat. But then I had no idea of that, and no one was there to truly help me.

"Do you have a boyfriend?" Dr. Goldstein asked me. "Do you see your sister much? Do you smoke cigarettes?" He was a portly man and wore a white coat, pressed white shirt and tie. The air conditioning was on full blast, and I shivered from the cold. He didn't look at me when he asked the questions, but just pretended he was checking my reflexes the whole time. I didn't like him. I answered "kind of" about the boyfriend since Michael and I had seen each other once the last week, had sex but it was perfunctory and quick; it wasn't making love, and "yes" that I saw my sister and shrugged my shoulders about the cigarettes. I didn't want my parents to know I smoked.

Why did he keep tapping my knee? My knee kept jerking up, and he kept asking questions. *Get me out of here,* I screamed to myself.

How could he help me with my panic?

Didn't he think I would know he was trying to suck information out of me? The grand inquisitor. That's what he was, just trying to label me and let my parents know I was weak and messed up.

Dr. Goldstein didn't look so happy when I left his office. I knew he would report right back to my parents. That I was sullen. Uncooperative.

I tried to be polite when I left. I knew the appointment had been a "professional courtesy" as I didn't sign anything or pay. I should feel lucky. How many people get to see a famous psychiatrist/neurologist in a big, plush office? My parents were concerned. They made the appointment for me.

I left his office on Central Park East, the walls covered with his huge perfectly framed diplomas. I walked across the gray pavement flecked with white, glittery dots. I wanted to glitter, to be beautiful, my eyes shining with joy, not pupils expanding from terror, my hands trembling, heart racing, de dum, de dum, de dum. I could hear it, hear inside my body. I remembered hearing that if you went into a soundproof chamber, you could hear the hum of your nervous system and the thump of your heartbeat. Those were the two main sounds of the universe, a high-pitched screech and a low da dum, da dum, da dum. How many heartbeats would we have in our lives?

If I kept moving in the summer heat, maybe I could outrun the panic.

I passed the Central Park Zoo. My father took me and my sister there on Sundays when we were little. "The polar bear has such a great warm coat," he would say when we visited in the winter. "I wish I had a coat like that!" In the summer, we watched the seals racing around and around in circles. Annie and I would giggle.

If there was a baby animal, like the time we saw a baby kangaroo, inside its mama's pouch, we'd all stare transfixed and not say anything for a few minutes as if we all knew: life was miraculous. One being neatly tucked inside another, just a heartbeat away.

Daddy would get us hot dogs. Sometimes ketchup spilled onto my shirt, and he didn't care. I liked that he didn't care. My mother cared too much that we looked perfect, nothing stained.

Maybe she wanted people to stare at us and not at her disfigured face.

I didn't want to let down my daddy by being crazy. He had told me to go out into the world. And my mother, facially disfigured. She had gone back to work, smartly dressed in a tailored tweet jacket and skirt, put on Ferragamo shoes, picked up a leather briefcase in her terribly scarred and claw-like hands, and picked up her life. She warded off stares and kept marching on. "She's so strong, what a heroine," people would say.

No one made another appointment for me.

A week later, I wasn't any better. Panic sped through my body as if something was suspended inside of me, lurking. Fish swimming in my bloodstream, little slippery movements that startled me. A fire not completely out, ashes that sparked. I couldn't take a deep breath.

"Mom, Dad, I need to talk." We had finished dinner. My dad was about to go into their back bedroom to read. My mother had just finished arranging and rearranging the dishwasher to perfection. I wanted to be perfect too, like the dishes.

"Okay, let's go into your room," my mom said uncharacteristically. Both of them sat in chairs near my desk. I sat on my bed and tried to sit up straight. My skin itched and I scratched a patch of eczema on the back of my neck.

"I need to see a therapist," I said. Tears flooded my eyes.

I had my friends, my mother repeated again and again after the accident. *I didn't need a psychiatrist.*

What was wrong with me. Weren't my friends enough?

"Your father saw a psychiatrist for four years," my mother said. My nervous system calmed down. I never knew that. "When he was thinking of becoming a psychiatrist." There it was again. He saw someone because medical school required it. My father said nothing.

"We'll help you with this," my father said, finally looking up and looking at me directly. His eyes were sad. He squirmed in his chair. Maybe he didn't want to believe that I was injured on the inside. My mother lit one tiny match and cascades of hurt swept down, even to the next generation. My father was right beside her holding the flashlight. Nothing was normal. I was the evidence. All the facades in the world couldn't cover it up.

They didn't say, "Oh I'm so sorry about the panicky feelings. That must be hard. We'll do anything to help, anything!" Like the time when I was assaulted, alone on the couch, I now sat alone on my bed, the two of them looking at me, my mother my father. Not wanting to face what I was feeling. That what happened to them had happened to me. That my dad's Ivy League education couldn't protect me. That my mother, who had pulled herself up from Salvation Army homes into the upper middle class could not stop my panic.

"How about Dr Bonime," my mother said. She was good at solutions.

"I'm not sure. I heard about someone, a psychiatric nurse. A friend told me about her, Lynne. She's just a few blocks away." My parents said nothing. From the way they looked at me—staring and silent—they didn't want to stop me from getting help, any kind of help. For that I was grateful.

Dr. Bonime was too connected to my parents. They might talk about me, together. I wanted something all my own.

When I went to bed that night, my body melted into the mattress, some of the trembling gone.

I called Lynne the next day to set up an appointment.

CHAPTER SIXTEEN

When I first saw the fan in Lynne's cluttered waiting room, I wanted to put my hand in it. Whirring flesh and blood. Spilling like drops of rain all over her messy table. Blood on *People* magazine. Blood on *Newsweek*. So red, everyone would know I was wounded.

Smells of sickly antiseptic mixed with the stale air as I walked to my mother's room at night after one of her many operations, her wounds covered over in gauze. I brushed my thin, not burned arms against the cool white walls.

"Mommy, Mommy, are you alive?" I'd say, trying to find her eyes that were not wrapped in gauze.

"Yes, sweetie, go back to bed." I turned around, my arms against the walls, and went back to bed.

Once when my mother was in the hospital I ran fast at the Playground after school, faster than all the girls and boys, my lanyard with my key around my neck, and then purposely slid on my right knee. "Ouch," I cried out. Blood seeped through my thin blue cotton pants. My sister saw me from across the yard.

"What did you do that for, Weezie? Let's go upstairs and clean it off."

I have scars, too.

Now, so many years later I was in a therapist's office. Lynne, a psychiatric nurse, had no air conditioning. It was hot. The fan in the waiting room made a loud, whooshing sound. Why didn't I go to Dr. Bonime, my parents' friend?

He was a kind, skilled psychiatrist, open to all sorts of alternative ways of seeing the universe. He once showed me a book on "energy fields," bizarre photos of how plants received energy, showing white lights surrounding a potted fern. Like an x-ray of a Martian ship. Maybe if I had seen him first, instead of Dr. Goldstein, I would have stayed with him and healed.

But this was my choice, seeing Lynne. I had to get away from my parents. I might get trapped, sucked down a hole I couldn't crawl out of. Plus, the generation gap was a huge gulf. "Don't trust anyone over 30" was the mantra of the time. I'd be suffocated. Thrown off course, even though I didn't really have a course.

As I sat in Lynne's cluttered waiting room with the whirring fan, I wondered if I had made a mistake.

A few minutes later, the previous patient walked out of her room and Lynne greeted me quickly. She was pretty with long dark hair, slightly heavy and moved slowly like a ship entering port. I sat down and proceeded to entertain her: what I had done, whom I had been with, what poems I had written. She wrote some things down in a notebook. Papers and books sat chaotically on top of her desk. She nodded at my outpourings: the shows at the MOMA I saw with Ken, my mother taking me out to an Italian lunch, the independent movies I saw, my new boyfriend, Sarkis, eleven years older than me, a good man, a solid man with a huge extended family, an Armenian filmmaker, whom I met on the IRT train. We were drawn to each other on that subway ride and talked briefly. He gave me a piece of paper with "Sark" and a phone number on it and said, "Please call." I kept thinking it must be Mark. I had never dated an Armenian man.

I talked about my father: that he was a brilliant doctor, Yale, Columbia, scoring first on a test that 700 doctors took to work for the New York City Fire Department, that my mother was second in her graduating class at Teachers College at Columbia. That I had just average math SAT scores, that kept me out of the top colleges though my verbal scores were good, and my grades were great. I worked hard, but I couldn't measure up. That was another hole in my heart.

I talked about my mother, her determination. I talked about the accident that burned them: the scars, the hospitalizations, and the pain. *Their pain.* Never my pain. She nodded. I told her I was privileged, I was okay. I felt sorry for the people without those opportunities. I wanted to change the world, to work with people who had less than me. She nodded.

I talked about my sister who drew dancers with limbs that intertwined in ways that were impossible, drawings my mother didn't like. "Anne," she would say in a sharp voice, after looking at the drawings. They didn't all look happy and cheerful and that's what my mother wanted, for us to be happy and cheerful. To be perky. "What are these supposed to be?"

Lynne nodded. She nodded until I thought she might not be able to nod anymore. She took the money my father sent, insisting I come three times a week. I could hear the fan still whirring in the next room. I could hear people coming in through the door and sitting in the waiting room. I could hear keys jangle, or the pages of a magazine, *Newsweek*, crinkle.

I could even hear the sound of breathing, but that was all in between my outpouring of what I'd done. Lists and lists. What I wanted to do. How Ken and I visited the Metropolitan Museum of Art the other day, how we reveled in the art. The poetry readings. The words, the words. She nodded. "Time's up."

The panic attacks had threatened to derail my life. Even though so many of those sessions with Lynne felt like nothing happened, just talking helped. The icy cold hands, the trembling inside, began to diminish, only a small ripple through my system.

On one visit, I stared out Lynne's dusty window on a bleak winter day and turned to face her when she said: "Your parents were adults when they were burned, but you were only four years old at the time of the terrible accident." I put my head in my hands, and saw myself, little pudgy hands, short bangs slightly crooked, a navy blue dress with a white collar, and I cried, finally, for little Weezie.

Years later, when I spoke at a burn convention, I found out that everyone in a family with someone burned is now called a "burn survivor." But then I didn't know that, and I couldn't understand the strange ache in my chest, the feeling that life could blow up at any instant, the terror about getting close to anyone. My parents' upper-middle-class life offered great opportunities and comfort but could never truly shield me from the torrents of buried grief.

By fall after college, my life started to stabilize, to congeal. My wandering molecules glommed together and began to create a "me." I got a job working for the Brooklyn Court Employment Project. My mother offered me a job at the American Journal of Nursing, where she worked. Her best friend offered me a job in her advertising company. If I had worked with my mother, perhaps we could have gotten closer, but I wanted to do it all myself, and I did. The late sixties and early seventies were part of it. Creating a new world meant breaking from our parents. My boss, Gene, was married to a woman who went to my high school. That sealed the deal at the interview.

Most of the people working there were ex- heroin addicts. It was a city job, so the pay was good, and I had benefits. I rented an apartment on Perry Street, my rent a perfect quarter of my salary. It was a few blocks from where Ken lived. A small studio, fifth-floor walk-up. Now I had help with the panic, a decent job, a filmmaker boyfriend, and a beautiful little apartment.

One weekend Ken helped me rent a sander, which we lugged up the five flights to the top of the building. We sanded and polyeurathaned my painted floor. We toiled all day in the humid heat both wearing shorts and t-shirts. Under dirt and gobs of paint, grain emerged, beautiful wood grain, shining like invisible words becoming visible when put into water. How wondrous that such beauty was so hidden.

I helped Ken sand his floor on his apartment, gorgeous wood grain appearing like a miracle, something fresh and new.

We also both painted our walls white. Pristine. Pure. Anything could be written on the walls. Tabula rasa. The wood and the white walls shone and glowed. Poems poured out of me in my little sanctuary, five flights up on Perry Street. I even tried to write a Villanelle, with specific rhymes. *You cry baby/like night gone crazy/Just cradle music child and lazy.*

One Saturday afternoon, I went to a psychic down the block from where my parents lived, a small, woman with a flowered dress who looked like a reverend's wife. She didn't know I was a poet.

"I see the poet Elizabeth Barrett Browning sitting on your left shoulder," she said. "On your right shoulder, I see an elephant, your spirit animal." Before I left, she said, "You're a happy person, but fear gets in the way." I wondered if fear was the invisible wall I built around me. That I was sealed in.

"You're not James Joyce," my boss, Gene, said. "Just write a clear report why this participant should get out of jail. Don't make it so flowery. This isn't creative writing."

At the Brooklyn Court Employment Project, where I flourished in my new job, I wrote two-page single-spaced reports to the judge. Young people arrested on misdemeanors and some felonies faced fines and jail time. They were brought into our program and given psychological counseling and career counseling. I had to convince the judge that they had changed, just like characters in novels born in difficult circumstances faced obstacles and then overcame their past. The arc of life. Bingo. I loved my job; that my writing could change people's lives.

High school dropouts from crowded one-room apartments with absent fathers and drug-addicted brothers, they had grown up without opportunities or safety net. Our program gave them a chance: a job at the A&P supermarket, and a "life plan" with a counselor. Check-ins by phone every day. Check-ins in person once a week. Paperwork, tons and tons of paperwork for the program, for the court. For some of them, life was looking up. They could change, really change forever. School—new skills. This felt good. I was privileged. They were not. I was doing decent work, not working in a bourgeois advertising company.

One day after work, a friend from work, Ron, and I rode the train together from Remsen Street in Brooklyn to 8th Street in Manhattan. We both held on to the pole, the train packed, bodies heaving back and forth. He stood a little too close to me, though personal space was at a minimum at rush hour. He also knew I had a boyfriend. He could be a new friend. We'd have dinner together. I liked that I had a friend from work. I could merge my worlds.

His flute was in a case, attached to a huge leather strap that slung over his shoulder. He played at lunchtime at work. He was good, really good. We got off at Christopher Street and walked to Perry Street and then west six blocks, almost to the water, and climbed up the five flights to my apartment: my sweet apartment with the newly sanded floors, my bed covered with a nubby white comforter and a few posters on my wall, Degas' dancers and a portrait of Isadora Duncan. A huge bookcase held poetry books, a few novels, some self-help books and little black journals with my scribbling and bits and pieces of poems. This was my first "grown-up" after-college apartment, and it was decidedly me: the splashes of primary colors, the books, my new yogurt maker, an attempt to do it myself and save money on all the yogurt I consumed. September was still warm. I opened the window gate to the sound of car noises and the voices of children. I turned on the fan. I liked having him at my apartment. Someone from work, from my other life. He was short and lithe, the kind of flute player that would make you cry all over your body it went so deep.

"You're quite a reader," he said, looking at my shelf of poetry and novels. "I have lots of catching up to do." He had been on heroin for years. Most of the counselors had been on heroin. But they had kicked it, had overcome huge obstacles. My struggles, trying to live up to my parents' lofty expectations, seemed paltry in comparison.

Before heroin he had been in music school and was going to "go somewhere big." He might have said something about his mother pushing him to get a scholarship since the family had no money, which he did, a sister who dropped out of high school and he couldn't find her. He talked quietly once at lunch, months ago, but the table was crowded and Gene, as usual, was holding court, about his crazy heroin days, about literature and about movies, so Ron hardly got in a word. He was sweet, a kind soul.

My parents, who lived off Fifth Avenue just ten blocks away, would probably not approve, because of the drugs and his lack of high-paying employment. They wanted my sister and me to make a good salary and to have peers that reflected that.

"He took heroin?" they would say. Even though my parents were quite liberal, they just stereotyped too much. People got off drugs and rehabilitated.

I had some chicken and salad in the fridge, and I pulled out two plates from the cabinet. We ate at my tiny kitchen table. We talked about some of the participants in the program and a little about the village and the music scene. "Hard to break into," Ron said. "But I keep trying." I was sure he would make it. He had the skill and the personality. I wanted to make it as a poet—poets/musicians, that's what the village was all about then. I put on the radio and Dylan crooned "I Shall Be Released."

I wasn't sure what I wanted to be released from, but I loved that song and sang along. Little did I know that years later I would move from the east to the west.

After dinner, after I had cleared and washed the dishes, Ron pulled out a joint. "Do you want a hit?" he said. "It's really good." I had no couch, just one maroon beanbag chair and the bed. We were both sitting on the edge of the bed, and I wished I had sat in the beanbag chair. Our backs were to the window, close to the window gate, which my parents had paid for. "A security measure," they said. The bars dug slightly into my back. He moved closer to where I was then and lit up. The smoke curled thickly in the air. The smell was strange, a metallic, shiny smell.

I didn't really want him to sit so close to me. "My boyfriend, Sark, is a filmmaker," I said. "He lives on MacDougal Street. I spend most weekends with him in the country, but we take a few days off from each other during the week. I write a lot at night." Hint. Hint. Boyfriend, close proximity to where we were. I wanted him to inch away from me or get up. He started to lean toward me, his shoulder moving toward my shoulder. I gently moved away, hoping it didn't look too abrupt. He took a deep puff from the joint and passed it to me. I took a puff—he took a puff—I took another and then he put it out on an ashtray and then stuffed it into his flute case. Smoke swirled around our bodies.

"Very strong stuff," he said. "Think that's enough." He got his flute out of the case, stood up and played a piece. The high notes sounded jagged, piercing, not lyrical as I remembered. I wanted to rock back and forth, close my eyes and smile like I did when he played at work, but the music screamed through my system. A loud, dizzying sound, trapping me, detaching me from my room. I was also terribly thirsty. As if reading my face he said, "Do you want something to drink?" and got up and poured me a huge glass of water. "Ice?" he said.

"Yes, that would be great." When he turned on the water, it whooshed too loudly. But he was being so kind, getting me a glass of water. I held on to the kindness, but the walls held their suffocating breaths with me; the beautiful grains in the newly sanded floor looked too thick and deep as if the wood had been slashed open.

"You're having a hard time?" he said, handing me the glass of water, and came closer to me. "Maybe this will make you feel better." I took five gulps, but that's not what he meant—the water. He sat next to me and moved closer and tried to put his arm around me. I could see his hand reaching for my shoulder, so close but not quite there.

"I want to go to my friend Ken's," I said, jumping up from the bed. "Right now." I was surprised how the *right now* came out, so demanding, sharp like my mother's voice could be. I had just begun to feel in control of my life. I had placed everything in my apartment where I wanted it. Books, stereo, bean bag chair, new yogurt maker. Now I felt out of control, like I was on speed. What was in that joint? I didn't ask him though. I just wanted him gone.

"Okay, okay, I'll take you there." I tried not to look at him but when I did, he looked disappointed. I should have known he wanted to have sex. How could I be so stupid, after all I had gone through the past years? Thank God he didn't push himself on me. He quickly put on his jacket and gently placed his flute back in the case. I was already out the door, and when he came out, too, I locked up and almost stumbled down the stairs I was moving so fast. The marijuana must have been cut with speed. I wanted to jump out of my skin, the skin I was just feeling secure in, finally, after months of panic.

A siren sounded from up the street, and I covered my ears. My hands were cold on my ears. The concrete rose into my feet; I liked the grounding hardness, but getting to Ken's took forever, like stepping in molasses, my body trying to stay attached to my feet while my mind buzzed.

"Louise, come in," he said, a big smile on his face. I was so distraught, I didn't even introduce Ron, who quickly said goodbye to me and walked down the stairs.

"Who was that?" Ken said.

"Someone from work. I took two puffs of something he gave me. I'm scared."

Ken held me for a minute, and I cried. I didn't want to feel out of control, foreign particles spinning through my system, particles that I couldn't get rid of. Ken gave me some orange juice.

"You're going to be okay," he said. "Just remember to breathe. You don't want me to call your dad, do you?"

"No, please no."

"Hi, Dr. Nayer. Your daughter just had a guy she knows from work up to her apartment and he gave her a hit— oh, that means a toke—oh, she smoked some marijuana— maybe cut with amphetamine. She's turned into a speed demon. Otherwise, things are going great!" I giggled and that released some of the tension.

Then he put on some Bob Dylan, and we talked for a while. He had met a new guy, he said. "He might be the one."

Then Ken walked me back to my apartment, "just to make sure you're okay."

The next Sunday, at 8 p.m. the air had cooled, and I passed couples murmuring to each other in the twilight, one block after the next toward my Perry Street sanctuary. I had taken the bus home from upstate. That weekend Sark told me he wanted to sell all his film equipment and move to the country. He wanted me to come with him. I knew I wouldn't. I held on to the image of my apartment, something solid, my sanctuary, the gorgeous, sanded floors, poetry books lining one wall, my jillaba that I'd carried on my back from Morocco hanging in the closet and my bean bag chair. My bed, so inviting, my pillows fluffy. The book I had been reading still lay on top of my wooden nightstand. I had forgotten to bring it with me—*The Book of Daniel* by Doctorow, loosely based on the Rosenbergs. Lightning entered their bodies. They never returned to their children.

On a shelf in the fridge, some leftover curry chicken salad waited patiently for me. My stomach growled. I imagined the salad and could taste it—chunks of chicken and the creamy curry sauce on top. I needed to eat soon, or I'd begin to feel faint, but decided I'd take a shower first—then eat, read and go to sweet sleep. I thought of Sark. His eyes were pleading when he asked me to move upstate with him. Knowing the end was in sight made me sad for him and for us, like a scarf that frayed. He was a good man.

I climbed the five flights slowly as I carried my backpack with clothes, cosmetics and a purse. My too-tight sandals hurt my feet.

As I reached my door, I saw it was ajar. I stopped and listened for a sound—anything—an echo in the silence. When I heard nothing, I cautiously pushed open the door and saw it—the wreckage. My dresser drawers open, socks, underwear chaotically collapsed on top of the beautiful wooden floor with its perfect grains. My stereo was gone, just an empty socket next to the bookshelf. My jazz records were gone. My yogurt maker was gone.

I had just started making my own yogurt. I loved seeing it sprout in the little cups like potatoes hidden in the earth sprouted out of the soil on the farm in upstate New York where I lived when I was four. Why would someone take my yogurt maker?

Methodically I started putting clothes back in the dresser and checked the window gate. It was open. Someone must have escaped out the back, down the wall; maybe there were two or three people. I was too stunned to cry.

I closed and locked the window gate, my "security measure," shut the door and walked to Ken's where I crashed on his couch for the night.

The next day I had the locks changed. That night I tossed and turned up on the fifth floor. I got up a few times to make sure the front door was closed and bolted and that the window gate was locked. Locked in. All locked in. I kept hearing phantom noises coming up the stairs. I told my parents what had happened that day. They called me before I went to bed. "The new lock works well, right?" my mother said. She could have been asking if I had put new toilet paper in the bathroom. Her voice was matter of fact.

Many years later, I would realize how hard she worked at sounding like that, at holding it all together.

"Get a good night's sleep. Everything should be fine, now." The "should be" set my nerves on edge.

"Good night, Mommy, good night, Daddy," I said and hung up. I got out of bed and checked the window gate again. I counted sheep jumping across a white wooden fence, like I used to do when I was little and scared of the tree shadows menacing the ceiling. When that didn't work, I got up and wrote. *It's an owl's dream, seeing in the dark.* Finally, I went back to bed and slept until 7 a.m.

The next day at work Gene told me, "Ron is back on heroin." I never saw him again. Perhaps he robbed me. I'll never know for sure.

I'd ask for some money for a new stereo for my birthday, three months away. I had the radio for music. But my yogurt maker. That's what I missed the most. I had just begun to use it, plugging it in and putting in powdered milk and starter. The next day I had velvety yogurt that I made myself. I never got another yogurt maker. I'm not sure why. My beautiful apartment had been invaded.

If it was Ron, he would probably never be a famous musician, even though he had the talent. I was sad for him. He had worked so hard to get off of heroin. But if he robbed me, I was angry. I had just started to feel the ground beneath my feet and now suddenly, I knew the earth could swallow me to a dark place. Poetry saved me.

For the next nine months, I wrote poetry every day and began to look at MFA programs. I wanted to go on in school; I wanted to make a life as a poet and teacher.

Months after I left the Brooklyn Court Employment project to go to graduate school, one of the participants murdered someone. The head of the organization terminated the participant before it hit the news, but the whole organization shut down. The program had helped so many young people. I had been part of that. Something bigger. Something that made the darkness brighter.

CHAPTER SEVENTEEN

At St. Marks Church in the Bowery, the center of poetry in the East Village, I studied poetry with Tom Weatherly. Our little group of eight followed him like the Pied Piper to his Brooklyn home and in rooms of St. Marks, dark rooms with small windows. We saw snow fall in the winter and trees blossom in the spring. Many of the people in that class dedicated themselves to writing for the rest of their lives. Every night on Perry Street after work, when I wasn't going out and even if I was—I'd write poems. They poured out of me. The words soothed me. The words unsealed places inside me, hidden places. I was a thief of my own history, stealing back to rooms wrapped in cellophane and plucking words from buried grief. Poetry was my refuge, my haven, and my solidity. *In the middle of pain, there's a day with a heart in it. A red carpet moving through a green universe.* I wrote a poem called "Transformation," about Sark shaving after many years; it was published in a small, well-known magazine, The Remington Review. My sister, who ran a small press, published a broadside of my poems in Montreal. I was published! Maybe I *could* be a poet.

Words and music spun in my head, and I wanted to capture them, like a player piano that wouldn't stop. I applied to graduate schools in poetry and got accepted to SUNY at Buffalo. Robert Creeley and John Logan, two famous poets, were both there and would be my mentors. Later, reference letters from Robert Creeley would help to set me on my course as a writer and teacher.

Maybe my Uncle Philip, from the Jewish side of my family, who died of kidney failure at 22, was looking over my shoulder, pressing me on. My dad said Uncle Philip wrote poetry too. My mother was happy I wanted to teach, too, so I could actually make a living. My father loved poetry and Robert Creeley was a big name.

I ended my sessions with Lynne. I got tired of entertaining her. I didn't need her anymore. Just talking had helped my panic. I now had a direction for my life. However, my time with therapists was far from over.

If I kept writing, maybe I wouldn't hurt so much.

I drove up to Buffalo with my parents in the front seat and me and my two cats, Ishi and Flow, in the back. I had gotten the cats after the breakup with Sark. Plus, when Sark moved, he let me take over his one bedroom apartment so the cats had more space. They had comforted me for months. They both pooped madly, and the car stank. My father held his breath. My mother kept turning back and looking at the cages as if she could will an animal not to poop. "This can't go on," my mother said. "This stinks. We've got to pull over then have Weezie clean the cages."

We stopped at a rest stop on the New York Thruway, the only small car at the moment in between huge trucks, and I tried to extricate the poop without the cats running away and without them scratching me as I could get "cat scratch disease," which my father warned me about a lot.

That would mean my legs could swell up like elephant legs.

This extricating the poop was all up to me. As I saw cars whizzing by, I knew I had to be as skilled as a surgeon. Ishi was despondent when I put my hands in the cage and caught the loose poop with pieces of newspaper that weren't soiled. My mother called out, "Be careful," a few times. Though she hated the smell of the poop, she was an animal lover and didn't want them to run away.

Flow wanted to bite me. She was very vain and pretty and obviously didn't like the move and that she had to be in a stinky cage. I couldn't blame her.

My mother had brought some kind of weird sanitary spray that I sprayed above their cages after the poop was gone into a trashcan right near the restrooms. It felt very artificial and both cats sniffed and sniffed into the air. I lugged the cages back into the car.

"Now that's better," my mother said.

"Yes, definitely," my father said, and he turned on the ignition and we were off.

For the whole ride I wondered why I was still with my parents. Trapped in their car, my precious cats in their cages. Everyone trapped together. I had graduated from college. I spent two years in New York City. I was 23 years old. Some women at 23 had careers and husbands and babies or at least significant others and didn't have their parents drive them up to graduate school. Why did I still need my parents?

I had gone up a week before with the mover who had a

truck and was cheap. I called it the Grapes of Wrath special as my stuff was thrown haphazardly in the back and tied with a thick rope, thank God. I sat up with him in the cab and the car jolted all the way on the New York City Thruway for hundreds of miles. I watched my urban landscape spread to suburban sprawl and then country, some of it the country I knew from my relatives in upstate New York.

That gray, hot and lonely August, Buffalo was the end of the world to me. No buzz like New York City. No subways to rush me to see friends, museums, poetry readings. No lovers with me. I was stuck on a precipice, the outer edge of my state, New York. My neighborhood had scary, growling dogs, no cafes or restaurants. I didn't own a car or possess my driver's license; you didn't need wheels in Manhattan. My father's attempt at teaching me to drive ended after I almost hit a hot dog truck and my dad coughed up blood.

That first week in Buffalo, words stuck inside me like I had swallowed concrete. I couldn't even write poetry. I had wanted to go to Columbia University, like my parents, be an Ivy Leaguer, or The University of Massachusetts, but my GRE's sucked. Even my verbal scores were dismal. I never even studied. I got four rejection letters and stifled tears. I didn't measure up, again. SUNY at Buffalo didn't require GRE's. That first week at what I felt was the end of the world, I almost rushed back home to New York City. I didn't care about all my stuff. I'd just take a backpack and my two cats in a crate and board the train. I was homesick.

Only my cats saved me from spiraling into a depression.

Ishi licked my face at night, and purred in my ear, trying to revive me from a psychic hell. Flow sat at the bottom of the bed preening herself. The heat was excruciating. I had no air conditioner. I sat in the kitchen, slumped over a chair, drinking coffee and eating little. My stomach hurt, morning, noon and night. I woke up three or four times to sharp pain. I thought I had an ulcer or appendicitis and went to the university clinic. "If it continues, it could be serious. Check in next week," the doctor said. He gave me a list of foods to eat. I looked at it and forced myself to eat something, spoonfulls of yogurt and berries.

My sister was going to visit but didn't. I kept hoping she'd take the long bus ride from Montreal to Buffalo and rescue me. I waited for her calls, morning, noon and night then realized she wasn't coming. I called Ken. He was busy and happy. He always said, "I love you" at the end of the calls, but he couldn't rescue me either. He had his life. I spoke to my parents a few times. I didn't want them to know how desolate I felt. My father asked about my health. What could he do from 400 miles away? If my stomach got worse, I'd tell him. The distance from home made me sad.

Sitting alone in the kitchen at a white Formica table in a strange city, I was four again, that morning in Cape Cod, my parents gone. A two-dimensional world, all the life sucked out of the stale air. A week before, when I told my mother that I felt scared about going to Buffalo, she said, "You always make friends." I held on to her words.

I had been dating someone after Sark in New York

City—serial monogamy—as I longed for a boyfriend always, but nothing ever stuck. With this new man, who I knew from college, there was always a wall, not only mine but his. Grief outweighed the joy. He had a shelf in his refrigerator where he asked me to put my food. The separation in the refrigerator was a metaphor for the distance between us. Nothing merged. I knew it wouldn't work, but we hung on for six months after I left for Buffalo, calling each other weekly. I talked to him that first week, but our conversations were short. I had left. Our love wouldn't survive the distance.

I didn't know where to go each day until classes began, but I wanted to see the poetry collection, started in 1937 and holding one of the biggest collections of poetry in the world: Established poets and poets on the margins. I stood at the bus stop on Baily Avenue, the only person waiting for what seemed like hours. Out the bus window I saw banks, liquor stores and funeral homes. No little cafes, independent movie theaters, at least in that part of town.

The collection was my sanctuary. I walked into its sacred space like I'd walk into a cathedral, awestruck. Books and chapbooks rose from floor to ceiling, even audio tapes. I listened to some of my favorite poets, Gallway Kinnell, Sylvia Plath and Robert Creeley who I would study with. The words and voices cradled me and eased my fears. My stomach, which had been hurting morning, noon and night, settled down in that room, the pain just a slight whimper. I also had my own box at school for my mail with my name proudly displayed. I was one of the graduate students now. I was on a path.

The nighttime was different. Darkness scared me. I didn't want to shut my eyes. The sounds on the streets were alien sounds, people I didn't know.

What was considered the city in Buffalo seemed like isolated suburbs to me. My neighborhood was filled with scary dogs. Only months later, the corner store would be guarded by a pit bull that growled viciously whenever I walked by.

When I first arrived, a young man, Dan, appeared from across the street—solidly built, blond hair, from Long Island—an engineer with a driving energy. One night we went to Niagara Falls at midnight, and we kissed in his car before he drove me home. We played together a few more times, made-out a few more times, and many years later when I moved to San Francisco, he looked me up and took me to the Golden Spike Restaurant in North Beach. I think he thought it was the beginning of something enduring. But either I wasn't ready or scared or his energy was too crazy. We only saw each other a few times, and the last time kissed lamely. And a year later, he called me from prison. He had done some kind of weird hacking, a white-collar crime. He didn't ask me to help him, but I didn't come get him, or work all night to raise his bail, and I often wondered if I was his only phone call.

It was Jacob who I spent the most time with. "I live right near the bus that goes to New York City," he said. "You can always stay here for the night, and I can drive you to the station." We had a friend in common from Madison. Jacob was constantly dating different women. At the Central Park Grill, the English Department/hometown bar, he would buy drinks for longhaired artistic women musicians and poets. He was dealing with a disintegrating marriage—but we seemed to find each other—at bars, in class, and at our houses. I babysat his son sometimes. He left spaghetti all made on the stove and I read to Ben, two or three books sometimes, the sleepy little blond curly-haired boy wanting desperately to stay up until Daddy returned. I was there enough that he attached to me like a mother, and I longed for that. I loved it when his head rested on my lap, and I didn't want to move an iota to wake him up. Sometimes Jacob would come home from a class and find us on his couch together, sleeping soundly. He would pick up his son and then offer me his hands and I would slowly walk to his bedroom, take off my clothes and fall asleep or sometimes we'd make love, a slow and solid lovemaking. At Jacob's house, a large one-bedroom apartment on the west side of Buffalo, the cool place with cafes, restaurants—near where I studied with the poet John Logan—I began to feel a sense of order—and of course family. In the morning, I helped him get Ben ready to go to the babysitter, or sometimes I left right away for class. We wrote poems, furiously. We skirted the edges all the time of real "commitment." An apartment right underneath him became available and I thought about moving in—getting away from my neighborhood that was increasingly getting scary. But I didn't. Maybe I was scared to be so close to a love that could work.

That meant it could blow apart.

During my second month in Buffalo, Maureen, my downstairs neighbor, sat across from me in my living room. I met Maureen the first day I arrived in 95-degree heat. She came upstairs with a glass of water and a huge smile on her face. "Welcome!" she said and disappeared back to the bottom floor. She was a nurse with a welcoming heart. We began to go back and forth to each other's houses, and she talked about co-counseling when I told her I had been having panic attacks. She took me to a class a few times, a room full of mostly women, where I learned how to "discharge," and the basics of a co-counseling session. It was so different from "talk therapy." I could access my feelings almost immediately, crying, hitting a pillow in anger.

Now at my house, with Maureen giving me my first full session, the gray wool couch felt scratchy, and I began to itch. When I stopped scratching myself, she took my hands and looked right into my eyes so I could see the brown flecks in her irises. It felt too intimate. My hands began to sweat and almost slipped out of her grasp as if my hands and my body wanted to disappear into the floor. I wasn't sure how I felt about her being so close to me and holding my hands; Maureen was a nurse/earth woman with long dark hair and kind eyes, one of sixteen children. Her mother had a huge map with darts on it showing where her adult children lived. How else could you keep track of sixteen progeny?

"Start with what's new and good," she said. I rattled off quite a list of all the things that were going well: some poetry publications, a radio show I hosted with a line-up of poets, a few parties, lists of things I had done, one after the other. Life was good. I'd have my master's degree soon, at twenty-five. My parents sent me a check each month for food and paid my tuition. I was lucky. I wanted to go on because stopping scared me, just as her eyes looking so intently made me turn away. That was part of the process, to look without judging or saying anything. Why was she staring at me? I wanted to leap out the window into another realm. I looked at the tree out the window. Since it was the fall, the green leaves morphed into red, yellow, and green. I focused on all the leafy colors. She kept gazing at me and squeezed my hands a little. "Look at me. What do you want to work on?"

No one had ever asked me that question, even in all the months of therapy with Lynn. I gazed out the window again. When I did turn back, my cat, Ishi, now right behind me on the couch, perhaps sensing that something important was going on, purred as he put his head next to my thigh. "The explosion," I said, finally finding my voice. She kept holding my hands, though I took my right hand away, momentarily, to scratch my face. The Dylan song "Forever Young" began to play in my brain.

I wished that I was still four years old, joyfully going on five, holding up five fingers to my mother in Cape Cod that fateful summer to show how big I was going to become. I wished time had stopped, then, forever young, five fingers up in the air, thrilling with anticipation of a vanilla birthday cake to come. When I *really* turned five, both my parents were horribly burned and in the hospital. They never made it to my party at the farm. They didn't see me blow out my six candles, one for good luck.

Maureen didn't flinch at the word "explosion." I started to talk, slowly, about the cellar that was below our rental house, the rickety ladder steps my parents had to crawl up, their bodies on fire, after the flash fire when they tried to light the pilot light. The gas that had no smell had been escaping for hours. The fire that I didn't see, except I did see the horrible ropey scars that lived on my parents' bodies, especially my mother's face, all covered with scars for eternity. "They were gone for nine months, and I was four years old and didn't know where they went or why they would leave me so suddenly."

"It's okay to feel it now, I'm here," Maureen said, holding my hands tighter and moving even closer to me, and I cried, not just noiseless tears running down my cheeks kind of crying, but an explosive sobbing for what seemed like forever but was only 15 minutes. Being with Maureen was so different from sitting across from Lynne. I could really feel her, feel from the pit of my stomach. That was her job, to keep me feeling. Every time I started to talk, she said, "Feel it now, cry if you want to," and floods of tears as big as the Great Flood rained down from what seemed like the sky but really from inside me. How could I have so many tears? My life was good, right?

That was the grief that was a fist in my chest. That was the darkness that kept pulling me down.

"You have one minute left," she said, handing me a Kleenex to wipe off my face. "Tell me what you're looking forward to. This is a way of coming back to the present."

"I'm looking forward to petting Ishi," I said, smiling broadly, and took my right hand out of hers and pet his soft fur as he purred louder and louder. He had been eerily silent when I cried. "I'm also looking forward to taking a warm bath and going to the party tonight."

"Now look around."

I took a deep breath and looked again at the tree out the window. It looked more brilliant than before, as if it were breathing too, breathing color into the leaves.

Maureen hugged me and then I gave her a session, too. I held her hands and then let go of one hand as she punched a pillow, screaming out the name of someone who hurt her feelings. When she finished, her face looked calmer.

Co-counseling had entered my life.

CHAPTER EIGHTEEN

A group of eight of us sat in chairs or on the poet John Logan's floor on the west side of town. We sat in a circle as he politely introduced us to each other that first class and never forgot our names after that. He was kind and gentle with his critiques.

Logan wrote long narrative poems, some about the death of his mother in childbirth with him, a guilt that wasn't his to carry but it infused all his work. He had nine children, but he and his wife had divorced. He was gay. He was always looking for connections, a longing that filled his eyes.

My poems got longer. I gingerly wrote about my parents and what happened to them but skirted the edges of the fire, as if I was walking on only a few shiny embers. I also wrote poems about my time in Europe, a few about Spain. *Let's hold vigil/in the blue crease of night/watch the ocean/ phosphorous/and the crimson light/that ribbons Africa/in a satin flush/to Algeciras and Seville.* After the workshops in the evenings, we often all went out to a bar, Jacob, my best friend Cynde and four others. John Logan got too drunk and sometimes we'd walk him home down his street canopied by elm trees.

Robert Creeley would hold court in his classes, tall, one-eyed, and handsome, rambling on about various famous poets, bars they frequented, anthologies they started. I remember little of those classes except I liked him and loved his poetry. Later I had independent study with him, and he talked about his partner at the time who lived in California and sometimes we went over my poems. He wrote me two glowing recommendations that opened doors.

I studied Fairy Tales with Leslie Fiedler, a well-known scholar. He talked about Little Red Riding Hood and that her hood represented menstruation. My class in the bible delved into the Book of Job and I cringed reading about the boils appearing all over his body. Scary images of my parents' burns flashed like mini explosions when I read those passages. I hosted a radio show and brought on poets I loved as guests.

I was living my life as a poet, a big cheese, following my dreams, with the good fortune that my parents could support me through the program. I even taught a free poetry class at my house, trying to get teaching experience. Forty years later, visiting Buffalo, my niece knew one of the students in that class. He said he never forgot that class. I was doing what I loved. I could have stayed there, put down roots.

When Jacob and I drifted apart from time to time, I dated other men but nothing stuck. One younger man, who was in my private poetry class, broke up with me, and I pined for him as I listened to Joni Mitchell sing *California* on the juke box at The Beef n'Ale where I waitressed. I looked for his blue truck, red jacket, chiseled face and wavy brown hair and wondered why it had to end. I wrote poems about him, his blue truck and red jacket. When we were together, sometimes we woke up dreaming the same dream. He had a twin brother. I felt twinned with him. "We're too much alike," he said to me one morning when he came by. I wore a red silk Kimono, and it was cold on the steps where we sat. And then he disappeared. Like twins who must separate. The next day I was desolate, and snow fell all night. My friend, Cynde, braved the snow drifts to come sit with me while I cried.

I didn't know then that I would actually move to California. "Take me as I am."

When I left Buffalo and moved west, Jacob and I wrote letters to each other, sometimes three or four times a week—with poems, thoughts, little fragments of his life in Chicago, mine in San Francisco. Sometimes his poems said "love" at the beginning or at the end, and I wasn't sure if he was calling me "love." Once on one of my crazy drives across country when I stayed with him in Chicago, I made eggplant Parmesan for dinner and pretended that I lived with him. He was surprised that I knew how to cook, but less surprised when I got in my car and sped away, again.

When I first came to Buffalo, I thought it was the end of the world. I missed New York City, my home. That first month I had constant stomach aches that almost turned into an ulcer. I clutched my stomach, morning, noon and night. When classes started, when I met new friends, I began to settle down into this new landscape. Writing continued to save me. Writing was my joy and my grief, all wrapped up together.

By the time I left Buffalo, I was a poet with credentials and publications. My thesis was a book of poetry, *Dancing Through the Rapids*. Even though I had found a path, I was dancing on swirling water, a dervish spinning too fast.

CHAPTER NINETEEN

One afternoon, about a month before graduation, the phone rang. I was working on my book of poetry, my thesis. It was due in a week. I had a cup of coffee in one hand and grabbed the phone in the other. "Louise, this is Mary. Do you want to move to Berkeley after Buffalo? You can take my room. I'm moving to Oregon!" I hadn't talked to Mary in a few months. We met Freshman year at our dorm in Madison. We both loved the book *The Little Prince* and especially the line, "And now here is my secret, a very simple secret: It is only with the heart that one can see rightly; what is essential is invisible to the eye."

I had no idea what I would do or where I would go. I didn't have a job. Mary's words came fast like they always did. Mary was tall and from Connecticut. Her father was a judge. He had a framed mallet on the wall. Her mother was a lanky blonde who drank too much. Years later I found out Mary's brother tied her up in a chair attached to a tree and left her in the freezing Connecticut cold when she was seven. On the outside, she looked perfect. On the inside there was darkness that I couldn't see then. Later, after selling houses in Oregon, she moved to an Ashram and stayed there for 30 years. Neither of us had any idea then, that her journey would take her to Muktananda, her guru.

"Yes, I'll take your room," I said, the words tumbling out of my mouth before I could even think. Creeley talked endlessly about Bolinas. Lots of poets lived in California.

Why not? Something was pushing me away from home. I wouldn't know why I had to leave for many years to come.

"I'm moving to Berkeley," I told my mom when I called later that day. There was a moment of silence. "Do you have a place to stay? A job? This has all happened rather quickly." Her voice was steady, but I could hear a catch underneath. In that moment of silence, I looked around my apartment. The clock was ticking too loudly. I started to sweat. It was suddenly too hot inside the apartment. I saw my life in boxes. Another journey, away from home, away from the perfect order, away from my parents' expectations of who I should be and what I should do.

"I have a place to stay. Mary is leaving her apartment." My parents had met Mary a couple of times. "A nice big room. I can just move in." A moment of silence again. "I don't have a job yet. But I'm sure I can get something. I have some money saved up." There I was again, even at twenty-five trying to justify everything to my mother. I imagined her in her apartment, posh Greenwich Village. She had just gotten a new stove and told me all about it in her last letter. "Electric this time." Gas was something we didn't talk about much in our family.

She had also gotten new flowered wallpaper for the bathroom. Yellow and blue. "It's very handsome," she wrote me. I was often bored reading about her house renovations. So many things felt more important.

"When do you leave? You'll come back to New York first? You have clothes here, things you need. Things in the basement that you can go through. Make sure you leave enough time to go through things." She kept repeating the word *things*.

I took a deep breath; grateful she didn't ask me anything more or put my father on the phone. When I heard his voice, I knew mine might crack. He might get upset. "Why go so far? Why not come home, come back to New York," though my mother would be nudging him not to say that. "Don't be such a worry wart," she would say to him. It seemed so definite now. Carved in stone.

My mother hadn't even tried to stop me.

"I'll be back in three weeks. Classes end at Erie Community College." I had gotten a poetry class there, a real feather in my cap. I felt proud to be a teacher. "I'll give notice at the Beef n'Ale. I'll come home for a few days." I caught myself saying *home* and stopped for a minute.

For that month, before I drove west on an impulse, I listened to Joni Mitchell sing "California" on the jukebox, playing it again and again and again at the Beef n' Ale where I worked as a waitress. As if California were a mythical place. As if California could save me. As if the words "coming home" were spoken directly to me. As if "Will you take me as I am, take me as I am" meant that I didn't have to be anyone particular or fit into a groove or a puzzle piece.

I thought of my parents' apartment, so organized, so neat, and how sometimes I wanted to smash things when I was there, a dark impulse to destroy the perfect order. "Take me as I am, take me as I am." Did my parents even really know me? Did they even try to understand me?

When I walked into my last classroom for the semester at Erie Community College, I got teary eyed. This was my first class, and I knew then that teaching was a calling. I loved my students. Saying goodbye to them was the beginning of many more goodbyes, a domino effect, leave-taking, going away. They were all there, all thirty-five of them, waiting for me. Seventy pairs of eyes. Only one person had dropped out in the whole semester. This was a poetry class, and I was lucky to be able to teach at this level. I was only twenty-four, but my mentor/poet Robert Creeley had written me a great recommendation. The first day I walked in with my syllabus, consisting of mainly white male poets with a few women, I was still in a white Eurocentric world and the class helped me begin to change. I saw that the class was primarily African Americans with one Polish nun who always sat in the front seat, so I changed my syllabus to include more poems by Amiri Baraka, Alice Walker, and Nikki Giovanni. I kept Allen Ginsberg and we read part of Kaddish out loud, a prayer for the dead. Even the nun read out loud and crossed herself after the reading. We all had had people we loved who had died.

"I'm moving to California," I told them two weeks before. They looked shocked. "Why?" some of them asked. I didn't have a good reason. "It's an adventure. It's beautiful." I told them I didn't have a job yet but was sure I would find one. I also told them I was driving across country by myself. The nun looked horrified.

Many of them had never left Buffalo.

When we began our last class, a series of presentations and readings by six diverse groups who had met for the past few weeks, I listened intently, proud of what they had learned. The shy man in the back read a poem by Baraka with a booming voice and talked about line breaks. Two women who hardly ever raised their hands at the beginning explained the theme of a poem. Another group found all the similes, metaphors, and images in a poem. During the break, they talked to each other in hushed voices in the back of the room. After the last presentation, right before class ended, the nun came up to me and gave me a card. I was stunned. "Open your card," one man in the class said. Inside the card was $200 they had collected. They had all signed it. Many with "Bless you" and "Stay safe" and "Go with God."

"I can't take money from you," I said, the bills almost spilling onto the hard floor. It seemed downright immoral.

"You don't have a job. We insist. We're not taking it back." Many of them crossed their arms in front of them. "No, we're not taking it back," one of the women in the back said firmly. Some of them had husbands, wives, and children waiting downstairs to drive them home. I could see some people in cars out the window, looking up expectantly. And I would be alone in the room. I knew the janitor was in the building, thankfully, an older man who, without making a big deal about it, always came up to the classroom allegedly to clean up, but I think, also, to check on me. I didn't want to keep him late at work. I began to erase the board and heard more people speaking.

"We'll miss you so much!" one man said, an older man who had finally come back to school after thirty years.

I turned around to face them again, my class, my first real class at a college. They were so kind and good. Tears dripped down my face and I wiped them off with my sleeve, which made me look like a four-year-old, but I didn't care.

"I'll miss all of you, too," I said tearily, looking at a sea of faces, students I had grown to love.

"Don't talk to strangers. Be safe." More people spoke to me as they left the room, some hugging me and holding on for a long time. I wanted to run away with them, get into one of their cars and live in their houses.

I could hear them talking as they went down the stairs. From the first class when they silently left that night, now they had developed friendships. Some of them carpooled together.

One young man stopped and gave me a card. "Open it," he said. He was only a little older than me and I think he liked me, but we were worlds apart, or so it seemed at the moment, especially with me about to go 3000 miles away.

"It's beautiful!" Inside was a pressed flower.

"To remember me." He wrote:

To a person who is beautiful on the outside and on the in-side. But I think you are sad. I hope you find what you are looking for.

Your student,

Julio

I gave him a big hug and we both almost started crying.

I watched him as he left the classroom and ambled slowly down the stairs, shoulders hunched.

"Goodbye," he called out again from the landing.

"Goodbye, Julio. Keep learning," I said. And then he was gone.

The classroom was suddenly empty. It was already 10:15 p.m. The janitor, Bill, came up and helped me put the chairs back in the right place. "Bye, Bill, and thanks for everything," I said, as I gathered my books and papers in my briefcase.

"My pleasure," he called out as I walked down the stairs with the $200 and the cards in my purse and a hole in my heart.

I tried to sing the Joni Mitchell song to myself: "California" *coming home* but I only got to the first few phrases and stopped. *It's an adventure*, I said to myself. *I'm going on an adventure.* But as I got in my car and drove home, my home in Buffalo for only the next month, I wondered.

Jacob drove my two huge suitcases and me to the train station. He came inside the train and helped me put them high up on the racks. "I'm sure you can get some help when you get off?" I was leaving some things at my parents' house, books and clothes that I wanted to keep but not take with me across country. They could mail things if I needed them.

"Yes, I'm sure I can get help," I said, though I didn't feel sure of anything. I wanted for a minute to be sure of Jacob, but we had drifted away from each other over the past two months. He was going out with a famous poet and seemed smitten. But I was leaving. Neither of our hearts were open to each other. Jacob kissed me on the cheek. We hugged and then he stood for a minute on the platform as I waved goodbye. He was always there to help me and then wave goodbye.

"Are all your dirty clothes in one place?" my mother said after she pecked me on the cheek. "You look exhausted." I had taken an all-nighter from Buffalo, catching only snatches of sleep as the Amtrak train barreled through upstate New York, from trees and water to the streets of Harlem. A kind older man mercifully had helped me get my luggage down from the rack.

Now, at home, I took a three-hour nap on my old bed in my blue room and woke up groggy. I could hear my mother and Evelyn talking in low voices, probably about me.

When my father came home, his eyes lit up but then drooped. "California," he said. "That's far away."

He made me a screwdriver and we talked for a while about poetry. The next day I took some books and clothes down to the storage room and sorted through some "things" my mother wanted me to get rid of; books I never looked at anymore and clothes I never wore.

"There's just not room to put more stuff down here unless you get rid of some stuff." I wondered what it would be like to have a home where you had a storage space for all your stuff. Stuff. It seemed that it just got moved from one place to the next, but I wasn't quite ready to divest of everything.

I only had one suitcase now that I was taking back to Buffalo. My train left at 10 a.m., and my parents both had to go to work early. After we had all gotten dressed and ready to leave, the three of us sat down in the living room for a few minutes, my parents on the couch and me facing them in a chair.

"Do you have enough cortisone for your eczema?" my father said. Instinctively, I started scratching my chin then stopped myself.

"I have a couple of small tubes. I should be fine." But I wondered. My dad would be very far away.

"Make sure you don't smoke marijuana or drink alcohol when you drive," my mother said. That took me by surprise. She didn't look directly at me, but I could feel her presence all over me.

"Oh, Mom," I said, embarrassed she even knew I smoked marijuana. "Of course not."

"Call us every day. Don't forget." Her voice was steady, but she looked fragile, as if her eyes might break apart. There was so much she must have wanted to say. But I just wanted to get out of there, really get out of there, out of the apartment with its perfect decorations, paintings on the wall, new wallpaper in the kitchen, food stored in the freezer, everything parceled out and marked with a black marker.

Their perfectly ordered lives just underscored the chaos I felt inside.

I had to push off, really push off.

Just like the time my mother said goodbye to me on the deck of the student ship, the *Aurelia*, when I left for France, now many years ago, I knew she wanted to say loudly, and my father, too: *Stay alive.*

"I'll be careful in the car," I said. "I'm a good driver," though that was suspect as I had just started driving a year ago. I was about to drive across the whole United States by myself. Women rarely did that if ever.

But I was still annoyed they didn't trust me.

"If I don't have enough cortisone, you can send some to me." My tone was adolescent, spoiled, like "duh, you can send it." I had no idea what they were really thinking, and I didn't really care or didn't want to care as they both lifted themselves up out of their chairs.

"Call when you get back to Buffalo," my mother said. For a second, I thought I saw a few tears rim her eyes.

She kissed me and then my father gave me a hug and held on longer than usual.

"You might want to think this over more," he said and then they both left the house. The door shut. I took the train back to Buffalo.

The day before I left Buffalo for good, my friend Cynde had a party for me. So many people came that both her house and garden were packed. Lanterns were strewn across the trees. The weather was perfect, warm but not too humid. I flitted from person to person. "You're driving alone?" many people said and wondered why. "On the road," I said and laughed, "a female Kerouac." How incredibly free to be alone with only my thoughts for hours and hours and hours on the open road. Trees. Buildings. Water, the sky turning to dusk and then dark. Small cafes that I'd never heard of and would never visit again. A waitress as my only connection to humanity for the whole day. "Honey, do you want a piece of pie?" Gas stations. Snacks. Sometimes meals. Too much coffee. I could see it in front of me, and it was all my choice. Where to eat. Where to stop. How long to travel each day. How much I would write. How could I tell my friends and my family that I craved this? Why did I crave this? No connections. *Like a rolling stone.*

But when I saw Jacob sitting solidly in a chair, a few women around him, he looked up and caught my eye. He said, "Talk to you later" to the group of women and came near me. I could smell alcohol on his breath, a fruity smell. There was something that loomed large about him and smelled of home.

"How are you feeling?" he said. No one had asked me that. It reminded me of our teacher, John Logan, who said he had only one friend who would call him and say, "How's your soul?"

"I'm okay," I lied and then added: "a little scared." We sat down under one of the lanterns. He held my hand. "You know you can call me anytime, anywhere. And as soon as you get there, send me your address." For a minute I wanted to curl up in his lap. I wanted to go home with him to his shelves stacked with spaghetti and sauce, to his curly-haired sweet son who loved to hear books read two or three times. But I didn't. We had our chance and it passed. Or that's what I thought, among all the swirling thoughts that night.

By that time, it was 11 p.m. I didn't want to stay much later as I planned on leaving at the crack of dawn.

Jacob and I stood up at the same time. He kissed me lightly on the head and walked away quickly. He almost turned to look back. I could see the slight shift in the movement of his torso, but he didn't.

The next morning my alarm went off at six am. I got up, had a cup of coffee and started packing the car. Maureen helped me. She was the first one to greet me with water and cups when I arrived in Buffalo on a humid summer day, and the last person I saw when I left Buffalo. She gave me a huge round mirror with "I trust myself completely" written in lipstick. I placed it carefully in the back of my trunk and covered it with blankets.

My friend Richard had sold me a '68 Camaro with mag wheels about a month before. It was low to the ground with a stick shift that was hard to manage, especially to get it in reverse. When I got in to drive, he said, "I thought you'd drive like a grandmother. You drive fast and have good re-flexes!" I felt proud of that.

My olive-green car had a racing stripe and a shag rug and a crucifix hanging from the mirror that I removed and put in the glove compartment. I wasn't sure who I was, but definitely not 100% Christian, though I had been baptized and confirmed, as my mother repeated. My dad is Jewish, I said again and again. I'm 50% Jewish.

The car had no air conditioning and no radio. I would have to get some other talisman to keep me safe. The mirror cracked when I got to Berkeley, but knowing it was there all the way out west comforted me, especially as it came from Maureen who had helped me break open my grief.

"Eat well and get enough sleep." My mother called me early that morning. I was looking at my apartment and how empty it suddenly looked, devoid of books. I also had had to make a terrible decision to give my cats away. A few months before, raging, itching eczema spread over my whole body and wouldn't let up. My skin bled from all the scratching I did at night. My allergist said I was highly allergic to cats and couldn't keep them. I had to say goodbye to my precious babies. I gave them to a shelter that promised they would go to good homes. They were beautiful cats. Ishi looked at me with desperate longing when I walked away.

No animal pals would come with me on my journey.

I took a sip of coffee. "Be careful, sweetie, and don't leave valuables in the car." It was a short, practical call about what I should and shouldn't do. She didn't ask me "How's your soul?" or "How are you feeling?"

"Bye, Mom," I said. "I need to get going."

"Call every day you're traveling."

"Not every day. I'll call." I felt annoyed. She could have

said, "We'd love a call every day." I didn't want any demands on me.

I went into the bathroom and gazed at myself in the mirror. My eyes looked tired and dull when I washed my face. I had had too much to drink the night before at the party of lanterns. I threw some cold water on my eyes and hoped they'd brighten up. But I wasn't going on a date. All I needed to do was drive and drive and keep myself caffeinated. I'd need my eyes to see well for the trip. I planned on driving even into the night, maybe even late at night.

I panicked as I thought of flashing headlights coming towards me, and huge, scary trucks on the road. My car was small. What was I doing? This was crazy. I let that thought go, as I was letting go of Buffalo, of New York City, of the East Coast, of everything I knew.

I knew I wouldn't take my mother's admonitions to heart. I was going to go fast—to make it to California as soon as I could.

I left Buffalo by 7 a.m. My hand was on the gearshift. The car was already hot inside. No local stations with smooth voices, weather reports and news of the day. No music, except what I could hum to myself, Dylan coursing through my veins.

She's got everything she needs, she's an artist
She don't look back.

That's how I felt, a poet not looking back toward my

home. I would paint the world in the colors I chose, transform the night and the day. I was in no-man's land, a place between countries, a place with no borders, no checklists, no uniforms, and no schedules. It was this space that I had been wanting to inhabit for months as I sloughed off the grief of loves coming and going, the grief of geography— where to land? I was in perpetual motion, an insect hovering over flowers but never getting close, a hurricane that never finds landfall. But there was something safe in that, like the calm eye of the hurricane.

I just hoped I wouldn't get swept away.

Many years later, at 66 years old, a San Francisco transplant still missing New York City with an unexplained ache that has never completely gone away, my parents long gone from this earth; one evening, I wept for a long time seeing the image in my mind of my mother dressed in a blue ultra-suede A-line skirt she made herself, a silk blouse and a blazer, her black patent purse draped over her shoulder, everything so neat except the tears falling softly down her face, tears I rarely saw. She lifted up her scarred right hand and waved goodbye to me as I pulled out of the parking place, a prime parking space right in front of their house in Greenwich Village, my car filled with books, and some new clothes my mother had bought me.

At that time, I had come back to New York for three months, "to test the waters" and see if I could find a job. But when a California Arts Council grant for a poet-in-residence at senior centers came through, a chance to live as a poet and to help the elderly give a voice to their lives, I decided to go west again. This time I did not come back. She must have known I wouldn't return, just as you know something that rises up out of the earth and swirls through your veins.

But I wasn't a mother then, and I was too young or too filled with myself to see how deep her grief was and how she seemed to want to keep waving as if waving could bring me back. But she turned back toward home as she had on the deck of the *Aurelia* so many years before. I wished I could have run after her; I wished I could have fit in her pocket like a baby kangaroo, so close, so warm inside, but I turned on the ignition and drove away toward California, so far away that she might not even be able to find me.

CHAPTER TWENTY

My car was a bug scurrying across the continent. The thick, hot air swirled inside the car even though the windows were open. No air conditioning. An old Coke bottle that I'd filled with water rested precariously on the passenger seat. I hoped the water wouldn't spill. Solidly safe in fourth gear, I picked up the bottle and chugged now lukewarm water down my parched throat. In fifty miles or so I'd have to stop for gas and then I'd get a cold drink. I desperately wanted a Coke. I needed a Coke.

Many years ago, when I was twelve, I also desperately wanted a Coke. After a summer camp canoe trip, I fell asleep on the hump on the floor of the back seat of the car. I rose from the floor to see that we had stopped for drinks. My lips parched and dry, I walked into the store and reached for my friend Carol's Coke in a pleading kind of way. Then I fell onto a bunch of boxes. Everyone laughed until I fell again, my legs buckling and the room spinning madly like a tornado. My blood sugar must have taken a nose-dive. Two counselors carried me outside and the clouds whirred in white puffs, whirring and whirring in a light blue sky. I wanted a Coke; I wanted it so badly.

I always wondered why my friend didn't just give me a sip of Coke. Why she didn't see my need.

Now, I had to take care of my own needs, driving across the country, the windows completely rolled down. Balmy air flooded the car, but at least it was a breeze. In the silence of the humid air, the hum of the engine, the whoosh of passing cars and the landscape, the concrete highway, and leafy trees, I made my way to Detroit. I had just now burst forth on the surface, living in the present moment, my body and soul buoyant. My eyes glued themselves to the road, looking ahead in this very moment: not back to past griefs, past loves. No noise at all except a hot wind whooshing through the open windows of the car, the loud whir of the engine, the noise of the gears shifting from one gear to another, little sips of water or Coke going down my throat and bits and pieces of poems floating through my mind. If I listened carefully, I could hear my heartbeat. I didn't want to hear it too loud, ba boom, ba boom, ba boom, because I knew the panic was living down there, hiding out in the soft tissue of my lungs, maybe swimming in my blood, lying in wait.

A soundless world except for my own thoughts. Bits of poems floated continuously inside me. A poem from my professor, Robert Creeley.

Love, what do I think
to say. I cannot say it.

He was living in Bolinas part time, and California called to me, just as his poems called to me and all the words I could never say out loud.

My mind went to Jacob, slowly rising from his bed, putting on his glasses and shuffling to the kitchen to get his coffee. After he showered, he'd walk into his son's room and gently say, "Rise and shine" to his sleepy tow-headed boy. He'd get him breakfast, cereal, milk, and some juice. While his son ate, he'd get his lunch together. He'd quickly eat some cereal himself and then go help his son get dressed, brush his teeth and out the door they'd go.

How safe these morning rituals all sounded, how ordinary, how repetitive, like my parents rising to get dressed, my mother putting pancake makeup over the lines where her flesh was sewn on to her face; putting on her lipstick over lips that would never be lips again; but with all the scars, everything still so ordinary. What would they eat for breakfast as they both sat opening different sections of the *New York Times*, poached egg on toast, or cereal with milk, each a cup of coffee, maybe talking about their daughters, maybe wondering where I was but not wanting to say anything to each other?

Rush hour in Detroit. I grabbed my water bottle and took a chug just as I heard a sizzling noise and plumes of steam rose from the front of my car, shooting in the air like a geyser. Dreaded panic flooded my body. Even in the extreme heat, my hands were moist, fingers slipping on the steering wheel. My heart raced. I could die on some anonymous stretch of humid highway in Detroit. I hadn't even called my parents the night before. My sister didn't know where I was.

Where could I pull over without getting hit by cars going at least 20 miles over the speed limit? I was in the middle lane and the steam obscured the road, but I kept my eye on the right side, sped up, as the plumes shot higher; I made it to the shoulder. I slumped in the car, stunned.

This is how people die; they do nothing.

It's okay, I repeated like a mantra: my car was not on fire, and the plumes of steam got smaller. Tears flooded my eyes. I took a sip of lukewarm water, which didn't quench anything.

I debated my next move: this could be life or death, to open the hood or not, to even get out of the car or not. A cop car pulled up behind me.

"What's going on, miss? Can I help you?" I almost started crying but stopped myself. I wanted to pretend that I was just going home from work. I felt embarrassed to be a lone woman on the road with an overheated car. But maybe he'd be impressed, the Camaro with the mag stripe. A strong woman, a woman Atlas holding up the world. Liberated, independent, able to take on the world.

"Looks like you ran out of water!" He had already opened the hood and taken off the radiator cap. "Can't drive without water –especially in these temperatures. Got water. But you better get to somewhere soon if it happens again. Get it checked out." I thanked him profusely, watching his sturdy body, head down, concentrating as he filled up my radiator with water. Every cell in my car was overjoyed at the cool liquid nourishment. "Follow me," he said after he closed the hood. "Dangerous pulling out. You follow me," and he led me out onto the highway and sped off.

I tried to take a deep breath, but my breath stuck in my chest like a small piece of cement. I was so alone it hurt. And it was so hot. I had to pay attention to the signs for Ann Arbor, which I knew were coming up. When I got off at the exit, I finally breathed. Traffic was thinner. Huge trees lined the highway, their canopy of leaves shading me.

I parked near a big house a mile from campus. Jeff, in my poetry class, whom I'd dated a few times in Buffalo, had good friends in Ann Arbor and put us in touch. "She looks just like you," he said, a bit wistfully. Seemed like he had had a crush on someone, but she married someone else. Maybe he thought I was her when we dated briefly?

I rang the bell and Rachel did look like me—long thin neck, thin face, long nose, dark eyes and a body that was thin on top and more zaftig below. She and her husband welcomed me with open arms and gave me a small room, the bed neatly made. "There are towels for you in the bathroom. Take a bath! Rest!" I soaked in their tub and put some lavender beads in the water and watched them pop open like speeded-up photos of flowers opening. For a moment, I forgot I was between places, on the road. Maybe I could stop here? Ann Arbor?

My mother had taught classes in nursing education in Ann Arbor when she was in her twenties. She took the train from New York City. I imagined her huge brown leather suitcase filled with clothes and books. Perfectly packed. She left New York after a long-term boyfriend broke up with her. "He was Jewish, and his mother wanted him to marry a Jewish girl." That's all she said.

Later he married a Puerto Rican woman. She told me that, and I could hear a catch still in her voice. Years later, I heard her say to someone, "At least my kids graduated from college. His didn't."

My mother had saved books inscribed "To Dorothy, from Saul." She told me they wrote "penny postcards" every day when he lived in Washington, D.C., for a while.

When she was horribly burned, her face and hands a mass of bandages, she told me a bouquet of flowers arrived with "Get well soon" in his handwriting and no signature. She rarely shared anything personal with me. He must have been important.

The next morning, I bought some huge banana nut muffins for the household. We sat around the table and chatted while Rachel made us all cups of steaming hot coffee.

"Stay longer if you want," Rachel said as she put her knapsack with books on her back and left for school. David, her husband, kissed her goodbye. "Yes, stay longer!" he said as he left, too, in the car. He was working at the other end of town.

I wondered what it would be like to have a husband already. To have the same person kiss you goodbye in the morning. The same house to live in. I hummed Cat Stevens's *Wild World* as I started to pack my clothes into one small bag.

Rachel had a look of longing when she said goodbye to me, as if she could simply change one life for another one.

Between the lavender bath the night before and the

morning muffin and coffee, I had completely forgotten that all the water had mysteriously emptied out of my radiator the day before. The highway patrol man, who saved me from potential highway death, had filled it but warned me to have it checked.

When I opened the hood, I hoped for a full radiator of water. To my dismay, the water had all drained out, a huge dark puddle on the driveway. This was the second time I had had a car disaster. The first one was when I stopped briefly at my cousin's house in Norwich, New York. My cousin's husband, a car mechanic for years, said he thought he smelled gas in my car. He descended under the car, his compact body barely fitting. "There's a leak in your gas line," he said. He fixed it but told me: "Be careful. If you smell anything or something doesn't feel right with the car, take it right in." My cousin, Jean, whom I had lived with on the farm when my parents were burned, looked alarmed. "Wow. Thank God John found that leak."

I had escaped being blown up again.

Now it was water leaking. I filled the radiator, again, and drove to the nearest gas station.

The mechanic opened the hood and looked for only a few short seconds.

"The hood that goes over the radiator—the thing that keeps the water cool—must have blown off somewhere! It's an unusual model. We don't have anything like that here. Don't know where you can get it." My eyes filled with tears.

"There's a car part place—a junkyard, about three miles

from here. That guy has everything, and I mean everything!" He wrote down directions. "You have a safe trip,"
he said. "Wherever you're going."

The car part place looked like the end of the world. I
knew cockroaches would take over the world after a nucle-
ar explosion and imagined albino ones crawling across the
world. I had had albino cockroaches on MacDougal Street
in Greenwich Village when I lived there until I talked to
them. "Please don't show your little white shells and whis-
kers when I'm around. I don't want to spray toxins." Mirac-
ulously, that seemed to work.

I wondered if car parts would come in as a close second
to what would be left after the mushroom cloud.

This place was massive, bigger than any graveyard I had
seen. Broken-down cars sat like skeletons, turned up, and
turned down. Pieces of cars littered the landscape, bright
shiny metal and red rusted metal. The silence was deafen-
ing. Where was I?

The man who worked there saw me come in and looked
surprised. How many young women drive into a place like
that alone? For a minute I felt a sense of pride, like I was a
pioneer. I didn't think anyone in my family had ever done
this—gone cross-country, alone. Gone to a junkyard, alone.

"Young lady, what can I help you with?" He had already
looked my car up and down as I drove in. Everybody did
that—the stripe down the middle, the mag wheels. It was
worth something to car enthusiasts and later, when it really

broke down and I sold it, I had almost twenty calls the first hour and offers of cold cash.

I explained the problem, and he opened the hood. "I see, yes, not sure I have this, but maybe." I saw myself, for a moment, going from one car graveyard to another, my "on the road" experience aborted as I searched for the radiator hood, such a small little piece and so important, like looking for the Holy Grail.

The man disappeared down a hill where I could hardly see him as he rummaged through mounds of what looked like litter to me but must have had some crazy order in his mind.

The temperature that day had soared to 95 degrees. I had forgotten to bring water in the car, which as usual was like an oven. My lips were parched, my throat dry.

"I'm hoping, just hoping, young lady, that this does it. You can't drive this thing without it."

"Do you happen to have any water?" I asked, with a pleading voice.

"Oh, yes, please go inside." He pointed to a little house. "Some clean cups next to the sink. Help yourself."

"I'm so grateful," I said, and I was. When I filled the glass and drank the water, I grew taller, like a plant. Out the small window at the top of the door I could see him fiddling with something. I tried to catch his expression. I also wondered what this man's life was like, rooting through mounds of broken-down cars and car parts, searching for treasure. Did he have a wife and children? The little house looked neat and clean. No photos on the refrigerator, though. Maybe he lived upstairs like a lighthouse keeper. The keeper of the junkyard.

I washed my cup and placed it on the drying rack, then walked back out to the car.

"Got it on there. It'll work. Not exactly the right size but it'll do. I attached it good. Now you might check, next 400 miles or so, but it's attached!"

"Thank God," I said a little too loudly. "It was scary when the car overheated on the highway."

"Bet it was, bet it was," maybe he was thinking, and she's alone and all. But he didn't say anything. His hands were in his pocket, and he was surveying the driveway. Another car was pulling in.

I paid him the twenty dollars he asked for, got back inside the car, and looked at my map. I was on my way.

On the road again, the black hood neatly over the radiator, protecting me, protecting the car, a new talisman of sorts. New York City, where my heart had started inside my mother's body and outside her body at New York Hospital, now faded away. The further I went, with the change in time, the earlier it became, like being born again.

What was freedom? Lack of restrictions? Out here on the road, no one was telling me what to do or what not to do. School, a boyfriend who would become a husband, a job, enough money, a place to live, a bank account, publications of my writing in the right magazines, the ones that would lead to bigger and better magazines, everything always bigger and better, as if life were to be one great crescendo, rising to some peak like Everest where I would stake my claim, drape a big flag that I'd made it to the top! Voices swirled in my head at times—the "shoulds" of life.

In the car between places, the voices descended to a soft whisper.

The time inside my Camaro was all my time. Crazy images spun through my brain, trees like dancers, the blue sky a silken robe, the cars in front of me huge beetles, the road an alleyway to the heart, my heart not broken on this stretch of road; maybe my heart had never really been broken when my parents disappeared. I wanted to believe that. I was always trying to get to an unbroken heart.

These thoughts, Olympic runners of the air, like a spinning wheel or a player piano, went so fast I couldn't catch them, but I knew they were there and all mine.

CHAPTER TWENTY-ONE

That night I stopped at a Motel 6. I lugged my typewriter and my suitcase into a room that smelled vaguely of mold. I started a poem: *Her fear was a long black line/a mesh stocking/a panther stalking a burning tree.* I wanted to start getting a few lines down each day, new lines that spun through my brain. I had eaten a few hours before at Denny's and watched families buzzing around each other, the children little spin-offs of their parents. I was very far from my family.

Now, at 9 p.m., an overwhelming fatigue claimed my body; my legs and shoulders ached from being stuck in one position, hour after hour. I hadn't called my parents in two days.

After I put everything safely in my room and locked the door, I walked to a phone booth near the road. The road was dark with no cars. The air was chilly. A full moon hung down low. Maybe that's why I felt that I could just take off into the sky, a crazy, weightless feeling. I walked into the booth, dialed my parents' number.

"Oh sweetie, I'm so glad to hear from you. Where are you?" First, I heard my mother breathe. A deep sigh. Then I could hear her whispering "Hank" to my dad, who might have been coming out of the bathroom or in bed. They both had to get up at 7 a.m. It was late to call. I'm sure she held the phone near to him, too, so he could hear my voice.

"I'm not sure. Somewhere between Ann Arbor and Madison. I'm staying at a Motel 6." I didn't tell them that everything looked bleak. That the full moon made me feel crazy. That if someone wanted to shoot me or hurt me it would be so easy to do because there was no one around to protect me and besides yelling and screaming there was nothing I could do. "I had a good dinner and want to get a good sleep. I'm going to try and make it to Madison tomorrow." I had covered all the right bases.

"Well, we don't want to keep you on too long. Say a quick hi to your father."

"Weezie. So good to hear your voice. I'm glad you're fine. Take it easy. Are you feeling well?"

"Yes, Daddy. I'm fine." I wanted to complain to him about my neck that hurt from all the driving, about my legs, which sometimes went to sleep, about my skin that often itched and especially in the heat. I wanted to complain forever, but I didn't do any of that because I was trying not to need my parents anymore.

"Be careful."

"I will, Daddy." I clutched the receiver a little too hard. Telephones. Receivers. Disembodied voices.

"Bye, sweetie," my mother said. She always got on the phone last. "Get a good rest and call us in Madison."

"Bye, Mommy."

I walked slowly back to the motel.

For a minute I couldn't find my room and pulled the key out of my pocket. Number 2, it said. We lived at apartment 2B growing up in Peter Cooper Village in New York City.

I turned to the right and saw the number two, a phosphorescent 2, shining even brighter because of the moon. I entered my room and turned on the light. The braided brown and yellow rug covered the whole floor. The bedspread, green and quilted, matched the green and white curtains. But these were not my colors. I liked pinks and reds.

I turned on the shower, and when I felt the warm water rushing over my shoulders, I let out a sigh, a whole body sigh. I wished I could stay in the shower forever, the warmth falling on my skin and into the tired inside of my body. I had driven over 400 miles that day, all by myself. Why don't they have diplomas for that? I smiled. Only a few more days and I'd be in California.

When I went to bed, crickets chirped out the window; they were rooting for me too. I curled up in fetal position, clutched my pillow to me and pretended that the pillow was Ishi, purring softly, licking my face, and pressing his furry body into the crook of my arm, the two of us so safe.

When I woke up, I reached for Ishi. He wasn't there.

The hotel had a free breakfast. I stood in line and filled my plate with plastic-tasting eggs and got a cup of bland Folgers coffee that I filled with fake creamer. A few middle-aged couples sat in chairs reading the paper.

Six hours to Madison. Caffeinated from cheap Folgers coffee, my stomach full from the eggs, I drove for hours in the 90-degree heat. Sweat poured down my face and little drops settled on my lips, which I brushed away. I finally entered Chicago, thank God not at rush hour.

Eight years ago, in August 1968, I found safety in a church on the University of Chicago campus. We were protesting the Vietnam War. The Democratic National Convention was about to start. Hubert Humphrey was already in Chicago. Police sirens screamed outside the stained-glass windows. We all held hands and sang, "Where Have All the Flowers Gone," imagining the senseless killings of young men, imagining the mothers' unimaginable grief. Imagining a world without war. The assassinations of hope had broken our hearts. Martin Luther King Jr. was assassinated in April. I had been a sophomore in college and huddled in my dorm with others, crying and shell-shocked, in a sterile common room with orange plastic chairs and a glaring turquoise couch. Many of us had marched through the streets of New York City, Madison, and places all over the country singing, "We Shall Overcome," Black and White students locked arms together. We would usher in a new era of peace and love and equality, and then boom! The streets exploded with violence. Only months later, Robert Kennedy was assassinated, and something died in so many of us as if winter had descended on the earth like after Persephone was abducted into Hades, the dark underworld. And winter came.

As I drove through Chicago, now over six years after the killings, these memories of all we stood for—peace and love—what I had carried in my heart for so long— and all we had lost, flooded my brain. I didn't want to think about the violence, the fires raging through neighborhoods, people hosed down, dead and maimed.

I still felt my eyes burning in Madison, 1968, at the Dow Chemical protest. I ran to the lake with my friend Joanne, to save our eyes and even our souls, and then prayed none of our friends had cracked skulls after the police beat students and carted them away in paddy wagons. We just didn't want napalm dropped on innocent people. Why did people get their skulls cracked for that?

Chicago brought all this up: hope and despair threaded together.

But I had to live in present time, moment to moment, keeping my eyes on the road. Sleep, eat, drive. Sleep, eat, drive. So simple.

A "Food" sign flashed in front of me, and I veered off the exit and drove to a small diner. When I sat down, watching the waitress move quickly from table to table with pots of coffee, every part of my body was utterly exhausted. I fidgeted with my napkin, feeling very alone in a big booth. "Where Have All the Flowers Gone" played in my mind like a loop tape. Freshman year of college, Joe came down with me to Chicago from Madison a few weekends, and we spent an afternoon studying at the high-ceilinged Gothic library, then went back to my friend Judy Clark's room and made love on her bed under a huge round mirror, which felt too revealing.

At night as Joe and I lay in each other's arms those weekends in Chicago, shadows from the window fluttered across the mirror. Judy was often gone, doing political activity, from Students for a Democratic Society meetings to the Weather Underground, which turned violent. Later she would end up in prison for life; she was the getaway driver for a Brinks Robbery. Three police officers were killed.

She would train dogs, finish a master's degree, start an AIDS education program. Over forty years later, she would still be on the inside looking out. Until one morning in 2019 when she walked out of prison: 68 years old, a free woman.

When I got to Madison, I lugged in my typewriter, my small suitcase, and my sleeping bag to Joanne's apartment. Joanne was a dear friend from Madison, still living there and in law school. She shared a one-bedroom with her boyfriend and had a pullout couch where I dropped my sleeping bag. "Hey, Louise! Welcome." Joanne was short, energetic, and talkative, a New Yorker like me. Her father was a famous civil liberties lawyer. I took a deep breath. Her boyfriend was shy but friendly. He excused himself to do some work. He was in law school, too.

"There's chicken and vegetables. Plenty to eat!" I got there at 8 p.m. as I had hit traffic going around Chicago. Joanne sat with me at her round Formica table as I ate and for an hour we talked: about her internship up north, the long drive home each day, the classes she was taking. Her days were structured by work and school and eating with her boyfriend.

"Hey, you're a real poet, now!" she said, when I talked about getting my master's degree and studying with Robert Creeley and John Logan. That my thesis was a book of poems, *Dancing Through the Rapids*. How leaving Buffalo was wrenching even though I couldn't stand the town when I first arrived.

When I looked at Joanne, I remembered the time we lived in the same dorm. We used to meet at the vending machines downstairs. I snacked all the time on junk food and sodas. I remembered how a bunch of us went skinny-dipping, and Joe lifted me up in the water and threw me down into Lake Mendota. I felt so light then, as if I could touch the stars.

"Any new guys?" she said, as if reading my mind.

"Oh, no one special, now," I said, turning my face down for a moment. I remembered the week we spent in Block Island one summer when I was dating Joe.

"Are you going to marry him?" she had said so many years ago. I wished I could have said "yes" with certainty. But I just shrugged.

"Pretty brave to do what you're doing—go across the country alone! I don't know if I'd ever do that." I got that a lot. That I was brave.

"Kind of scary at times, being alone, but I like just thinking to myself for so many hours each day. Sometimes I say poems out loud to myself or sing rounds my sister and I used to sing."

She had a puzzled look on her face. "I wish I could think

for myself! Law school is the opposite. Lots of memorization!"

"You don't have too much more to go, right?"

"No—just one more year and supposedly each year gets easier." She started to yawn. She had things to do.

"I have to get up at 5 a.m. There's coffee and donuts. Milk in the fridge. Help yourself. Then just close the door. It locks behind you. Wish I didn't have to get up and work. We could play! "

We gave each other a big hug. "Good luck," she said. "Be careful. Let me know where you're living in California. Maybe I'll visit."

She smiled and then walked to her bedroom and closed the door.

As I lay on the couch, alone, I had trouble sleeping, even though I knew I needed to sleep well.

I could see the kitchen table—a bowl with lemons and oranges waiting to be sliced. Shadows fell across the wooden floor. I wondered how many students had walked across the floors in this apartment. I imagined Joanne crawling into bed and Bruce's arms opening up for her. I thought of Joe and how we fit together like puzzle pieces a long time ago in this very town.

I fell into a deep sleep.

In the morning I called Ken when I stopped for gas at around 10 a.m. He was about to go to graduate school at Yale for his Ph.D. That's what my parents would have wanted for me. Years after my dad died, I found a journal that I had given him. He struggled with depression. "You should write, Dad—might make you feel better." But when I read the journal, he wrote he was disappointed that neither my sister nor I got a Ph.D. He wondered if he was to blame. If the accident was to blame. He was too preoccupied.

I shouldn't have read it because it made me sad, that he was sad and that I didn't measure up. Plus, it was his private journal.

"Louise, Louise, where are you? On some road somewhere in the middle of nowhere, USA? How are you doing? I miss you."

"I just left Madison." My voice was flatter than it usually was when I talked to Ken. I felt so different from him now. So far away.

Madison was where we had met, if only briefly, but something we shared.

"It was so weird being there," I said. Tears sprung to my eyes. Hearing Kens' voice, I suddenly felt exhausted. That I had nothing to share.

"When will you get to California?" he said. "I wish I could talk longer, but I have an appointment at Yale. I've got to register for classes." I imagined him taking the train down to Yale, my father's alma mater. My father said when he left for Yale, his mother, Lena, cried when he went away. He must have looked through the window and watched her waving. Though it was only an hour and half away from New York City, she must have felt like he had fallen off the side of the earth.

She was only 58 when she died. I never met her or my Jewish grandfather and uncle, who all died young.

I wasn't going to Yale, but at least I had my graduate degree and a letter of reference from Robert Creeley. But I'd probably get a Kelly Girls job while Ken got a Ph.D. and a solid academic appointment. I could have been a French professor, on a track, waving my hands in the air at some university, students looking up at me adoringly as we read the poets Verlaine and Baudelaire, my accent parfait, all the work I put into French, listening to Edith Piaf, le petit rossignol, the little nightingale, my imagined life expressing itself on this alternate path. But I didn't, I hadn't gone that route. I had taken what felt like a harder route, a route of the heart that paid dirt.

"Should be there in two days. I've been driving till about ten at night." I wanted to hang up, get a cup of coffee and keep going.

"Call me any time and especially when you get there. Be safe. I love you."

"Love you too. Good luck with registration."

We both hung up and I felt desolate. I wished I were registering for classes. That I was back east where I belonged, that I could see Ken soon and talk to him for a long time about the way my heart ached at odd times during the day; sometimes even when I looked at trees on the road, so leafy, a canopy over the highway. Why did my heart ache when I looked at trees?

CHAPTER TWENTY-TWO

As I drove through Iowa, endless, green-furrowed land spread out like angels' wings along the sides of the road. Wispy clouds dotted the sky; I wanted to hop from cloud to cloud, so free, out of the metal machine that I felt soldered to, with my racing stripe, my car racing past the cornfields, the blood in my system pumping too fast from the effect of three cups of morning caffeine.

I passed a church at the side of the road, red roof, red steeple, and white walls. My grandpa, Reverend Daubert, swept me up in his arms and called me "my little buttercup." I held on to those words when I felt sad. My mother wrote to me that he had died while I was in France. I had just gotten him a wooden saint candleholder in Barcelona and carried it home in my backpack. It still hangs on my wall fifty years later and I think of him when I see it.

Huge birds, vultures, circled the sky. I imagined them swooping down for carrion and thought about how many things died each day. Bits of Galway Kinnell's poems floated through my brain, from *The Book of Nightmares*. "You scream, waking from a nightmare. When I sleepwalk/ into your room, and pick you up, /and hold you up in the moonlight, you cling to me /hard,/as if clinging could save us. I think/you think/I will never die, I think I exude/to you the permanence of smoke or stars, /even as/my broken arms heal themselves around you." I thought of my father's broken soul after the accident and maybe even before. His mother, father and brother all died early. I thought of how he hadn't really healed. Do people ever really heal or do they just go on?

Iowa faded away as I entered Nebraska, flat as a line. I only hit traffic a few times, in Lincoln, near the capitol building that rose from the earth like a white knight. I imagined Apu, Ishi or Flow on my lap then, purring, cheering me on, further and further across the country. My mother had driven across the country with a friend after she was married, and my father was a physician in the war in Persia. She hadn't told me anything about that drive, but I imagined she loved the adventure.

The summer before the accident, when I was only three and my sister, five, she would put us in the back seat of the car and say, "Let's get lost!" and we'd drive up and down hilly roads in Sea Cliff, Long Island, blue and red geraniums exploding out of gardens. The next year my sister and I were lost to them for nine months, and I never wanted to get lost again.

After the accident, I was always waiting for my mother to come home from her 37 operations, face pressed against the windowpane in summer, autumn, winter and spring. I wanted to stay put. If she was even one minute late to meet me, my whole body shook.

Now, so many moons later, maybe I *did* want to get lost or know that I *could* get lost and be found again.

A Hershey's bar along with the Coke, sugar and caffeine, lay on the passenger seat. With the clutch safely in fourth gear, I ripped open the chocolate bar; the creamy chocolate melted into my mouth—all that sweetness like a piece of heaven.

Twilight came on quickly, a thief stealing the sunlight. I passed fields speckled with just a few trees, under a big sky, which suddenly got pitch black. I heard thunder. I saw lightning, a huge luminescent crack through the windowpane. My hands felt cold, and my heart raced. *Panic begone*, I screamed to the sky. I didn't ever want that panic grafted onto me like my mother's flesh from other parts of her body grafted onto her face and neck. What if lightning struck my car?

You're supposed to wear rubber sneakers when lightning strikes, but I didn't know what to do in a car. The tires were rubber, but there was so much metal inside. I pulled to the side of the road, the rain thick stripes of water now. I put my hands in my lap so I wouldn't touch metal and prayed. "The Lord is my shepherd; I shall not want." My dead grandpa appeared in the seat next to me. His tall, calm presence slowed down my heart rate. I imagined my grandma, too, sipping tea out of an English floral teacup. And then the rain stopped, and the lightning stopped. I unfolded my hands as my grandfather disappeared into the Nebraska sky.

It was almost 8 p.m. I was ravenous and exhausted.

For the next thirty miles there was nothing except what looked like a truckers' stop, trucks parked in a huge lot and a diner. I stumbled out of the car and entered a place full of men—except for the waitress. She caught my eye and smiled. I sat down at the counter.

"Sweetheart, what can I get you?" About twenty truckers sat at the counter or at some tables nearby. Some turned their heads towards me, and they all looked nice, but the waitress glared right back at them. I was protected. No one was going to do or say anything to upset me. My mama savior.

"A hamburger and fries," I said politely. "Thanks."

One of the older truckers sat next to me. He seemed fatherly.

"Where you off to?" he said, taking a sip of coffee. I figured he would probably be driving all night and needed the caffeine.

"On my way to California. Should be there in a couple of days." I felt like a proud lion, sitting at a truckers' stop on my way to California, all by myself. Junkyards. Trucker stops. Something my parents would never have done. Or wouldn't have approved of.

My hamburger and fries arrived. Even though I had been alone all day with my thoughts, I didn't really want to talk to anyone. I just wanted to know that the waitress was there, keeping an eye out for me. Being a trucker was a job that must age people fast, I thought, driving thousands of miles through the night, your circadian rhythm, the 24-hour cycle, suddenly out of synch. Was I getting out of synch? *Get rest along the way. You're not in a big rush.* My mother's voice whispered into my ear.

"Well good luck to you!" the older trucker said and opened the *Lincoln Star*. I briefly glanced at the news. A Japanese woman had reached the summit of Everest. The first woman to get there. Twenty-nine thousand feet up on the roof of the world. My father took me to see the movie about Sir Edmund Percival Hillary and Tenzing Norgay, the first climbers confirmed to have reached the summit of Mount Everest. They were a team, a bridge between continents. I also saw that the Symbionese Liberation Army had planted pipe bombs under cars at the International House of Pancakes in L.A. The bombs didn't explode. I shivered for a minute. Suddenly California sounded scary.

Out the window a long stretch of nothingness was punctuated by a few outcroppings of rocks; the sky was dark as a gutter but filled with the brilliant light of millions of stars. Even when I was in summer camp in the Maine woods, I had never seen so many stars at once.

The Motel 6 was down the road about ten miles. I checked in, double-locked the door, took a warm shower and crashed. I didn't wake up until 9 a.m. In the morning I looked at my map and decided to take a slightly longer route through Colorado, to see the Rockies. Soon I would be more west than east, backwards in time zones and forwards towards something I could not even imagine. I turned on the ignition, rolled down the window and let a soft, warm wind cover my body like a radiant gown.

In Colorado, everything became gigantic, like an Alice in Wonderland transformation, as if the sky, the rocks, and the trees multiplied themselves by four. Something caught in the pit of my stomach. I was west. I was no longer East anymore. The road was strangely empty, too, so I felt small surrounded by so much space. Voids usually get filled, or that is what I remember hearing, but here on this highway, I wasn't so sure.

I stopped at a restaurant, more of a shack than a restaurant, and bought a turkey sandwich and a Coke and took it outside, looking for a tree or some shade, as it was over 90 degrees. A tall man in jeans, a plaid shirt, even in this heat, wore a wide-brimmed cowboy hat. He stood still, looking over at a barren field nearby. At his feet, chickens ran around in circles. He didn't look at me, and I felt small in the blinding sunlight. I found a lawn chair, sat down and ate my sandwich, gazing at the Rockies and wondering why the rocks were so jagged, and how many eons ago they rose out of ancient waters. Suddenly the man turned his face away from the sky, touched his cowboy hat in some weird western ritual, walked into the shack and must have gone out the other side to his car because he was gone. The chickens broke from their circle and ran around chaotically, searching for food dropped on the ground. They made high-pitched noises in stark contrast to the silence of the barren fields and the endless sky. The cold Coke slipped down my throat like heaven. I had been thirsty for a long time.

I finished my sandwich and got back into my car, heading toward the Great Salt Lake. What was thirst? What was

I thirsty for? I sang the song, "I know where I'm goin'. And I know who's goin' with me" by Judy Collins. But I didn't know either.

Since I was driving alone, I never stopped for hitchhikers, as I traveled Interstate 80. Morning, afternoon and even in the evening I saw mostly young men with backpacks, some upright, some sitting on the side of the road chugging water, some couples, standing along the highway in the highway silence I remembered so well from my hitchhiking days down the coast of Spain. Just waiting. Like waiting to be blessed and wondering if you would be chosen.

As much as I felt for all the hitchhikers I passed, I was afraid as a single woman, afraid of being snatched from life into the shadows. The darkness from the assault might be lurking in the eyes of a hitchhiker. Just common sense, my parents would say. *That would be too dangerous. Why would you do something like that?*

I longed for company, even small talk. When I passed people with their thumbs stuck out, I imagined myself, not that many years ago, standing along empty highways, hoping for human kindness. I sang Randy Newman's song. Maybe I *should* be giving someone a ride? Maybe I *shouldn't* be so scared.

Bright before me the signs implore me
to help the needy and show them the way

I gazed quickly at a face or backpack, while trying to keep on the road. When one hitchhiker saw me turn his way, he moved forward, eyes pleading as if I would save him. But I didn't. I saw his disappointed body cave in on itself as I kept going in my self-sufficient metal fortress, something no one was going to penetrate.

As I got nearer to Salt Lake, my body worn out, I stopped at a diner for a hamburger and diet soda, which made me buzz. A spacey, lost feeling overwhelmed me. My soul didn't feel good. My right foot touched the pedals of the car, my hands gripped the steering wheel, but I felt detached from my body.

My thoughts powered across the interstate, thoughts I couldn't stop. They spun too fast: lines of poetry, songs, voices of my mother, father, and sister fragmented, voices decorating the rooms of my brain. My mother, "Where are you, exactly where are you now?" and my dad, "How are you feeling? Are you feeling okay?" and my sister, reading me a passage from a book or a poem, maybe one I had just read because we seemed to read the same things, swallow the same words. I saw Ken, too, with his list of classes, his syllabi, so stable, on his path. I tried to hold on to the thoughts or one of the voices. My eyelids felt heavy and my limbs dead weight. Soon it would be dark.

It was already 7 p.m. Salt Lake City was ten miles away. I had to slow down for traffic. Out of the corner of my eye I spotted a hitchhiker, sandy hair, glasses, a scholarly-looking type with a friendly face and neat-looking backpack. As my car got closer to him, I gazed at his eyes to see if they were hard pebbles. When he gave me a broad smile, I impulsively pulled over. Without opening the passenger seat door, I rolled down the window.

"Hi, where you going?"

"Just need a ride to Salt Lake." His voice wasn't smooth, scary, or sticky. "Happy to give you some money for gas." He seemed a bit shy. Nice. I let him into the car.

CHAPTER TWENTY-THREE

He said his name was Bob and I liked that Bob waited for me to lean over and open the door and that he didn't ask anything of me, to scrunch his backpack in the loaded-down backseat or put it in the trunk which had my huge mirror with "I trust myself completely" written in red lipstick. I was always worried the mirror would break. He held his backpack, his little house, neatly on his lap. For a moment, we both breathed together, two strangers immediately comfortable. I was happy for the company and began to wish Salt Lake wasn't just ten miles away but hundreds of miles away so I could just have him next to me, so that we could talk. Turned out he was in graduate school, studying to be an engineer, but when I told him I was a poet, he said he loved poetry.

"I'm not a Mormon," he said, "in case you're wondering, though I have good friends who are," and we both laughed. As we got closer to his house, I suddenly felt afraid. Not afraid of him, thank God, but where was I going to sleep? My mother would have all her itineraries, trips planned out months in advance, phone numbers of each hotel sent to my sister and me, "in case of an emergency." Always able to be tracked down. But now I was the opposite, like a tumbleweed, a rolling stone. At night, when darkness fell like a black gown, I longed for my parents' house, for the weekly menus on the refrigerator, for the smell of cleaning antiseptic, all the microbes gone. As if life could be sanitized.

As if picking up on my fears, Bob blurted out, "I have a pullout couch in my apartment. A lot of friends have slept there. You're welcome to…" And he was looking out the window, perhaps wondering how I'd react as we just met ten miles ago. I could see he didn't want me to have to refuse him. This would be so easy, so cheap, too, "Yes," I said, "yes," and he started pointing out the mountains that loomed above us.

"Twin Peaks is over 11,000 feet. I've hiked up there. Went up Broads Fork. Had to scramble on rocks towards the top." I thought of the time when I was 12 years old and went with my camp group from Maine up Mt. Washington. We trudged up Tuckerman Ravine, careful not to slip.. The weather shifted fast on that trip, rain smearing across the Presidential Range, and we never made it to the summit that year. But I remembered sitting with a group of spiritualists who believed that Martians had contacted them! If I were a Martian, that's where I would go, it was so beautiful.

I wondered what this peak in Utah would be like. Would I ever ascend it?

I could see shadows on the Great Salt Lake, a chiaroscuro world. I was getting so sleepy, though, it took all my energy just to drive. We entered the west side of the city where he lived. How would I even have the energy to brush my teeth? I just wanted to crawl into bed. Sleep, sweet sleep. My hands hurt from clutching the steering wheel for so long.

"Can I help with your suitcase?" he said, getting it from

the backseat and lifting it up his front steps while I carried my typewriter, my precious typewriter. A relief to have some help. My muscles were sore from lifting things in and out of the car. I could hear my mother's voice, "Make sure to protect your things." What would she and my dad think about my staying with a male hitchhiker I picked up as twilight fell in Salt Lake City? But this was my life, not their life. He didn't look like a rapist. He looked the opposite. Curly hair. Glasses. Friendly blue eyes and freckles that danced.

His apartment was small and neat. He handed me a glass of water. "Food in the fridge if you're hungry. Help yourself." He made up the couch bed, put out a bath towel for me, went into his bedroom and shut the door.

I was so grateful for his generosity. A bath. Floating in warm water. No need to put my foot on the pedal, or gaze at a map, or wonder where I would eat and sleep or plummet through the dark. If it had been practically any other moment in my life, I would loosen my tired arms and limbs into the water. I lay down on the bed, neatly made with cotton sheets and a thin blanket. I fell into a deep sleep, comforted that Bob was in the next room. I didn't realize how lonely I had been feeling.

In the morning, Bob came out of his room all dressed for school. "Coffee is made if you want some. Food, too."

I got dressed in the bathroom and got myself some coffee, my mind racing to the next place I would get to. How far could I make it? *California coming home*, I sang to myself. "Just coffee, thanks! Think I'll eat later."

"Since you're here, thought you'd want to see the Mormon Temple? We could drive there, and you can take off from there."

How could I not stop and see the Mormon Temple even though I was aching to get back on the road?

"Okay. Yes, the temple it is!" The Mormon Temple rose out of the ground like a great gothic building, reminding me of the library at the University of Chicago. I thought of my friend Judy again. A beautiful soul who would make a terrible decision. The Weather Underground. The fight for peace and love turned violent. *There but for fortune* how a life goes.

This was a different gothic structure. I was far from Chicago. As we walked into the Mormon Temple, I was sure I saw Jesus lit up in blue, though years later, I couldn't find a photo of a blue Jesus and wondered if I imagined it. Maybe I had been on the road for too long or somehow was thinking of the Indian gods in my art book from France, maybe Krishna, the god of protection, compassion, tenderness, and love, who would protect me on my journey.

On the bottom floor was the baptismal font, which sat on the backs of twelve oxen, representing the 12 tribes of Israel. I had been baptized at nine years old at St. George's Church in New York City, my godfather the organist. My Presbyterian grandparents were thrilled; my Jewish dad seemed to accept it all and my mother was happy for a community and must have thought some kind of religious education was better than nothing. I went to church camp and sang in the choir, wearing a long red robe with a white collar, a different life from most in my progressive radical private school. I prayed at night, but when I turned fourteen and said the lines "Almighty and most merciful Father; We have erred and strayed from thy ways like lost sheep. We have followed too much the devices and desires of our own hearts. We have offended against thy holy laws," I suddenly knew I wanted to leave the church. I wasn't a sinner. I was a pantheist, believing all things compose an all-encompassing, immanent god or goddess. I read Spinoza. I didn't believe that the mind and body are separated. I believed that God is in nature. I didn't believe in original sin. That was a mean-spirited thing.

Bob and I walked through the rooms—the creation room, and the garden room—paintings of green trees, where the lion and lamb lie down together—my favorite room. Then we moved to the Telestial Room, the opposite of the Garden of Eden, fallen trees, and animals fighting each other. One of the signs said that if people lead sinful lives, they would end up in spirit prison. Spirit prison. I suddenly wanted to get out of that church quickly, but Bob insisted we go up to the top, "the Celestial room, the highest room on the path," he said, "soft light, the sun shining on everything. You'll like it up there. It will be nice to see it before you get back on the road." He was right to take me there. It *was* peaceful. But I still wanted to get out quickly.

Plus, my blood sugar was taking a huge dive after two cups of coffee. Bob told me the lake had 10,000 miles of shoreline. The salinity was so high, he said, you could float more easily than in any other salty lake in the world. "It's amazing," he said to live here. I liked that he knew these facts as if the facts anchored him.

I'd always loved floating in the water. Years later, before I had children, I dreamt that I was nine months pregnant, belly filled with life, and I was floating in the middle of the ocean, about to give birth, surrounded by cerulean blue. I wasn't afraid anymore.

"Time for class," Bob said as we descended from the sky, "and I guess for you to get closer to California."

"Thanks for everything."

"And thank you for picking up a solitary hitchhiker! Good luck." He looked a little teary-eyed. Maybe I could have stayed, gotten to know him better. Maybe I could even have put down roots in Salt Lake.

We hugged right in front of the temple, people pouring in, as it was June. Then I walked to my car and got back on Interstate 80. The south side of the Great Salt Lake spread out like the word infinity.

When I had left Buffalo to begin my trip, I saw a boxcar with the writing *Danger, Eternity Ahead*. I had felt it was an omen, though I wasn't sure of what.

Now, on the road, hunger gnawed at me. I stopped on the outskirts of the city at a Denny's. I sat at the counter, as I wanted to eat quickly and be gone. Denny's was busy, families with young kids pouring in for summer break, the sun glowing through the window, waitresses scurrying to and fro. I scarfed down my eggs and bacon and raced back to the car. I'd lost some time by going to the temple. I wanted to make it to Nevada before sundown.

Night driving felt too hard. I got that from my dad who had night blindness. The night of the explosion, he let my mother drive home down the curvy Cape Cod roads in the pitch-blackness. The lawyers for the gas company said he was drunk. That was why he let my mother drive. That was unfair. He had night blindness. I had it too. The lights of cars from the opposite lanes and shadows of trees threatened to steer me off course.

Maybe my dad and I were both just scared of the dark.

As I drove further west, away from my home in the east, I felt things slough off me, like a snake shedding its skin. Who would I be now? I wanted to believe that I wasn't attached to anyone. Being attached meant people would tell me what to do, and I didn't want to be told. And being attached meant being part of a circle, and I wanted to get out of a circle because something might pull me down, like Persephone was pulled down to Hades, like my parents were pulled down to that fiery cellar and came out screaming, with fire on their bodies.

I walked to the crowded Denny's parking lot, got back in my crazy car with its mag wheels and racing stripe. A few men eyed the car and then me and then turned away. I was used to that. The steering wheel was burning when I placed my hand on it. I grabbed my canteen on the passenger seat and put luscious cool water on a paper towel to coat the steering wheel so I could drive. I rolled down all the windows, got out the map. Straight shot to Nevada.

I would reach my destination soon. The place I was going to. What would the apartment be like? What would my new roommate be like? Susan had said to me on the phone in Buffalo, "You'll take over my room. I have a roommate." I knew nothing about her. I didn't even ask. *California coming home.*

Eighty miles later, I pulled into a gas station and reached into my purse for my wallet, messy with Bic pens and some crumbs from a chocolate chip cookie. Where was my address book, my pink-flowered square precious book that I carried everywhere, the book with all the names and addresses and phone numbers of everyone I knew and loved? I looked at the seat and felt all over the floor of the front and back seat of the car. I picked up a pair of shoes to see if it was hiding, lying in wait for me under something, like a child in a dark closet waiting to be found. *Gotcha,* I would call out in Peter Cooper Village when all the kids would play Ringolevio and hide. *Gotcha, gotcha.*

My address book *had* to be somewhere.

I spilled out of the car into the oppressive heat while the attendant filled the tank and opened the trunk thinking it must have fallen out somewhere. It couldn't be lost. Not my address book. Anything but that. Take my makeup— lipstick, eyeliner, or even my dry skin cream. That was all replaceable.

I had no backup. This was 1976. People's lives lived in

their handwriting. I pulled things out of the trunk in an adrenaline haze, poetry books, a small cosmetics case, and a stash of dirty laundry in a pillowcase. It was hard to do because the mirror Maureen had given me sat on the top of everything. I didn't want it to break. I liked peeling open the blanket that covered the mirror and seeing "Trust yourself completely" written in red lipstick. I relaxed. Yes, "Trust yourself completely."

Then I remembered. At Denny's, I pulled out my address book to look up Gene, my old boss from the Brooklyn Court Employment Project, who had moved to San Francisco. He told me to phone him while I was on the road, so he would know when I was arriving. "My wife and I will have you over." I must have left it at Denny's. Now I couldn't call Gene. I couldn't call Ken anymore on this trip as he had moved so many times, I forgot his number. Of course, I knew my parents' and sister's number and would have to slowly figure out how to get in touch with people to find all the numbers again. But some would be lost forever. Names of people and streets suddenly vanished. Why was this happening to me, now, alone, on the road?

"All filled up," the attendant said as I handed him the money and waited for change. He came back with six dollars, which I stuffed into my wallet and put back into my purse, my purse which now felt too light.

My address book was either thrown into a garbage can at Denny's along with leftover scrambled eggs, pancakes and syrup, or perhaps held for a week or two waiting for me to come back. But I never did. When I got back on the road, the panic had vanished, replaced by feelings of freedom sweeping over me. I took it as an omen.

That I would have to reconstruct my life and leave people and places behind.

CHAPTER TWENTY-FOUR

The landscape on the drive toward Elko Nevada was barren, dry, so different from the tall trees in the country landscapes I knew so well: the Maine Woods and the aroma of pine needles, Long Island and the waves of the Atlantic that I rode into shore. Places I took the train to as a child. Now, the sky spread over me like a huge light blue umbrella dotted with white cotton ball clouds. Sky and earth such strange playmates, always one on top of the other, never swerving or veering off the road. At night I even pinched myself. *Stay awake, stay awake.* Even though I was going a little over the speed limit, drivers shot past me. I stayed to the right, in the slow lane, timid, defensive, not willing to go faster and compete with the huge trucks. After stopping at the truck stop, I came to see the truck drivers as so human, their jobs so difficult. But maybe they were a little like me—like how I felt? The rush of freedom in a suspended no-man's land between places? Like a sailor at sea, landing for a time but always pushing off somewhere else.

Peter Cooper Village, the housing development that I lived in until I was twelve, seemed so very far away. Apartment 2B. My childhood kitchen was tiny with a white Formica table where my sister and I ate dinner with our babysitter until I was almost eight as our dad came home late from work. My mother kept his dinner warm on a hotplate. They ate together when he got home. Each floor had eight apartments, everyone squashed together, but that was what I knew, and it was comforting to hear the flood of family voices every day and the familiar sounds, my shoes padding over concrete city streets, noises of sirens and the planetary voices of my parents and sister. When I rode in the back seat of the car on trips to upstate New York to visit my aunt, uncle and cousins, I fell asleep easily, lulled by the familiar cadences.

Now, barreling across country by myself, I clutched the wheel tighter, terrified for a moment by my anonymity, so different from the anonymity of New York City teeming with millions of urban dwellers. In New York City most people I knew were just a breath away. Here, empty space devoid of people surrounded me. The window was rolled down as far as it would go, but the air was hot. My left arm had a sunburn, and I couldn't seem to get enough water in me. I kept going, with only a short stop in Elko for some real food, a hamburger and fries. I filled up my canteen with water; I got a Mars bar for the road and kept driving through desert country, through mining country, only tiny tufts of green reminding me there were places where trees grew. The Humboldt River flowed to my side, the water thin trickles, not a rush of white froth.

It began to get dark. When night fell, the terror came on, like a dark swelling.

But like an orphan heart, I had to develop a hard shell, and this was my proof: I was traveling for thousands of miles alone. "I'm all right." I repeated that to myself like a mantra when things got tough, when night fell and I didn't know where I would stop, or when a car almost hit me on the road at night, a drunken swerve, where I could have disappeared from the earth in an instant.

I felt free.

My brown hair flared out the window in a humid wind and twilight slid into a scarlet sky like the time in Ibiza with Ken when we took LSD, and I felt part of everything: part of the metal car, part fleshy hands on the steering wheel, part breath going up and down, part feet on the pedals, part petals of all the flowers in the universe and I didn't want to stop. I wanted to drive until the stars coated the blackness with their galloping light.

But I was tired and hungry. I couldn't make it all the way to California that night. Reality set in like a clock.

The Motel 6 in Reno, Nevada, had two lights broken so the Open sign said "pen" and I thought of a pen, or the penal system, my mind still dancing through the rapids. When I opened the door, I practically fell out of the car, my legs lead-heavy, so tired from the long drive from Salt Lake. The stark whiteness of that lake now seemed so remote as I made my way down a barely lit path to the motel.

A huge clock hung behind the reception desk, a reminder that I was leaving the "zone" I had been in. It was 8 p.m.

"A room available?" I said, my voice too high pitched, like a child's. I wanted to grab my typewriter and suitcase out of the car. Though I had hardly used the typewriter at all on my road trip, it was my talisman, my comfort. Poems danced through my mind and the words soothed me, even if I didn't write them down.

"Yes, we have a room," the clerk said. He was older and spoke slowly.

"Thanks so much and a place to eat?"

He handed me the key. "Take a right down the road. There's a Denny's."

I lugged my stuff in, again, to a generic Motel 6 room, washed my face, brushed my hair and drove to Denny's, almost missing the turn.

As I ate, I pulled out my book of Galway Kinnell poems from my purse.

"The first step...shall be to lose the way."

Was I trying to lose my way, reveling in a clockless universe? Was I waiting, finally, for "our scars (to) fall in love"? Did I have scars too? The scars coated the open places, the wounds. Would I ever truly find and give love? I never liked to sleep alone. When I was little, I often waited up for my sister to come to bed when she was allowed to stay up later. Hearing her breathing nearby soothed me. Now, no one was breathing next to me at night.

I closed the book. I had poetry, words breathing inside of me. That was my comfort. I rested my hand on the shiny cover of Kinnell's poetry book.

I finished my food and drink, paid and left a good tip. I had been a waitress too, and knew what tips meant to a life. I drove back slowly in the Nevada dark and collapsed on the bed.

I left Nevada in the morning, driving through dry desert spanning both sides of the road, brown tufts popping up from the ground and bits of greenery and yellow flowers in small clusters. Every once in a while, I saw a cactus jutting up from the ground, a green dancer in the dry brush. It was hot as hell, an inferno inside the car. I guzzled water, rolled down the windows and knew that today I'd get to my destination. I began to sing, "I'm getting married in the morning," for some weird reason. But I wasn't getting married. I was getting to Berkeley to a new life. Marrying my new life. I laughed. I'd be near the Pacific Ocean with its phosphorescent life. The ocean.

Back east, I'm four years old. My father's hand in my hand, the briny smell of seaweed and sand beneath my feet. "Look for the magic bubbles," Daddy says, a small red bucket with a plastic shovel in my left hand. Wellfleet, 1954.

How could a whole town, a whole set of memories be etched into my brain forever and also disappear forever? The accident. I would bury it six feet deep like an amputated limb. No one would ever find it.

Many, many years later with a family of my own, I would find the house again, the little cottage with the cellar that burned my parents, but I wouldn't even go inside. A family was living there. A swing set, rafts, a kiddie pool on the lawn. What would I say to them?

I needed to stop for gas. The tank was below half full, too hot out to run out of gas. Running on empty, the needle at zero, my life at zero, so hot I could hardly take a deep breath. Thank God a gas station ahead sang to me like a mirage, *you're not going to run on empty*, and I pulled in, filled up and warded off stares as usual of men wondering what I was doing in a hot rod with a racing stripe.

I parked near the small, attached grocery store and got a Coke and a chocolate bar, sustenance to transit Donner Pass. I also squirreled away some nuts in the car in case I got too jittery.

"Two dollars, miss," the cashier said, glancing at me and looking out the window at my car as if I came from another planet, a whirling dust planet. Or maybe he wasn't thinking anything at all. Maybe I was putting words in his mouth or in everyone's mouth.

I'd been alone for too long.

As I clutched my chocolate bar already melting from the heat, a wave of sadness washed over me. But it was temporary.

I had to pay attention to the road.

As I got into the car, the words Donner Pass terrified me. Crush of cars, ghosts of the dead sweeping— "human flesh marked so we don't eat our own kin," I read in a book. I turned on the ignition, soon to be driving across the Sierra, which I could see, snow-tufted granite mountains that I got to drive across in comfort. The mountains so stunning I wanted to fly up and around them, spin around the necklace of snow. Here I was—so many years later and so many miles later surrounded by beauty. But how about the Donner Party?

When did they stop believing they would make it? A snowstorm, five feet fell, and all their dreams dashed. Many of them never escaped.

As I began ascending the mountain pass, I quickly opened the Hershey's bar and followed the signs. Why didn't I call anyone? My parents? My sister? Ken? They'd all be at work or school. But I wanted to tell them that I loved them. That sometimes I thought of flying in my car, flying off the mountain like a bird because I wanted to soar. But I knew my bones weren't hollow. How could I soar without hollow bones?

Donner Pass on Interstate 80 still had signs that said "Icy" though it was warm. Beyond the green pine trees, the highway lifted and sank like a huge roller coaster. I felt so small, so low to the ground, huge trucks swarming around me as I passed them, or they passed me. I prayed their brakes worked. That there wouldn't be runaway trucks. Runaway. Was I a runaway? From my previous life?

I sang "White Coral Bells," the round my sister and I sang together as children, praying I could drive safely over the pass. This was the scariest road I had ever been on. I was still a new driver. I wanted my sister with me, close to me.

White Coral Bells
Upon a slender stalk
Lilies of the valley deck my garden walk
Oh, don't you wish that you might hear them ring?
That will happen only when the fairies sing.
That will happen only when the fairies sing.

I sang it again and again and again as I drove back down the spectacular Sierra Nevada Mountains, passed Sacramento and followed the signs for Berkeley, Ashby Street. I was so proud of myself for getting off at the right exit. Here I was, California! Adrenaline rushed through my body.

The house stood back from the street, nestled in trees, a beautiful street, College Avenue, the street that leads up to the University of California Berkeley campus.

As usual, I picked up my typewriter first—then my backpack and walked up to the front door and rang the bell. No one answered. I rang it again, taking a full deep breath. The weather was beautiful. Sunlight shone through the trees. A woman about my age walked out. She didn't smile at me. She was curt. Maybe she had an appointment to get to.

"Oh, you must be Louise." That's all she said, not even looking directly at me. She wore a t-shirt and jeans and seemed distracted.

"Yes, you must be Katy." I looked at her and smiled, ready to give her a hug. She would be my new roommate. She knew my dear friend Mary. I had driven 3000 miles to get to this very moment, but she didn't smile back.

"I'll show you your room and then I have to go."

My heart sank.

She led me through a cluttered dining room, papers, books, coffee cups spilling over all the flat surfaces, up some back stairs, to a tiny room with no dresser. Just a bed. Mary said there would be a bed. I didn't remember if she said no dresser.

"Bathroom's on the first floor. Four of us share it, so make sure to clean up after yourself. Gotta go." And she was gone. No one else was home. No, Are you thirsty? Hungry? How was your trip?

I drove across country to live with a stranger.

I took four trips from the car up to my tiny room. My mirror with "Trust yourself completely" had cracked. I had to be careful not to cut myself as I grabbed my stuff out of the trunk, my stuff that had traveled with me for thousands of miles. Upstairs, I unpacked my suitcase, but I had nowhere to put my clothes. I spread them out on the bed to sort through. Tonight, I would have to lay them on the floor until I could get a dresser. My room didn't have a closet.

I wasn't sure about the phone, whether or not I could use it, so I took a walk down College Avenue until I found a pay phone right next to the 7-Eleven. After I made the call, I'd get a diet soda and maybe some cheese and crackers. I was too tired to think about food shopping. I didn't even know where to go.

When I called my parents, my voice cracked. "I made it," I said and almost burst into tears.

CHAPTER TWENTY-FIVE

Three months after I arrived in California, my mother came out to visit to attend a nursing conference. She stayed in a hotel on University Avenue, not too far from my house. I was working as a secretary at University of California Berkeley, writing poetry every day, sometimes during work when no one was looking; poems on napkins, small pieces of lined paper, or on index cards. I was volunteering to teach one poetry class for senior citizens, but I felt deflated. I didn't have much money and no prospect of a teaching job that would pay the bills. Berkeley was for students and what seemed like the homeless and mental health patients. I'm sure there were families, neatly tucked into apartments and homes, but their lives were different from mine, too. My family was all back east—except for my cousin Lew, whom I saw every once in a while.

Whenever I saw my mother, I also saw high expectations walking towards me in her put-together outfits and Ferragamo shoes. I didn't have a Ph.D. or a steady, stable boyfriend. I now lived in a part of town where drug deals went on until late at night in front of Dunkin' Donuts (I would later get robbed for the second time). And my job—I was a secretary, doing what I had done at Kelly Girls for years since high school, typing up documents and sometimes correcting my bosses' spelling errors. Plus, there was the marijuana and sex, but I didn't talk about that.

I *was* writing poetry furiously, possessed by words, and

I had had some poems accepted at magazines. Doors had opened for publications and later part-time teaching because I had a recommendation from Robert Creeley. That was something big. But could I make a life out of that? My mother seemed to be waiting for me to do something else or at least stop living from hand to mouth as she called it all the time.

After work, I rushed home to get dressed and drive over to my mother's hotel on University Avenue. It was a chilly day in October. I wore actual navy-blue pants (not jeans) and a lavender silk shirt that I prayed had no coffee stains on it. I wore a camel coat over everything, hoping one of the buttons wasn't loose. I was sure my mother would find something to complain about—a thread that threatened to unravel the coat and perhaps unravel me—my hair not brushed enough, my nails cracked, my eyeliner too much like a raccoon as she once said.

Everything in my being wanted to please her and everything in my being wanted to do everything I could to not be her.

"Sweetie," she said, first drinking in my face, then my coat, then my shoes and then my hair, which I must admit, hadn't been brushed all that well. I gave her a hug and then lay down on her bed.

"I'm tired," I said, not asking her anything about her flight. We were going out to dinner on College Avenue.

"Rest for a little while, then, while I unpack and get ready."

I looked up at the ceiling, one of those egg carton ceilings with a fluorescent light. This was not a fancy hotel, but it was near to where I lived. I saw a few black specks on the ceiling and then I must have fallen into a deep sleep for fifteen or twenty minutes to the sound of my mother getting ready for dinner.

When I woke up, half drowsy, I heard my mother walk back and forth from her room to the bathroom. I heard her hang a few things up in the closet, the thin sound of a jacket draped over a metal hanger and put up over a pole. I heard a creaky drawer open and imagined she put her nightgown and underwear there, and then the sound of the drawer closing. I heard her getting some things out of the suitcase and putting them on top of the bureau. Probably her makeup, her pancake makeup to cover the place where the flesh was sewn on; without the makeup there was a red line which never went away.

I heard some people talking next door, an older couple and a young person. We were right near UC Berkeley and parents stayed at this hotel. I didn't like that I wasn't in school. School was what I knew. Even though I had a master's degree, I wasn't sure how I could make my way in the world except to type boring letters about things I didn't care about. I did have some poems published. I also cared deeply about my class with the elderly. One woman who had Alzheimer's, her memory shot, dictated a poem to me about dancing with her husband in Chicago in a room full of mirrors; she wrote that she glided across the ballroom floor and her eyes lit up. Even though her hair was gray, and she was so heavy it was hard for her to walk, I saw the young woman dancing with her love so many years ago.

I was volunteering to teach the workshop. My mother didn't approve of volunteering when I needed money. I hoped it wouldn't come up over dinner.

"Where do you want to go?" My mother was all dressed now, and I picked myself up from the bed, did a quick brush of my hair and we left the hotel.

"There's an Italian place, not too far."

"Fine, as long as it's good." I knew what she was thinking. I had led a starving poet life for the past four years. I got cheap slices of pizza out here or in New York and ate falafels on MacDougal Street. Or cheeseburgers at diners with jukeboxes. I would search through my purse for lost quarters and play a Beatles song. I loved diners and red vinyl booths and dreamed of having a booth in my house someday.

My mother had moved up in the world from her childhood in Salvation Army homes. Her father, who left her when she was nine, had worked for the Salvation Army. She had lived on hand-me-downs. Slipping into a booth in a diner was not her idea of eating out. For a minute I wondered if the restaurant was good enough. Would it meet her standards?

As my mother ate her eggplant Parmegiano, a piece of stringy cheese stuck to her cheek. She had no feeling in her face, and I subtly pointed to the cheek with the cheese, and she wiped it off. I had done that my whole life.

I imagined that she had so many questions for me or maybe they were the questions I had for myself. *Why California? Why so far away? Why don't you just come home where you belong?* Part of me wanted her to ask me that. "Just come home." Part of me wanted her to scoop me up like a baby, get me a one-way ticket to New York City. That was where I really belonged. Not in this godforsaken place at the end of the continent, the Golden Gate Bridge so spectacular and deadly.

"How is Ken?" she said. "How does he like his Ph.D. program?" She emphasized the word Ph.D.

"He loves the program. He doesn't like New Haven though." I didn't say much more. I knew he had been robbed, but I didn't feel like going into that. Plus, Ken and I hadn't talked much in the past two months.

"How is your job?"

I worked as a secretary for an architect at UC Berkeley. The office was big and beautiful with an oriental rug, paintings on the wall and a huge picture window; I didn't tell her that the architect asked me out one weekend, "to come on my boat with me." He was twenty years older and not attractive to me at all. I told him I had a boyfriend (which I didn't) and that we would be spending the weekend together.

On Monday when I went to work, I was told by a woman I had never met that I was being moved down to a basement office. Brick walls and no window. "You have a different job now," she said. I never saw the architect again. I gathered all my things from his beautiful maple wood desk: tea bags, aspirin, pens, some hair ties and a few odd papers that I had put in my special drawer.

No explanation. I never asked why I had been moved.

I hated the dark, cramped space with stale air.

"The job's okay," I said. "The usual. I'm such a fast typist they give me lots of work and they're happy with me."

She told me about friends' children who had married lawyers or doctors and had an apartment on the upper West Side and also a country house in Long Island. I nodded and turned away for a minute as tears rimmed my eyes. *I'm trying so hard to set up a life here,* I wanted to cry out to her. Why couldn't she see that my life was important, too? Or tell me she was proud of me?

She perked up a little when I told her about teaching the class at the nursing home and the woman with Alzheimer's who wrote such a beautiful poem.

I showed her a photo of me with my students. We were standing in front of the entrance to the Home for Jewish Parents. Three of my students were in wheelchairs, all proudly facing the camera. It was a sunny day. One woman had her arm around me.

"That's nice," she said, "but does it pay?"

"No, not now at least."

"Oh," she said and that's all. She picked up the check and paid. She never said anything about whether the meal was good.

On the drive back to her hotel, we said little. We talked

a little about Farouk, her dog, who had been my sister's dog, a sweet, well-trained white furry pooch that made their sterile house feel like a home. "I'm sure she'll need to be brushed!" my mother said. "Your father is not going to brush her when I'm away."

My dad and Evelyn, our house cleaner, would walk Farouk regularly, but it was only my mother who would diligently brush her hair at night. Talking about Farouk settled us both down. I dropped her off right in front of her hotel. She looked tired. I just wanted to get home and crawl into bed.

"Sweetie, let's have dinner on Thursday? We can try another restaurant."

"OK, Mommy," I said, my voice now thin. Thready. My sister and I still called her "Mommy," as if we were still four and six, the year of the explosion.

We hugged goodbye, and I watched her walk up the stairs and into the hotel. I knew she would never want to see my apartment, and I didn't invite her to come by.

She seemed so far away already.

I drove home, only a five-minute drive from the middle of Berkeley to the edge of Oakland where I now lived. I had moved into my own apartment only two months after I arrived in California. One street after another passed by, devoid of humans. I missed New York City. I missed walking from one place to the next, my shoulders almost rubbing the shoulders of other New York City dwellers. I missed the fluorescent lights of stores always open, the click of heels, boots, and shoes on the sidewalks. I missed the first snowfall, the pristine flakes that quickly turned into yellow slush and then brown slush. I even missed looking at the cracks in the sidewalks, remembering when I would play games as a little girl: "Step on a crack and you break your mother's back," such a strange game, trying to save our mothers' backs.

No one was on the street when I pulled into a parking place on Alcatraz Avenue, fortunately only a block from my house. I didn't feel safe walking too far in that neighborhood alone at night. As I opened the car door and grabbed my purse, my mind raced back to the meal with my mom. I wanted to show her how well I was doing, 3000 miles from home—that I was making it on my own. I had even driven cross-country in a car with no radio or air conditioning. Some of my poems had been accepted in magazines. But as I got out of the car and stuck my keys between my fingers, which I had learned to do in New York City on the streets late at night—an attempt at a weapon—the difficult last few months rushed back, a flood of bad memories.

My friend, Kathleen, glommed on to me at a poetry workshop in Berkeley. She had bright lilac eyes, I later learned from contact lenses. Her long curly hair gave her a wild, witchy look.

"You're an amazing poet," she said looking deeply into my eyes. "Let's do some readings together."

In a North Beach bar, drunken men falling off their stools, I got up and read my "America" poem. I had left the America I knew, my parents' apartment in Greenwich Village, their clothes neatly hung up, their diplomas neatly hung up, their expectations for their daughters in their eyes like a hunger that couldn't be tamed. I had left boyfriends, friends, and the familiar.

"America," I read again. What was this America where I was nobody's daughter, nobody's child, where the living was supposed to be easy, but even with the spectacular views there was a decadence all around? "America," I sang out again to the yells of "That a way baby, yes, baby, keep going, telling it like it is." One drunken man yelled out, "America," and he swallowed the word and his head fell on the table and he fell asleep.

Kathleen wasn't even listening to me read. She was in a tête-à-tête with a man. "I know I'm going to meet someone soon," she had said earlier as I drove across the Bay Bridge, always her chauffeur since she didn't own a car. "I know it. I can feel it. I can feel it in my bones." Her voice was soft and throaty, a mix between a hypnotist and a porn star. She also confided to me on the ride over that she had had two children that she had given away. Her voice sucked into itself when she told me that, almost a whisper. She didn't face me but looked out the window. She told me how she held her baby close to her and touched his hair and smelled his baby smell. "The girl I didn't even hold. She was taken away immediately at the hospital. I was stoned all the time. I couldn't bring them up. It was the sixties." I got very silent after that. I didn't know whether to applaud her for giv-

ing up her children—I hoped to good homes—or decide I
didn't want to be her friend anymore.

Give up your children? That would be like amputating
your arm. How could anyone give up a child because it was
the sixties? What a lame excuse! It seemed so heartless.
She moved around restlessly in the front seat. I didn't say
anything for a long time.

She was silent for a minute until she launched in about
finding a man. I was halfway across the Bay Bridge into the
city, listening to her talk. If it wasn't for the poetry reading,
the opportunity to share my new poem in a North Beach
bar, I would have told her I just wanted to go home and
hoped she could get back across the bridge by herself. After the reading, I searched for her all through the bar and
even checked the women's bathroom. Exasperated, I finally
found her outside with a drunken man with dark soulful
eyes and a chiseled face. "This is Paris," she said, "he's coming home with me." I drove them both home that night.
They didn't say anything to me. They sat in the back seat
kissing and fondling each other all the way to Oakland.

Over the next few months, I drove to her house a few
times in the middle of the night, the streets devastating-
ly empty, to help her get Paris to the hospital. She wanted
me to move in with her when Paris went to rehab, and I
even considered it. But when I saw the bedroom, all neat
and clean, waiting for my arrival, I panicked. If I lived with
her, I knew I would be sucked into a dangerous universe. I
wouldn't be able to crawl out. "No, I've decided to stay put."

Her face froze, lips curled downward in a terrible Medusa-like anger that blew over me like a tornado and blew over the huge oval mirror that showed our faces as they truly were.

When I left that day, I knew I had escaped something big.

By the time of my mother's first visit, I was done with Kathleen, and she had stopped calling. I had met some new friends who weren't so crazy.

Sometimes at night, though, as I lay in bed listening to the sounds of Oakland, the neon Dunkin' Donuts sign flashing through the white curtains of my studio apartment, I thought maybe I *should* just go home.

My mother's conference was not too far from campus. As I typed report after report in my windowless basement hovel, I thought about her during the day—that she was so near to me. That her face and voice were just a breath away like the strip of concrete, no-man's land between Spain and Morocco so many years ago.

Even though I dreamed a lot, and later in my life found scattered journals of dreams I wrote down about huge waves of water cascading towards me, lost keys, lost wallets, stolen cars, being chased, waking up late for classes, I never had a dream with my mother's disfigured face or even a dream with her face before the accident. It was as if her face was off limits, something I couldn't even bear to dredge up from my unconscious.

After I was married, after I had children and I was

writing a book about the accident, I found a picture of her burned face as the frontispiece of a plastic surgery book; my whole body started shaking, my hands so cold I rubbed them against my jeans. I was at the University of California San Francisco medical library sitting in a comfortable armchair, gazing out a picture window of San Francisco and the Golden Gate Bridge spectacularly spanning the Pacific. I opened the plastic surgery book. In the first picture her face was completely blackened, like charred meat. The other pictures showed how flesh was rolled up like a suitcase handle from her stomach and grafted onto her face.

I must have let out a small cry like the yelp of a newborn puppy when I saw my mother in that book because a few people turned my way for a moment. There were six photos in the book all in a neat row, from the initial charred flesh to the final face. There were no "before" pictures.

I tried to push away the image of my mother's face. The ropey scars. The gullies of skin.

"Turn anything scary into a flower. You can't have two thoughts at once." I read this in *Psychology Today*.

Two days after our first dinner, my mother and I went out again on Thursday, this time to a French restaurant in San Francisco, an upscale restaurant she had heard about through friends. I drove confidently across the bridge that night, my hands relaxed on the steering wheel and my mother, often nervous in cars, didn't stiffen or clutch the sides of the seat or tell me what to do.

At the restaurant, a beautiful room with oil paintings of the Seine and Notre Dame, I could tell she wanted to get back to New York. To my dad, to her dog, to the familiar. New people always stared at her face. Conferences could take a lot out of you. She looked tired.

At times, as I ate my chicken dish, she looked at me as if she didn't know me at all, as if I had morphed out of someone else's head into an adult like Athena sprouting out of Zeus. Other times, she looked at me as if she just wanted to whisk me on the plane with her, stick me in her pocket and tell me, "We're going home now, no ifs, ands, or buts." Sometimes I longed for that. She was always so good at telling me what to do. She was good at making plans. She was good at budgeting: "I've never bounced a check in my life," she often said. She was good at packing, folding things into small spaces. She was good at sewing, even with her terribly burned hands. She was also good at getting jobs and often said, "I never looked for a job in my life." She had an M.A. in nursing when few women of her time even went to college. My life felt like a struggle.

When I dropped her off that night, I didn't know when I'd see her again.

"Bye, sweetie," she said. "Get a good rest." She looked at me again with a mixture of love and confusion.

"Bye, Mommy," I said. "Have a safe trip. Thanks for the dinner." This time I was relieved that she was going. A man in my building with curly blond hair who was studying at University of California Berkeley had talked to me the other day. I had the feeling that he was single. Maybe it would lead to something?

Another man, Japanese American, had invited me up to the roof to have dinner with him. He said he'd cook for us on his hibachi. He was working with Bob Dylan on the Rolling Thunder concert. Bob Dylan. I knew the lines of most of Dylan's songs. Those songs got me through a lot.

I didn't even look back to see if my mother looked at me as I pulled out of the parking space. It was autumn then, though I didn't see the leaves turning like I did back east. Only two months until Christmas. I didn't know if I'd have the money to go home, or even if I could get a whole week off from work. For the first time in my entire life, I thought I might not go home for Christmas.

"I know we haven't seen each other in a long time," Kathleen said, as I heard her inhale on the phone line. She smoked almost two packs a day. "But I'm having a potluck on Christmas. If you're in town, come over."

"I might be able to. Thanks for the invite." And then we hung up. We had little left to say to each other. I stiffened up when I heard her voice. But she was reaching out, and I felt lonely. The curly blond-haired man and I did go out and I fell hard for him. He took me on adventures up to the Oakland hills where he jumped on a wild horse, and we went to dance places where we danced for hours. For two months, we got closer and closer. One day we were parked by the water under a full moon, and he told me he was going home to L.A. for Christmas. "I have a girlfriend there. I'm not sure where we're at." My face collapsed but I tried not to cry. I felt betrayed. He had never mentioned her before.

I crocheted a red-and-white scarf for him over the holidays. He called as soon as he came back from L.A., but he got sick and when I brought him the scarf and won ton soup I knew it was over. We saw each other a few times as friends, but I pined for him for three months.

The man with the Hibachi invited me to go with him on the Rolling Thunder Tour. To be his girlfriend. It was an exciting invitation, but I said no. I was still afraid of getting close to a love that could work.

For the first time in my life, I didn't go home for Christmas. I went over to Kathleen's even though I hadn't seen her in months. It was my only invitation for that day, and I ended up talking to no one. I heard a weird buzzing in my head that I couldn't get rid of. Panic crept into my body, as I felt detached from everything. All I thought about was New York City. That I wasn't there.

When I came home, my neighbor, whose girlfriend had gone back to Connecticut for the holidays, invited me over. He had a plate of stale crackers and cheese and I brought over some apples and oranges and a bottle of wine. He poured the wine into paper cups. We tried to watch T.V. but all we saw was static that looked like snow. At least we were together. It was still early when I went across the hallway to my apartment and went to sleep, for the first time in my life wishing Christmas would be over soon.

Four months later my mother came out to visit again. Another conference. We were sitting on a wooden bench, and it was spring, everything in bloom as if life should burst forth in joy and glory. Our arms did not touch, our voices talking about where to eat lunch and when she'd need to get a taxi to the airport sounded disembodied. Suddenly I began to sob, a heaving sobbing, like a little girl. I had been co-counseling sometimes two or three times a week and crying now came easily to me, but never in front of my mother. She didn't like crybabies.

But at that moment, next to my mother, I couldn't stop crying. My mother moved towards me, her shoulder touching my shoulder, but we didn't hug—she didn't put her arm on my shoulder and her voice didn't get soft. Instead, she turned to face me directly. "Why don't you just come home?" It was the first time she had said that. "Why don't you come home," she repeated, and all the familiar things thrust themselves in front of me, a parade of comfort.

And at that very moment I knew I wouldn't go home, that even though I had gotten robbed again in Oakland, that I lived from hand to mouth as my mother often said, that I had no regular teaching job or true love, that I still rang the doorbells of almost strangers to co-counsel, the grief from the accident still pouring out of every cell in my body—even with all of that or maybe because of all of that—I knew I had to stay put. But my mother had released me. She had asked me to come home and I could refuse. My tears stopped, but in an unusual moment, I saw tears flood her eyes. She knew I wasn't coming home now or anytime soon. She turned her face away and sat up straighter. So did I.

"The bus is coming," she said.

"Yes, it is." I had pulled myself together, too, and we climbed on board to go to downtown Berkeley, back to her hotel and to eat lunch. She would fly back to New York City that afternoon. After lunch when we hugged goodbye, she held on to me, so unusual for her, for a minute, like my dad had done before I left for California the first time when he said, "You might think about this decision."

After the hug, I looked at my mother's face for a minute and didn't see the burns, just a face, my mother's face, re-arranged by fire.

I went home to my own one-room studio apartment in Oakland on Alcatraz Avenue, across from the flashing lights of the Dunkin' Donuts, and I got out a pad of yellow-lined paper from my desk drawer, made myself a cup of tea, sat down at my kitchen table and began to write.

EPILOGUE

Three years after my mother left Berkeley, the day I sobbed on the bench, I camped in the Sierra Nevada Mountains with a boyfriend I had been dating on and off for a year. The stars dazzled the sky. Huge trees canopied the land. We crawled into his tent after the campfire went out. An icy cold spread over my body. "I'm cold," I said, "freezing cold. I'm not sure why."

"You're fine," he said and fell asleep. He didn't look for another blanket or offer to warm me up with his body. He just fell asleep.

Just like when I was deathly sick in Marrakesh so many years before, I imagined all the people who loved me. I tried to conjure up their faces and whispered their names over and over in the stark, chilly night.

That was the moment I knew: I didn't want to be an orphan anymore. This man never talked about his family. He disappeared for weeks. He often slept on other people's couches, house-sat from place to place taking care of plants. He had a child then whom he never saw. Who was he? Where did he come from? What kind of life could we have together? I wanted a different life. I wanted a family.

That morning, not long after sunrise, when we collapsed the tent, I was silent. I was even silent when we stopped at a diner for eggs and toast. "Is everything okay?" he said in an unusual moment. As attractive and smart as he was, and even as kind as he could be, I could never figure out his eyes. They always seemed to have roads inside them I could never travel on.

"I'm okay," I said, taking a final sip of my coffee, and that was enough for him. We drove back to San Francisco on a gorgeous, sunshiny day. When he dropped me off at my apartment I said, "I can't be with you anymore."

A couple of years later I met Jim, striking, warm blue eyes, endlessly curious, generous, smart and athletic. We shared a similar vision of the world. He and I had met briefly when I had just moved to the Bay Area and we both worked in the Tenderloin District. He directed the North of Market Senior Center. I was "the poet in residence," helping to give voices to the seniors, many who lived in residences, recovering alcoholics, alone and often cut off from family.

We began dating when he directed the Haight Ashbury Senior Center, where again, I had received a California Arts Council grant to write and teach poetry. I was supporting myself as a poet then. I was 32 years old. He was the first man that moved in with me when a roommate in my house left. I had always kept my distance from boyfriends. I always kept my own place. To be that close felt scary. Nightmares of the accident still entered my dreams. *Everything can blow up quickly.* Even up to the time when we decided to get married, I was hesitant, wary. "What if it doesn't work out?" I said to him, my voice nervous, anxious.

By the time I walked down the aisle, I knew we would stay together.

Jim would never let me be cold if he could help it. I knew

that. I knew that in my heart. And I would do the same for him.

One afternoon, sitting together, he put his arms around me, looked me in the eyes and said, "I think we're going to create something together."

I don't think I could have ever been with him if I hadn't expelled all that grief, grief that poured out of me in torrents of tears.

I never gave up writing.

Even when the children were little, Jim always encouraged me. Every Monday night, I would close my bedroom door and write all night as Jim treated the kids to pizza and a movie.

Words keep spinning around my brain just like when I drove across the country so many years ago. Words ride on my back, always with me, like the knapsack I carried through Spain and Morocco. There are still stories to be told.

Ken still remains my dear friend, even through the 3000-mile distance.

The panic attacks have gone away, only slight nerves sometimes in rickety, creaky elevators. But at the age of 42, the age at which my mother and father were burned, and my own daughters were four and six, I began writing about the accident. The panic attacks returned with a vengeance then, sometimes overtaking my body when I least expected them: camping, at the playground watching the kids in the sandbox or going down a slide, and especially driving to work. Rashes mysteriously covered my face as if I had been burned, too. I had tremendous help, though, and saw my way through the terrible fears.

I still get help when I need it.

The last sixteen years of my parents' lives were spent in Oakland, California. They moved to a complete care facility, only forty minutes away. They got to see our daughters regularly and my relationship with my mother softened and deepened. At the end of my mother's life, we talked every afternoon.

My parents died at 91 and 93 years old, after long lives that were not defined by that one terrible accident. My mother's puffy, grafted face got thinner with age. She had no wrinkles since the grafts were from her stomach. People still stared, but her world got smaller, mainly filled with people she knew. People who didn't stare.

I still write and teach and try and change the world for the better.

I'm still the same person I was so many years ago.

I just don't have to run away anymore.

ACKNOWLEDGEMENTS

A book is a journey, often a long circuitous journey of writing, revising, editing, sometimes hiring editors and wondering if it will ever see the light and launch into the bigger world. I'm grateful to so many people for helping me in so many ways over many years. Please forgive me if I've left anyone out.

Some early readers when it was just a personal essay include Laura Fraser, Julia Scheeres, Caroline Paul , Eleanor Vincent and later Roberto Lovato. Other early readers include Laura Glauberman, Alicia Tarlen, Jen Sullivan Brych, Jackie Davis Martin, Nancy Hobbs, Ken Silver, Emily Freeman, Leslie Lingaas, Rose Heller, Ginny Lang, the late Kathryn Olney and Dixie Morse. Dorothy Wall helped me with structure and going deeper. Melissa Kite spent months helping me hone and edit chapter by chapter. Anne Horowitz helped me with her great insight and attention to detail toward a final version. My daughter, Laura Patten, read a final version and expertly helped me with proofreading and editing by asking good questions. Pat Tollefson also generously helped me with the near final version. Janet Rosen stood by me for many years, and I thank her profusely for all her work. Kathy Seligman so generously read a final version. My daughter, Sarah Patten, helped me with art consulting. I'm grateful to Leslie Simon for recommending Spuyten Duyvil.

Thank you to the Writers Grotto where I spent many hours writing this book surrounded by community. My sister, Anne, as always, was with me through it all. My husband, Jim, has always championed my work and been lovingly by my side for over 40 years and always given me comfort during the rough spots. Finally, thank you to Aurelia and tt and Sputyen Duyvil for all your work and for the beautiful note that popped up in my email one lucky day.

LOUISE NAYER is a long-time educator and author of six books. *Burned: A Memoir* was an Oprah Great Read and won the Wisconsin Library Association Award. She received six California Arts Council grants as a poet and has taught for years in community colleges, senior centers and nursing homes. She now teaches at OLLI UC Berkeley and at the Writer's Grotto where she is a member. She has given readings of her work across the country at bookstores, colleges, and universities as well as on over 60 radio stations including NPR. She is the mother of two grown daughters and a step-daughter and lives with her husband and dog in Glen Park, San Francisco.

louisenayer.com

Made in the USA
Las Vegas, NV
16 May 2023

72131575R00194